POPS
FOSTER

the autobiography of a
New Orleans jazzman

POPS FOSTER

*the autobiography of a
New Orleans jazzman*

as told to
TOM STODDARD

introduction by

BERTRAM TURETZKY

interchapters by

ROSS RUSSELL

discography by

BRIAN RUST

*University of California Press
Berkeley / Los Angeles / London 1971*

University of California Press
Berkeley and Los Angeles, California
University of California Press, Ltd., London, England
Copyright © 1971 by The Regents of the University of California
ISBN: 0-520-01826-5
Library of Congress Catalog Card Number: 75-132414
Designed by Dave Comstock
Printed in the United States of America

Frontispiece: The last photograph taken of Pops Foster
in March, 1969. It is mounted on his headstone.

CONTENTS

Foreword / vii

Introduction / xi

1. On the Plantation / 1

2. Early Days in New Orleans / 12

3. The Magnolia Band in the District / 26

4. Gigging Around / 41

5. Lawn Parties and Funerals / 61

6. Jazzmen / 73

7. On the Boats / 105

8. Prohibition / 119

9. New York / 138

10. Traveling with Armstrong — and After / 158

Epilogue / 175

Chronology of Musical Groups, 1899-1969 / 177

Selected Discography / 180

Pops Foster Discography, 1924-1940 / 181

Selected Bibliography / 199

Index / 201

FOREWORD

One of the best periods of my life began in May, 1967; that was when I met George Murphy "Pops" Foster. At our first meeting, my wife Roberta and I were accompanied by our four children. Pops fell in love with them as he did with all children. A few weeks later Pops and Alma Foster came to our house for dinner and a deep friendship developed. Pops wanted to tell what he knew of jazz after spending seven decades as a bass player, from the very beginnings of that musical form until the late 1960s. I agreed to set it to paper for him.

While the problems of writing such a book were few and the pleasures many, it seems worthwhile to recount some of the things that went into it, in order to give the reader a better understanding of the book's limitations, emphasis, and construction.

My original plan was not to have a plan at all. I merely took my tape recorder to Pops's house and simply had him tell his story, only prompting him here and there with questions. I foolishly thought I could then transcribe the tape directly into a finished book. This method proved suitable for collecting a lot of basic material but was, of course, completely inadequate for anything else. This first stage finally resulted in about seventy hours of taped interviews that will eventually be donated to an archive so as to make these tapes available to other researchers. The tapes were practically all made at Pops's house at 427 Webster Street in San Francisco. I would generally spend two to three hours at a time recording about one and a half hours of tape. If I live to be as old as Pops, I doubt I will ever know more pleasant hours than these. Extracting and putting the material into final shape was a bitch of a job, and one on which I procrastinated far too long.

In the quiet of my home, with four raucous children, a two hundred-pound collie dog, and a wife who felt lonely whenever I put the tapes on, I began transcribing. After a slow start, I began to extract material by topical groupings. Whenever Pops started a new topic I left a blank line or two on the sheet. This method resulted in a pile of several hundred sheets of 8½-by-11-inch paper accumulating over almost two years. I then tore the sheets along the blank lines on the paper and grouped these into several large categories (McCall Plantation, New Orleans, the Riverboats and St. Louis, and a pile I called "way late.") The McCall material was very modest, but that became the first chapter and was easy to keep separate. The New Orleans material was about 30 percent of the whole and was the most difficult to thread together. As you will note, the material is arranged in roughly chronological order.

While transcribing the material from the tapes, I soon noted that Pops covered the same material a number of times and that the versions differed in some details. Usually, I felt I understood Pops and knew the story well enough to decide which was the most accurate version, and in all cases I tried to keep most of the details. Some seriously conflicting stories did come up, such as the time and place of Pops's last playing date with Freddie Keppard. In two or three instances it was at a banquet (pronounced "bonkay" by Pops) while at other times he remembered it as a parade with a brass band. In a number of instances I decided to leave both versions in the book, feeling that Pops erred only in the chronology, not in the actual occurrences. On other conflicting details, I consulted with Pops to check his story. I believe, however, the reader has what is probably the most accurate possible version of what happened.

The above is not intended to reflect in any way on Pops's memory. He was a very articulate man and had a most remarkable recall. He conjured up facts, details, names, and dates of events more than sixty years in the past with an ease that still evokes my admiration.

Pops's amazing recollection of the early jazz era is justification enough for this book. He had read and heard so much crap and claptrap about New Orleans and early jazz that he wanted to put the record straight, as he knew it. He wanted to title the book "The Whole Truth About New Orleans." It was this simple but profound desire to get the story straight which made him devote so much time and effort to it. This, I might mention, was not the first attempt to have him tell his story, but all the others somehow never came to fruition.

The reader will note on the opening pages that I have made a sincere effort to retell the book as Pops told it. The colloquial language is retained, the interesting phraseology and syntax are kept, and as many musical, folk, and regional expressions as possible have been left intact.

Knowing that readers would be interested in certain important personalities, I asked many questions about them. Thus, these individuals loom large in the book. Had not the questions been asked they probably would not have received as much attention. Ideally, it would have been interesting to put down only those things that came naturally to Pops's mind, without prompting him at all. It is, of course, too late now and Jelly Roll Morton, Buddy Bolden, and others may be cut a shade larger than life.

The book contains virtually all the material collected on the tapes. I have tried to work that material into a fairly free-flowing book; however, I have not been altogether successful in this task. A number of details that may be of importance to the jazz historian have been put in the book even though they may interrupt the flow of the narrative. For these lapses in reading pleasure, I apologize.

I expect to be deluged with correspondence regarding inaccuracies and errors. I realize that many things in the book conflict with "known" jazz history. But Pops was a historical source and was as entitled to say his piece as the cat who wrote that history. Frankly, after spending all that time with Pops, I would be inclined to accept his version of the story. There probably will be a number of points that I may have misunderstood or where Pops was just plain wrong. Anyone who thinks so may certainly write. I do not promise to answer all the letters.

Finally, I would like to thank Pops and Alma Foster for their patience and understanding, and for lots of snacks and coffee. Thanks to my wife Roberta and my four children Antigone, Hillary, Marcus, and Jana, for putting up with me during the two and a half years of this project. Several people also deserve my thanks for helping with the book: Bertram Turetzky for the excellent critical analysis of Pops's career; Ross Russell for the sparkling interchapters; Alain Hénon for superb editing; Brian Rust for his great reference book, *Jazz Records 1897-1931* and for his fine discography for this volume; and Sam Charters for his book *Jazz New Orleans 1895-1963, An Index to the Negro Musicians of New Orleans.* Thanks to these and the many others who helped and encouraged me.

Tom Stoddard
San Anselmo, California

INTRODUCTION
by Bertram Turetzky

The career of George "Pops" Foster is staggering to contemplate,
as it ranges from Congo Square to John Coltrane — some seventy
years. Foster was the first famous double bass player in jazz,
and he worked with almost all the greats, including Louis
Armstrong, Sidney Bechet, Duke Ellington, Earl Hines, and
Charlie Parker. The only other double bassist to rival his career
was Domenico Dragonetti (1763-1846), the Paganini of the
contrabasso, who was the first celebrated European bass virtuoso.
During Dragonetti's professional career of sixty-nine years, he
became a friend of Haydn and Beethoven, among others.
Both Foster and Dragonetti represent, historically speaking, the
beginning of a growing awareness of the importance of the
double bass in Afro-American jazz and European concert music,
and both had careers of prodigious length. Both maintained
a dazzling performance level from their genesis to their last
days, and left important legacies.

Foster, one of the handful of string bassists[1] to gain a place on
the bandstand for the double bass in the days of the legendary
Buddy Bolden, developed musically through the 1920s and
1930s and was still able to bowl over thousands of aficionadi at

---

1. A term used in the early 1900s to differentiate between wind
bass (i.e. tuba) and the contrabass or double bass.

the 1963 Monterey Jazz Festival at the age of seventy-two! Around that time he worked in a quartet, with Richard Hadlock, soprano sax; Elmer Snowden, banjo and guitar; and a "swing" drummer doubling vibes. They played a repertoire ranging from ragtime and Jelly Roll Morton pieces to Thelonius Monk tunes. Pops never faltered and, more important, never lost his own wonderful identity.[2]

The love of music and quest for knowledge permeated his entire life. This is one of the reasons why he outswung and outlived so many of his contemporaries. "I used to pick up ideas from everybody. Sometimes I would find an alley guitar player, playing only blues, and give him a quarter to play all those pretty chords they used to go through."[3] I have scores of letters and interviews that attest to the voraciousness of Pops's commitment to his art, ranging from discussions of harmony with pianists to informal seminars on classical technical concepts of double bass playing.

One of the most fascinating pieces of evidence of Pops's far-reaching musical imagination was related to me by two of the most distinguished traditional jazz bassists in New York City, Bob Haggart and Jack Lesberg.[4]

> At that time (ca. 1958) he was planning a recording with four basses . . . he was anxious to be part of this quartet idea. I believe he mentioned Milt Hinton, George Duvivier, and myself (since I was present) and why didn't I write something for the session (which never materialized).[5]

Needless to say the idea of a Double Bass Quartet (in any genre) was visionary at that time. Gunther Schuller wrote what is

2. Letter from Richard Hadlock to Bertram Turetzky, July 16, 1970.
3. See p. 92.
4. In a July 4, 1970, letter, Jack Lesberg said: "Pops was constantly after me to organize a group of four basses to get something of interest going; unfortunately, this never materialized, but we did get to play together frequently, along with many other well-known bass players such as Bob Haggart, Sid Weiss, Eddie Safranski, etc."
5. Letter from Bob Haggart to Turetsky, July 1, 1970.

*most probably the first significant quarter for four basses in
1947, and this piece had to wait until 1957 for its New York City
premiere. It is simply incredible to think that one of the original
New Orleans jazzmen, age sixty-six; Fred Zimmerman, the
"dean of American bass playing," who commissioned the
Schuller quartet; and Gunther Schuller, one of America's most
important young composers were thinking along the same
wavelength. Today, this idea is still new and radical in many
parts of America and almost unknown in Europe.*

*The more I did research for this chapter, the more I realized the
magnitude of the musical thinking and doing of Foster, and
so I decided to let the autobiography tell the story and to
concentrate on aspects of his playing style and conclude with
some discussion of his influence and some critiques.*

*A study of a large number of photographs, letters,
descriptions, and discussions of his playing clearly shows that
Pops had what his friend Jack Lesberg termed a "most
original technique."[6] His left hand technique was not of the
"German school," which still is the main fingering system
used in American jazz and symphonic double bass playing,
but something close to what the English refer to as the
"fisticuffs" technique. Let us explain the differences with
commentary on three characteristic photographs of Pops at
work and one of this writer. To begin with, in the classical
technique the bass is not held upright, but angled or
leaned toward the player in order to get the left hand
around the complete fingerboard with ease.[7] Pops held it
upright and therefore lost some of the physical ease and
power that occurs when the elbow and left hand are
almost level with the shoulder. The lowered elbow simply
gets in the way and the reader can experience this by
trying to emulate Pops.*

---

6. *Letter from Lesberg to Turetsky, July 4, 1970.*
7. *This is a simplification of the standing position and the
reader is directed to any of the standard methods of
double bass which have photos showing the positions, the
bow, and how to hold the instrument.*

In all the photographs of Foster, one will notice that his thumb is visible on the left side of the neck like a violinist or country guitarist.[8] The thumb traditionally is set behind the second finger[9] in the middle of the fingerboard and acts as a fulcrum, pivot, and guide. The fingers are arched[10] and the first, second, and fourth (the third is a pressure aid paired with the fourth finger) are employed to produce a half step each. The "fisticuffs" position necessitates an enormous amount of movement, whereas the "German school" position eliminates much shifting, as the player keeps his hand in proper "shape" and only moves from string to string. For example, in the one-half position,[11] the following pitches are "under the fingers" and the only movement necessary is to change the arc of the arm to move across

8. This substantiates Pops's statement that his violinist brother Willie "taught me more about playing the bass than anyone" (see p. 82). Therefore, the often-quoted notion that sister Elizabeth Foster, a cellist, taught him bass should be dismissed on the basis of Pops's words and his use of the thumb. The cellist's thumb is also in the middle of the fingerboard and not at all visible from the front.
9. String finger numbering does not count the thumb.
10. This is not an academic point, but a question of a most centered sound and greater projection.
11. So called because it commences a one-half step from the open string.

the strings, whereas the other method resembles the "hunt and peck" typewriter technique (although it can and does produce artistic results).

Pops, however, grasped one of the most significant elements of left hand technique, which is the necessity of depressing the string against the fingerboard with enough weight to get the fundamental overtone to dominate the sound. This gives the tone a center (low frequencies need to be perceived carefully) and greater projection. Another important aspect of this concept in left hand technique is its relation to the "attack and decay" pattern. The securely depressed string produces everything mentioned above plus a long decay time. The jazz bassist today has a prodigious technique that permits him to produce pizzicato (that is, plucked) notes that "ring" and sustain so long that the string community is looking and listening to the double bassists as the leaders in the realm of pizzicato playing.

Pops Foster was one of the few of his contemporaries who were "into" this aspect of bass technique, and it should be clear that the aforementioned results of his technique not only made Pops indispensable but helped the double bass push aside the tuba as the preferred bass instrument in jazz. Gunther Schuller[12] is the first to discuss the "attack and decay" characteristics of the pizzicato bass in print, but he only mentions the right hand, which is not nearly as important. He does also mention the lowering of the bridge, which helps the left hand pressure. In conclusion, Schuller articulates the most musicianly discussion of the superiority of the double bass over the tuba I have ever read.[13] This book is hardly the place for a rehash of that tired old argument; besides time has given us the answer.

There is no question that this aspect of Foster's left hand technique had a great deal to do with one of the most

12. Gunther Schuller, Early Jazz (New York: Oxford University Press, 1968).
13. Ibid., pp. 159-160.

significant components of his style — his powerful sound. "The greatest of these bass players [Al Morgan, John Lindsay, Wellman Braud, and Bill Johnson] is probably Pops Foster, for the extraordinary power of his playing, and his attack, are a precious stimulant to the musicians with whom he is playing."[14] Scores of others wrote and spoke about Pops's drive and power that inspired so many soloists and bands. But it was more than the big sound and the enthusiasm that mattered. There was also his extraordinary innate sense of time. "Pops's rhythm was so sure and firm, San Francisco Jazz pianist Vince Guaraldi once said, that he was really better to work with than most young, technically advanced, bassists."[15]

Let us begin a discussion of right hand techniques with the three basic sound generators used: (1) arco (i.e., bowing); (2) pizzicato (i.e., plucking with the fingers); (3) slapping. Thus there is in reality three different timbres in contrast to the usual one "big sound" pizzicato sound (and the occasional bowed solo). Slapping is the least familiar of these techniques and is executed in two different ways: the first consisting of slapping the fingerboard with the open palm of the right hand while grasping the string to be plucked; the second requiring the string to be pulled up away from the fingerboard. Its subsequent release causes the string to hit the fingerboard and produce the forceful slap (or snap) sound. It is important to note that "slapping" was considered a "hot" sound, like growling through a trumpet or trombone, which affected a timbral transformation as the string bass was then converted into a formidable percussion instrument. Slapping was an integral part of Pops's playing throughout his life. In the 1950s and 1960s he slapped less, but we will never know if this was a bow to the ever-changing aesthetic or purely a physical situation. We can, however, authoritatively credit Pops for popularizing this technique.

---

14. H. Panassie, The Real Jazz (New York: Smith and Durrell, 1943).
15. Letter from Hadlock.

Tony Parenti, who first met Pops in 1918, wrote: "Pops was one of the first original New Orleans bass players that made the slapping bass playing popular in New York City."[16]

Bowing was an important aspect of the Foster style. "I first learned to bow the bass, then started doing a lot of picking. . . . It seems like I've been switching like that all my life."[17] He frequently began a piece arco and then changed to pizzicato thus adding to the rhythmic crescendo that has traditionally been an important element in jazz. Pops used what resembles the "French grip" and utilized both French and German bows. The bow moved from the arm and not the wrist (as is traditionally taught), but it cut the string at the proper angle, and as he rarely played fast or exposed passages, it did not matter. The arco sound was not bel canto, but big and gutty. Technically he was the equal of any recorded jazz bassist before Jimmy Blanton.[18] "He could also sing a part in a vocal trio and bow the bass part at the same time . . . he did that day [in September, 1963] as a member of the Hines group."[19] Jack Lesberg says: "I doubt if he had any classical training, however he did practice and figured out things for himself, as many famous and accomplished players have done."[20] Bill Crow, veteran New York City modern bassist, recalls overhearing Foster holding forth on his harmonic approach at Jimmy Ryan's around 1946 or 1947, and he wrote of hearing Pops's voice, dripping with disdain, saying:

---

16. *Letter from Tony Parenti to Turetzky, July 11, 1970.*
17. *See p. 76.*
18. *Regarding Blanton, Pops said: "A couple of guys were better at playing melody than me, Jimmy Blanton and Junior Ragland. They could both play a whole lot of melody but had trouble keeping a rhythm foundation. Ragland was a guitar player and Blanton a cello player before they switched to bass. Blanton played string bass like he played the cello" (p. 147). This is one of the two moments of braggadocio to be found in the autobiography.*
19. *Letter from Howard Rumsey to Turetsky, July 16, 1970. Rumsey is a distinguished bassist and proprietor of the Lighthouse in Hermosa Beach, California.*
20. *Letter from Lesberg to Turetzky, July 25, 1970.*

"Hell, I just play any old go-to-hell note, as long as it swings!" To me, just beginning to hit what I considered the right notes with anything better than ordinary luck, this seemed sheer old folks bravado in the face of the wondrous new harmonic intricacies of bop, and may even have been just that. Now, however, after twenty years of learning appropriate bass lines for the changing fashions of Jazz, and having found three or four musicians, like Jim Hall and Hank Jones, who will take any old go-to-hell note one might play and make it sound like a brilliant and gorgeous choice by surrounding it with a heavenly chord, I am inclined to agree with Pops. If the notes you play add to the feeling of swinging together with the rest of the group, then they're probably the right ones.[21]

This interpretation of Pops's harmonic concepts would have pleased him, I am sure, and it is the most authoritative, articulate discussion of the nitty-gritty of the harmonic responsibilities of the jazz double bassist I have ever read.

Many writers have advanced what Rudi Blesh calls "the base canard that New Orleans jazz is a hippety-hop 'two beat' music."[22] The New Orleans rhythm section style of about 1920 was quite different and the concept of two-beat bass playing was only one aspect of what was a most sophisticated rhythmic style. In fact, after the 1920s, I feel, a great deal of variety — rhythmic, coloristic, and textural — had been given up to "pump out" the beat. Gunther Schuller refers to this rhythmic variety in discussing John Lindsay's performance on the 1926 Victor recordings of Jelly Roll Morton.[23] Pops tells us: "In New Orleans we'd have two pick notes in one bar, then you'd go to six bars of bowing, and maybe have one note to pick."[24]

---

21. Letter from Bill Crow to Turetzky, July 31, 1970.
22. Letter from Rudi Blesh to Turetzky, August 25, 1970.
23. Schuller, Early Jazz, p. 159. Lindsay alternates playing half notes, whole notes, and quarter notes in a most bright and variegated manner.
24. See p. 76.

Pops often did more than simply "run changes" . . .
frequently (especially if the tune or the chords inspired
him) he would build counter melodies to what one
or another of the horns was doing. There are not many
examples of this, unfortunately, on record, but I
have heard him do so many times.

On some such occasions, his bass counter melodies
would be projected pizzicato, but frequently — especially
in the blues — they would be arco. One good recorded
example is to be found in the bowed counter melodies
he extemporized with Dan Burley's barrelhouse
piano on the Old Circle "skiffle" record, Dusty Bottom,
from the 1946 album South Side Shake.

Dusty Bottom is a blues slowly and thoughtfully
projected by piano with antiphonal bass responses. It is
as pure as any Baroque duo — purer, I should say
and Haydn, I'm sure, would have loved it. Edgar Varese
did, anyway. Everytime he would visit me he
would say, "Play that Boogie Chorale thing!" and
I'd get out the old 78 rpm shellac disk.[25]

Also fascinating is Pops's statement of about 1967: "Now we
pick four or eight beats to a bar or full note."[26] This and
the earlier rhythmic ideas plus the melodic style referred
to above are clearly in the avant-garde (that is, those
liberated bassists who don't just play time in ensemble). It
would seem that jazz bass playing went around full circle
back to this wonderfully rich and varied style that Pops
helped promulgate in the early 1900s. One of the main
differences between this aspect of the Foster style and the
avant-garde is that most of the "new thing" bassists play in
the upper registers while Pops played in the lower positions
because he felt the bass was a foundation and not a solo
instrument.[27] Finally, Charles Mingus, Ray Brown, Richard
Davis, the late Scott LaFaro, and others brought new vistas
of velocity to double bass playing, but let us not forget that

25. Letter from Blesh.
26. See p. 76.
27. See p. 76: "I don't think the bass or the drums are solo
instruments; they're the rhythm and I don't like to play
solos."

fast bassists existed previously. Some of us may remember when Wellman Braud was written up by Ripley in "Believe It or Not" as the world's fastest bass player. This caused another bit of braggadocio as Pops responded, "I know Braud couldn't pick as fast as I could and I never knew anyone else who could."[28] Whether or not Pops was the fastest is not really important. What we most definitely know is that he was one of the most inspired and inspiring, steady, powerful, and consistently creative bassists in the annals of jazz history.

In the 1920s many New Orleans bassists played a two-beat style. Pops was playing a four-beat style then "when I went to New York playing that way, everybody wanted to do it too. Right after that . . . about 1929 or 1930 . . . they started writing arrangements that way, with a four-to-the-bar bass part."[29] That "wide" beat and booming, stomping sound dominated many rhythm sections, especially that of the famed Luis Russell Orchestra. The Foster sound and approach most definitely led to the bass dominated rhythm section that jazz history usually tells us Count Basie, Walter Page, and Jo Jones brought out of Kansas City in the 1930s. It is interesting to note that many of Jones's innovations simply lightened the "drum kit" sound ideal which made it easier for the powerful Mr. Page[30] to "walk on through," whereas Pops was pitted against some "experimental model" drum sets that really roared. Nevertheless, Pops came through and it can be said without fear of contradiction that Pops fostered the bass dominated rhythm section in the 1930s and this is still the preferred sound ideal in mainstream combo and big band jazz today.

Musicologists have traditionally evaluated performers through documented reports of their prowess from contemporary

---

28. See p. 147.
29. From an unpublished interview with Hadlock, ca. 1964.
30. Page got the nickname "Big Four" but it should be clear now that Pops deserved this appellation earlier than the famous Kansas City bassist.

sources. This time honored approach will be followed here.
Pops had a seventy-year playing career; it must be decided
when he hit his peak. Many musicians felt that Pops was
in peak performance from 1929 on, while others considered
the Luis Russell years (1929-1937) the vintage days. How
to settle this with scholarly accuracy? I decided to discuss
Pops at peak form from 1929 on. Recordings were of
some assistance, but, because of the acoustical nature of
pre-1950 recordings of the double bass in jazz and the
well-known psychological problems of studio recording in
general, and in the pretape era in particular, I personally
felt that the critiques of colleagues would help illuminate
many things that are not clear on the recordings, especially
for those readers who are not fortunate enough to have
heard Pops Foster "rompin' the big fiddle." [31]

> Pops Foster was the greatest of the New Orleans
> bassists, and perhaps the most flexible. He could swing
> a big band or trio and anything between. His only
> peers were Wellman Braud, his contemporary, and the
> much older Bill Johnson. His beat was an inspiration.
> What else can I say?
>   Don Morgenstern, July 14, 1970.

> I feel he had a lot for the bass as well as bass players. I
> always enjoyed him and was amazed when I heard
> him play . . . all bass players would go see and hear
> him play. He must have been taking care of business.
>   Eugene Wright, July 27, 1970.

> He was always the oldest member of our band [in the
> 1940s] but the most active and youthful in his playing
> and personality — when I featured him on the bass,
> he would always get the biggest hand from the audience.
>   Tony Parenti, July 11, 1970.

> I had the pleasure of meeting and hearing the great
> Pops Foster in the early thirties, with the Luis Russell
> Band. . . . He was known by the people who knew all
> about this kind of music to be the best of his time.

---

31. *"Pops Foster, Forty-eight Years on the String Bass,"*
Jazz Record *(March, 1947).*

He was a great gentleman, very humble, and when I
say "humble" I mean in a gracious, dignified way
(obviously he had not read Harriet Beecher Stowe.)
                    Bud Freeman, July 10, 1970.

Pops was one of the few greats on any instrument
one encounters in a musical lifetime.
                    Art Hodes, August 3, 1970.

Most of my recollections of Pops Foster are in the
form of indescribable musical sounds which I can hear
in my head (all I do is turn on the mental tape
and I can isolate short segments of bass lines heard
many years ago at Roseland or on the many great
recordings of Armstrong.) This big chomping sound Pops
Foster got out of a bass was a driving force and
inspiration to me for many years. There was a primitive
quality to this sound which appealed to me and it
played a large part in my background and influenced
my concept of bass playing. . . . The first bass sound to
catch my ear was Pops Foster and it was his approach
to bass playing that inspired me to switch to bass
[from guitar] and devote a life time to this instrument."
                    Bob Haggart, July 1st, 1970.

I don't suppose Pops Foster, technically, could compare
with the present generation of bass players, with its
symphony refugees and Julliard graduates. This
is not to put them down, but without him, they might
still be lost in the symphony forests, hoping, each one, to
be the second "serious" player — after the late
lamented Serg Koussevitsky — to get a solo spot. Pops
Foster may not have done 180 miles per hour on
the Super Highway. He just laid out the highway,
that's all.

                    Rudi Blesh, August 25, 1970.

1. ON THE PLANTATION

If I had it to do all over again, I'd do just the same thing I
did. But I'd want it like it was when I was a young man around
New Orleans, that was kicks. Musicians had fun then and
never had any Jim Crow. Sometimes in my life I've had it good
and sometimes bad. One time I had to pawn my bass for
$6.00 and then had to rent one for a long time because
I couldn't scrape up the money to get it out. So it gets rough.

I've always wanted to write down what I know about the times
in New Orleans. Some of the books are fouled up on it and
some of the guys weren't telling the truth. One of them says
Louis Armstrong played the District. Louis played Saturday
nights at Buddy Bartlett's tonk and didn't have no regular
job. Guys like Joe Oliver and Freddie Keppard had regular
jobs, but most guys around New Orleans didn't. The critics and
guys who write about jazz think they know more about
what went on in New Orleans than the guys that were there.
They don't know nothing. They're wrong most of the time.
We had a whole lot of trumpet players around New
Orleans besides Oliver and Armstrong. This book is gonna
straighten a lot of things out.

The guys that teach music, they're another bunch; they don't
know about it. Any of them that see you playing a string bass
want to show you how to hold the bow or tell you you
aren't fingering right. The teachers always want to tell you to

finger the strings with the tip ends of your fingers. You can't finger for tin can music like that, it's too delicate. You've got to grip those babies to get a tone. All your tone is in the left hand. If you just half muffle the string you don't get no tone; it's like playing with a mute on a horn. It's the same way with the bow. No guy can teach you how to hold it, but all the teachers try. You can't teach people to hold a pencil the way you hold it. You've got to pick it up the way that's most comfortable for you and it's gonna stay that way. All the guys I've taught, I told to hold the bow the way it's comfortable and go on and play.

Some of those critics and dicty teachers should see the first bass I had. My brother Willie did most of the work to make it. He put a two-by-four through the hollow of a flour barrel and nailed it on. We used some kinda wood for a bridge and carved some tuning pegs to stick in the two-by-four. Down on the two-by-four we pounded some nails in to tie the strings to. We couldn't afford regular strings so we used twine. It had three strings: we'd twist three pieces of twine together for the lowest, then two, then one for the highest. For two or three days we'd rub the twine with wax and rosin before we'd put them on the bass. The first bow was a bent stick with sewing machine thread tied on it. After awhile we got a regular bow without any hair in it. For hair we caught a neighbor's horse and cut the hair off his tail, but it didn't work, and we went back to sewing machine thread. My daddy made us use the bow on it, no plucking. I got awfully sick of sawing on it. We just played it around the house.

My older brother Willie was the first one to take up music in the family. He learned how to play the homemade bass, and then our uncle Wyatt on my father's side hired him to play cello in his little band. Uncle Wyatt was what we called a hamfat violin player — he wasn't so good and he wasn't so bad. Uncle Wyatt would get jobs playing dances around the McCall Plantation from eight at night until four in the morning, and Willie would play for him. Back in those days the band owned the instruments. They'd all put in to buy them and

Pops Foster in typical playing position

Bertram Turetzky in classical playing position.

Charlie Foster, Pop's father, about 1900.

Annie Foster, Pop's mother, about 1940.

Willie Foster, Pop's brother, about 1925, New Orleans.

Willie Foster and Henry Kimball, Sr., about 1925, New Orleans.

when you left the band you couldn't take the instrument. If the whole band broke up, whoever ended up with all the instruments could sell them. One day uncle Wyatt gave Willie a mandolin to play and I got the homemade bass. I've been playing ever since. The earliest I can remember playing, I was seven years old. After a while I started playing in uncle Wyatt's band too.

Later on uncle Wyatt sold a cello to my mother for $1.50, and I got to have it for my own. The first real bass I had was a cello. Even after that we didn't have real strings and had to use twine rubbed with wax and rosin. Willie is the one who taught me to play the bass. Willie first learned cello bass, then he was so fast he learned violin and mandolin too. Later on he picked up banjo, guitar, and all the other stringed instruments.

It wasn't too long after that that Willie, my sister Elizabeth who learned to play guitar, violin, and bass, and I started getting jobs for our little trio playing lawn parties and birthdays in the afternoons and evenings. It seems like we played a birthday every Sunday. I was so small at the time I had to stand on a box to reach the neck of the cello. My brother and sister were both better reading musicians than me, but I could play better and couldn't read so good.

My daddy saw that we had a good thing started, so he got Willie and me to start our own band to put on dances. We called the band the Fosters. None of the field hands around McCall Plantation played anything, but there were a few guys around who played. In our little band we hired a guy named Louie Budour to play valve trombone, and a guitar player. Willie played the mandolin and I played cello or bass. Elizabeth didn't play night jobs with us. Our first guitar player was a guy named Frank who came from around Fort Barrow, Louisiana. He worked on a dredge in the Mississippi River and he was a sleepwalker. One night he walked off the barge and they never found him. Our next guitar player was June Skinner who worked around the Plantation. He played mandolin too.

My daddy would throw the dances on Saturday nite. He'd rent an empty house. It would cost fifteen cents to get in and he sold beer. Anywhere from fifteen to twenty people would come to them. We'd play quadrilles, polkas, rags, and lancers. Our little band was very good, and we started taking uncle Wyatt's jobs away from him. Uncle Wyatt would have a dance at Richard McCall's plantation and we'd have one at Harry McCall's. We'd get most of the people at our dance and he'd get real salty. He started coming around telling my daddy that he was ruining us kids by keeping us up late playing dances. He carried on about how it wasn't good for us kids. My daddy and him had a big fight. My daddy told him it was OK as long as he was keeping us kids up, but when my daddy started doing it, it was bad.

Back in the early days, after we moved to New Orleans, we needed money pretty bad, so I sold the cello I got at McCall for $1.50 to a little white kid. Later on I tried to get it back, but he wouldn't sell it. I played the cello in my brother's band for awhile before I sold it.

My daddy, Charley Foster, was no good. He worked for the McCalls as the butler and spoke French. Everybody who worked in the house or the yard had to speak French all the time because they wanted their kids to learn it. I don't think he ever drew any money from the McCalls. They had the plantation store where you could buy anything, even a horse and wagon. It had a bar, drugstore, and grocery. My daddy put so much whiskey on the tab there he never drew no money and I don't remember him ever buying us kids nothin'. He went to work early in the morning and got off after he'd served supper. The McCalls usually cooked too much food and he'd bring home the leftovers to us or we'd go get them. I always said I'd kill my daddy. I stole his pistol once and if it wasn't for the coachman, I'd've killed him then. I wanted to practice with the pistol shooting a can; it wouldn't shoot because the safety was on. The coachman saw me and told my mama, and she took the gun away. I told my

daddy, "When I get to be a man, I'm gonna kill you."
Our house at McCall Plantation was about a city block from
the big house where all the house workers lived. It had great
big wide wooden planks for the floor, and boards on the
outside. There was a strip of wood over the cracks on
the outside and some places on the inside. The roof was
made of shingles and there was no ceiling. You could look up
and see the rafters. Once in a while we'd whitewash the
walls inside and the outside was just boards. There was a big
fireplace, a really big one. That's where you did all your
cooking and got all your heat. We'd make a stack of bricks
on two sides, then put iron bars across the center to cook on.
It snowed at McCall in the winter, and at night we'd put a
great big log in the fireplace to burn all night.

There were two huge rooms in the house. Most of the cooking
was done in our room where we had two big beds. Mama
had a stove, but most people didn't — they had big pots with
legs on them. You baked your bread in a round oven with legs
on it, and you put fires on top and bottom. My brother and
sister slept in one bed in the big room. I slept in the other,
except when my grandmother Martha Foster stayed with us,
she slept in my bed. The reason I slept alone was I was
always fighting. I'd even hide rocks in my bed so I could
throw them at my brother and sister after we went to bed.
When my daddy would stay out all night — he didn't hardly
stay home at all — my sister slept with my mother.

In the yard outside the house we kept chickens and washed
clothes. Back then you washed clothes in a big iron boiler that
had a fire under it. You made your soap from ashes from the
fireplace and lye. It was the strongest soap you ever wanta
see. Out in the yard we kept chickens.

On my mother's side everybody was musical. My
grandmother's name was Charlotte Williams. Her people were
all from around Donaldsonville, Louisiana. There were a lot
of Indians around there and my mother was nearly
full-blooded Cherokee. My cousin Clairborne Williams had a

band around Donaldsonville and Plaquemine, Louisiana.
Everybody in it was named Williams or related to them, and
it was called the Williams Band. Lucy Williams played piano,
Clayborne's youngest son played clarinet, his son-in-law
played drums (he was the only one not named Williams),
Clayborne played trumpet and clarinet, and his brother
Michael played bass. They played mostly ragtime music. It's
through my mother I'm related to that horse thief Clarence
Williams, but I found out about that way late.

My mama, Annie Foster, was 108 years old when she died in
1959. Her mother lived to be over a hundred and had
twenty-one children; mama was the youngest. She was always
knitting, crocheting, and sewing for other people to earn
extra money for us. She spoke seven languages, French,
Spanish, Latin, Italian, English, and God knows what else. I
only speak one and don't do it any good. I remember mama
sewing up a lot of gingham dresses around the plantation.
Gingham was the same as silk to the women in those days.
Years later on the road the guys used to say, "Don't give
me no evening dress, give me a gingham gown, they don't
want so much." I knew what they were talking about.

Martin Luther King's funeral reminded me of the funerals on
the plantation. They used to put the casket on a long wagon
drawn by four mules owned by the plantation. The family and
close friends would sit in chairs on the funeral wagon. Then
they'd have more mules pulling sugarcane carts with the rest
of the people riding on them. It was all very quiet with no
music; music was sinful back then.

There were two McCall plantations, Richard's and Harry's, and
they were first cousins. I was born on Harry McCall's
plantation on May 19, 1892. The ground around the
plantation was black bottomland, and there were at least a
couple of thousand acres on the place. Some of the people
would eat the black mud. They said they liked it, it's salty.
There were three or four hundred shacks where the field
hands lived about a mile from the house. They all kept

*chickens, hogs, and cows, and the horses and mules were
kept out there. The field hands didn't play any music, not even
guitars and sing blues. Up around Fort Barrow there were
a lot of guys who played blues on guitar. All of them
were colored, you never saw a white man with a guitar or a
mandolin.*

*Around the plantation there were all kinds of trees. There
were a lot of sycamores, a few big magnolia trees with
beautiful blossoms in the summertime, and some bay trees.
Around the big house there was a fence and inside there
were all kinds of fruit and nut trees. One big tree we
called a muskeydyne was like a big cherry tree. They had
bitter orange trees, big black fig trees, and pecan trees.
Us kids could ask to go through the gate and get the fruit
if we wanted, but we'd climb the fence and steal it. If
we got caught, we got a good lickin'. All around the house
there was a honeysuckle rose vine that smelled so nice,
and the bees would buzz around it all summer.*

*On most Saturday nights we'd play a dance at Harry or
Richard McCall's place. Near the plantations there was a
little one horse town called Philadelphia Point where we'd
play sometimes. Another place we'd play was Smoke Bend
near Fort Barrow. We played a lot of dances in the
Bouley where the Cajuns live. That's like the back woods.
They're mostly sharecroppers. Most of the Cajuns were
half-breed people, who were so mixed up you didn't know
what they were.*

*For the Cajuns we played mostly country or hillbilly music,
it's a lot like Jewish music. They liked their music very
fast and they danced to it. Some of the numbers they
liked were* Lizard On The Rail, Red, Oh Red, Chicken
Reel, *and* Tiger Rag. *They had a guy who called figures
for them. First you'd play eight bars of a tune, then stop.
Then the announcer would get up and call, "get your
partners." When everybody got their partners, he'd blow a
whistle and the band would start playing again. The*

announcer would call the figures like, "Ladies Cross, Gent's Right, Promenade" and all that stuff. You'd play three fast numbers then take it down to a waltz, a slow blues, or a schottische. The Cajuns would dance till four in the morning and sometimes just go on all night.

All of us kids went to a Catholic school at Donaldsonville about three miles away. After we'd come home, we'd do our homework and practice music. In those days I was crazy about horses. I just loved anything that had to do with a horse. I guess that's why grandmother Foster bought me one. I didn't want nobody using it but me. My daddy would try to loan the horse to a clerk at the store for whiskey. He'd send Willie out to catch it and I'd hear them talking. I'd go out and start shooting rocks at her with my peashooter to make her run off. Willie would run to catch the horse and I'd run and shoot again. Sometimes they wouldn't catch the horse; other times when they'd catch her, she'd be so tired she was no good; and they'd always be late getting her. One time Willie caught her and I threw a cat on her and she threw Willie off and hurt him pretty bad. I loved horses so much I really didn't want to start playing music. But after I started playing and all the little girls started coming around, I liked it. When I started playing, I was the youngest thing playing for a long time, now I can't find anyone who started when I did.

In 1900 Harry McCall's son Mac became a lawyer and moved to New Orleans. He got married and settled for a year, then he sent down for Willie to come and work for him. My mother didn't want him to go, but back in those days you did what the whites said to do. He went to New Orleans and that broke up our little band for a while. In about 1902 my daddy got so bad at drinking and not taking care of us that my mother wanted to leave. She got us out by telling him she was gonna take us to New Orleans to visit Willie. We were gonna stay and he thought so too, so he wouldn't let Elizabeth go. When we left for New Orleans we left with just what we had on. When we got there, we stayed with Willie at the McCall's, in his little old room. Then mama got a job cooking for the Wilmans and me and mama moved over there. I had the job of taking Harry Wilman to school and bringing him home so the other kids wouldn't beat up on him.

It wasn't long after that that my grandmother, Martha Foster, stole my sister from my daddy and brought her to New Orleans. Willie left the McCalls about then because they were gonna beat him up for not serving supper on his night off. He got plenty of jobs working other peoples houses after that.

For some reason the McCalls sold the plantation and moved to New Orleans right after that, and they brought my daddy with them.

Pops was ten years of age when he emigrated to New
Orleans, home town for dozens of famous jazz musicians.
Behind him Pops left the life of a Mississippi bottomland
plantation with its sprawling village of shacks, company
store (and bar), and great mansion house. The move to
New Orleans required a journey of some sixty miles,
sufficiently long at that time, actually a leap from the nineteenth
century to the twentieth. The feudal enclave of McCall
Plantation was replaced by a corner of the most cosmopolitan
city in America. At the turn of the century, when Pops
arrived, the population of New Orleans exceeded 300,000
persons. They came from a variety of cultural and ethnic
backgrounds — French, Italian, German, Portuguese, English,
African, and Caribbean.

In New Orleans music was heard at every conceivable
social occasion — at parties, dances, political rallies, store
openings, parades, picnics, outings, and funerals. The custom
had been established during the permissive rule of
governors appointed by the court of Versailles. After the
Louisiana Purchase, French gaiety, permissiveness, and love
of good times continued. An influx of peoples from other
countries served to add new colors, rhythms, and

melodies to New Orleans musical style, which became
progressively demotic and varied, less formalized, subject
to change and experiment. New Orleans was one of the
great melting pots of music history.

One heard snatches of melody plucked from the latest
tango or French music hall hit, from a schottische or landler,
from *Tannenbaum* or *Il Trovatore*, from John Philip
Sousa or Scott Joplin, from a country folk song or the country
blues — everything was grist to the musical mill. Melody
was always in great demand; New Orleans musicians were
not overly concerned with harmonic invention; the forms at
hand, simple ideas from band marches and gospel hymns
and ragtime, were sufficient. The main thing was to tailor the
material to the requirements of dancers, and, there, too,
variety was great: the upper classes still danced the
quadrille and other stately steps handed down from their
European ancestors; in the lowest tonks couples indulged in the
most outlandish and unabashed gyrations; and there was
every shade of the terpsichorean art in between. For a boy
of ten, with music in his blood, with something of a head
start as a string player, New Orleans was a most exciting city
in which to live and grow up.

2. EARLY DAYS IN NEW ORLEANS

On the plantation you didn't see anything but sugarcane and corn. When I first got to New Orleans, I saw wagons going everywhere delivering coal, selling vegetables, and doing different things. In those days the markets opened at three or four in the morning and stayed open till noon. They sold everything you wanted to eat at the outdoor markets. A lot of guys drove vegetable wagons around selling to people in their homes. The vegetable wagons weren't legal, and they had to have fast horses to get away when the cops chased them. When that happened, you could get all the fruit and vegetables you wanted for free; it would fly all over the street. A lot of kids made money driving the vegetable wagons. One guy got so big, he had twelve wagons going.

In the heart of town they had a big dump, and if you lived near it you sure could smell the rotten garbage and stuff. Later on they started carrying the garbage out in the Gulf in big barges. We used to have backyard toilets in those days and colored guys used to come around and clean them out. They'd put the crap in barrels, roll them out to the aggravatin' wagon, then haul them down to the docks and load them on boats, and they'd carry them off down the river. You could smell those aggravatin'

wagons for a long way, and the only thing that would kill
the smell was lime. The guys who worked the aggravatin'
wagons made more money than any of the other colored,
but most guys couldn't take it for more than a week. You
could smell those guys coming — they smelled terrible.
Those outdoor toilets caused some of the biggest roaches
you ever saw. They were big red flying ones and it really
hurt when they bit you. The mosquitoes were terrible too.
It was so bad in one place we played, named Howard's
Canal, we had to wear nets over our heads. New Orleans
in those days was a mess, very few streets had gravel,
and only the ones like Canal Street had cobbles; most
were just mud.

On Sunday afternoons I used to go out to Lincoln Park.
It was a big amusement park. They had a pavilion where
a brass band played in the afternoon and people would
dance. There were different kinds of things to do, like a
merry-go-round, flying horses, a roulette wheel, throw the
hoop, and other stuff. The brass band would play the
pavilion from about 1:00 p.m. to 5:30 p.m. Then they'd
have the hot air balloon ride. They'd get a big fire going
and fill this big balloon up with smoke. Buddy Bottle
would climb in the basket and go way up in the sky with
it. When it got way high, he'd jump out and land by
parachute. The balloon would turn over then and come
down. Sometimes it didn't work right, and it would take
them two or three days to find the balloon. They also had
a woman who went up, but I never knew her name.

After the balloon ride, they had a stage show in the
theater. It was a TOBA style show with comedians,
jugglers, and all that. John Robichaux's band would play
the show which lasted from about 6:00 p.m. to 8:00 p.m.
After the stage show, the people would come in and the
brass band would take over on stage to play a dance.
It cost fifteen cents to get in and I was lucky to have a
nickel to take the streetcar home, so I had to sneak in.
I'd hide behind a post then get mixed up in the crowd

and move on in. Inside I'd hide around the stage so I could peep at the band. The cop in the place would catch me sneaking around every Sunday and chase me off. Finally, he asked me what I was looking at. I told him I was watching Mr. Kimball play the string bass. He said, "Why don't you learn to play it?" I said, "That's what I'm trying to do." He said, "OK you can stay till 9:00 p.m. after this." So after that I could watch Mr. Henry Kimball play till nine. I always thought Mr. Kimball was a wonderful bass player. Years later I was asked to show him how to play.

After my mama got a job in New Orleans, we lived at 2523 Octavia Street. From there we moved up on Broadway. We lived there a little while and moved to Adams Street. When we lived there my brother started working for the Rites people and that's when he bought me my first bass. My mother and me got along real good, she was comical and had a funny name for everyone. My sister and I couldn't get along for one minute. My mother never had any restrictions on my brother and me — we could stay out as long as we wanted, but Elizabeth couldn't. I usually came home around ten or eleven at night. Us kids would spend the evenings playing around a corner under the street light until one of the cops came along and chased us off. Then we'd go on home or run and hide in the cemetery where we'd play hide and seek.

My father, my uncle Wyatt, and grandmother Foster lived together in New Orleans. My father used to come around to fuss and fight with mama. One time when he was there I got up behind him with a baseball bat to hit him, but my brother pushed me down. My father told mama I'd never be no good. Sometimes I used to go over to see my grandmother and take some money over. He'd be there. I'd tell him, "You ain't never been no good to us, and now I've got to take care of you." He'd say, "I'll smash you." I'd say, "No you won't, you used to do that,

*but not now." He also used to come around where I was
playing and want to talk to my boys, it made me mad.
He finally got so sick, we had to put him in the hospital.
They called his sickness TB of the throat, but I think now
it would be cancer of the throat. Papa finally died in
1906 at about fifty years old.*

*I went to school at New Orleans University on St. Charles
Street and Leontine. It cost mama a dollar a month for
both my sister and me, and we had to buy our own
books. I didn't do well in school because I was too busy
playing music. I used to sleep all day in class so I
could play at night. In those days if you could play music
they'd let you play and pass you. They even loaned us to
other schools like Leland University to play their shows. I
left school just when I was turnin' to go into the fifth,
I got a job with the Munson People in Audubon Place
and quit school. I always tell kids to finish their schooling
before taking up music professionally. I sure wish I had.*

*All the kids around New Orleans had a goat and a
wagon to ride around in. Kids used to get fifty cents to
buy a sickle and a shovel. Then you'd go around getting
jobs cutting grass to make a little money. You could buy
a goat in those days for about fifty cents and I bought a
gang of them. If I'd buy one for fifty cents and a half
hour later someone would offer me seventy-five cents, he'd
have a goat. You made your own wagon for the goat to
pull out of lumber scraps and old wheels. There was a
guy at Oak and Carleton that made harnesses for the
goats that cost you $2.00. It took me a long time to get
a hold of $2.00.*

*After I turned professional, I spent a lot of time at Lake
Pontchartrain. Sunday was your big day at the lake. Out at the
lakefront and Milneberg there'd be thirty-five or forty bands out
there. The clubs would all have a picnic and have their
own band or hire one. All day you would eat chicken,
gumbo, red beans and rice, barbecue, and drink beer and*

claret wine. The people would dance to the bands, or listen to them, swim, go boat riding or walking on the piers. The food was mostly every tub, that means everybody takes what he wants and waits on himself. The musicians had just as much fun as the people you played for.

Mondays at the lake was for the pimps, hustlers, whores, and musicians. We'd all go out there for picnics and to rest up. At night they had dances in the pavilions out on the piers. One night we were playing at the lake and we had a clarinet player named Leb who ate so much fried fish he nearly choked to death. We had to take him home and he was sick for a long time. He was from Breakaway, Louisiana, where Sam Morgan's from. Some people lived out at the lake all year long. The only time they had to be scared was in a storm.

When I went out at night around New Orleans it was mostly to hear different bands play. I only saw Buddy Bolden's band play once at Johnson's Park. That's where the rough people went. I knew all the guys in the band and later on played with them. Buddy played very good for the style of stuff he was doing. He played nothing but blues and all that stink music, and he played it very loud. Buddy got to drinking so bad they had to hire two trumpets and Joe Howard played the other one. Joe played on the riverboats with us way late. Jim Johnson the bass player was a very good friend of mine and I used to hang out with him all the time. He was an older guy than me. Jim liked working with the Bolden Band and stayed with Bolden till he [Bolden] went crazy. Then he went with Jack Carey's Crescent Band. Jim worked on the boats way late and was the last one of Bolden's band to die, in about 1957. He was touring Texas with Don Alberts's band when he got sick and died there. Brock Mumford was the guitar player. Brock had a barber shop at Cherokee and Ann Streets in the heart of what was called Niggertown. Most of the guys in Bolden's band were barbers. Willie Warner was on clarinet and Frank Lewis played another one. Frank Keely played valve trombone with the band for a while then Willie Cornish took over. Willie and I played with Freddie Keppard, and I played other jobs with him at Milneberg and around New Orleans. Willie was a plasterer and bricklayer. None of the band could read. Frankie Dusen never played with the band, but he took it over and named it the Eagle Band after Buddy blowed his top. Frankie was one of those cheeky guys. There was another guy around named Buddy Bolden, but he didn't play nothin'.

From about 1902 to about 1906, when I joined the Rozelle Band, I played with little groups and trios for lawn parties and fish frys. All over New Orleans on Saturday night there'd be fish frys. The lawn parties were usually Monday or Wednesday night. If the guys didn't have a job to play a lawn party, they'd put on their own and hire somebody's yard. When you gave a lawn party or a fish fry you had to go to the police station and get a permit to have one that cost fifty cents. Then you had to have a policeman on duty that cost you $2.50 or $3.00. Most of the time you just hired a policeman you knew, then you didn't have to take out no permit. To advertise, you'd get a carriage with the horses all dressed up, a bunch of pretty girls, and then the musicians would get on, and you'd go all over advertising for that night. Down at the Jackson Brewery or whatever one you thought was best, you'd buy kegs of beer. A quarter keg cost you eighty cents and you got three or four, then packed them down with ice to keep them cold, and sold it for ten cents a glass. The wife usually did the cooking in the morning. She'd fry catfish, cook gumbo, make ham sandwiches, potato salad, and ice cream to sell. The man would get the beer, wine, and whiskey. When it got toward dark, you'd hang a red lantern out on the front door to let anybody going by know there was a fish fry inside and anybody could go in. A plate of catfish and *potato salad, or a plate of gumbo was fifteen cents. It usually cost twenty-five cents to get in and it was a good way to make a little change.*

Around Chicago and New York they had the same thing but they called them "house rent parties." In New York you'd even get invited to a birthday party and they'd charge you to get in. After some of the guys from New Orleans went to Chicago, they started giving fish frys in the bars. At the door you'd buy a ticket and get a lucky number. If you won the drawing you'd get a bottle of whiskey.

The fish fry that had the best band was the one that would have the best crowd. The band was usually a string trio of mandolin, guitar, and bass, and sometimes violin, guitar, and bass. String trios would get a whole lot of jobs around New Orleans where they wanted soft music. Some guys were big stars on the mandolin and would draw a crowd to a fish fry. Buddy Kyle was one of them who played a whole lot of mandolin and was very hard to book. He played a lot of jazz. Elmer Snowden played banjo like Buddy played mandolin. It was a lot more pleasure for me to play in the string trios than in the brass bands.

There were always twenty-five or thirty bands going around New Orleans. There was all kinds of work for musicians from birthday parties to funerals. Out at the lake they had some bands in the day and others at night; Milneberg was really jumping. There were a lot of string trios around playing street corners, fish frys, lawn parties, and private parties. The piano players like Drag Nasty, Black Pete, Sore Dick and Tony Jackson were playing the whorehouses. In the District there were the cabarets, Rice's, Fewclothes, Huntz & Nagels, and Billy Phillips who had the best bands. Some bands played dances in milk dairy stables and the bigger name ones played the dance halls like the Tuxedo Dance Hall, Masonic Hall, Globes Hall,

*and the Funky Butt Hall. The bands played picnics out
at the lake; they played excursions on the riverboats and
for the trains. The restaurants like Galatoires on Dauphine
Street had bands. On Chartres Street there was Jackson
Square Gardens where they had two or three bands
going. There were tonks like Real Tom Anderson's at
Rampart and Canal, and Tom Anderson's Annex at
Iberville and Basin Street. Out in the country, like
Breakaway, Louisiana, or Bay St. Louis, Mississippi, you
played dances, fairs, picnics, and barbecues. We had
plenty of fun together and there was music everywhere. If
the rest of the world was like musicians, this would be a
great world. You should see musicians back stage when
one band comes back to see another. Jesus, there's some
noise and talk.*

*The first band I was with regular was the Rozelle Band.
It was started in 1905 by my brother, Roy Palmer,
Ovette Jackson, and a guy named Rucker. I started playing
with them in 1906 and that's when Willie bought me my
first real bass. They were a seven-piece band, and that
was a big band. We had some good musicians in the
Rozelle Band. Our first guitar player was Ralph Honis.
The last time I saw him was in Chicago in 1962, he
may still be alive. Ralph gave up guitar and started
playing trumpet so we got another guitar player, Joe
Johnson. After that Ralph switched to trombone and Joe
switched to trumpet, so we got another guitar player. Joe
was a very good guitar player, but my brother had an E-flat
trumpet and Joe kept borrowing it. Sam Dutrey taught
him how to play it and he switched about 1907. Joe was very
good on trumpet and took Joe Oliver's place in Frankie
Dusen's Eagle Band later on.*

*Back in the early days, all of us guys used to hang out
at Sam and Nora Dutrey's pressing shop at Cherokee near
St. Charles Street. There were four Dutrey brothers, Sam
who played clarinet, Honoré (we called him Nora) who
played trombone, Jimmy who played drums, and Pete the*

violin player. Sam and Nora always wanted us guys to hang out at their shop and Sam would give us free music lessons to get us to stay. I never will forget when the Dutrey brothers and me went to Joe Johnson's funeral in about 1914, the preacher sure did lay it on us, but that's later.

The Rozelle Band played a lot of lawn parties and milk dairy stable dances. In those days there were milk dairy stables all over New Orleans. Guys would hire the stable and clean it out for the dances. Most of the time the owner of the stable would put on the dance. They were on Saturday, Sunday, and Wednesday nights. Most milk dairy jobs you'd get 75¢ to $1.25 to play. You'd start playing at 8:00 p.m. and the dance would last until 3:00 a.m. or 4:00 a.m. A lot of parents would come to the dance, bring their kids and stay all night. In the morning you'd be playing along and outside you'd hear the cows start mooing because they wanted to come in and get milked. When that started you knew the dance was over. Sometimes we'd be romping real good and keep playing with the mooing going on. Those times they'd open the doors, bring the cows in and run us out.

Back in those days I was real small and still had to stand on a box to reach the string bass right. I always told Willie that the string bass was too big for me to carry. I'd carry his violin or banjo on a job, and he'd carry my string bass. Then one time I got a job and had to get there right away. Willie wasn't around so I carried the bass. He wouldn't carry it for me after that.

I remember that a bunch of us young guys heard about the Holiness church back then, where you went down and rolled around with everybody. We thought it meant you could go down there, pick out a chick, and roll around with her. So we went down and they threw us out. The Holiness church was the only one that didn't consider music sinful. Their music was something. They'd clap their

*hands and bang a tambourine and sing. Sometimes they
had a piano player, and he'd really play a whole lot of
jazz. You should've heard it. Way late they added things
like guitars, trombones, trumpets, and so on. The first time
I heard one of their bands was about 1930 in Washington,
D.C. We used to hurry to finish our theater job so we
could go listen to them play. They really played some
great jazz on those hymns they played. My sister,
Elizabeth, joined the Holiness church in the late twenties
and played guitar for them. She really thought they were
somethin'. The closest thing we had to religious music
around New Orleans was when the bands played for
funerals.*

*I was with the Rozelle Band for about two years.
Around 1908 we moved to St. James Street near St.
Thomas Street. The Rozelle Band broke up and we went
our separate ways. Down around St. James Street I met
Eddie Garland; we always called him Montudie. He was
playing with the Ory Band and got me a job playing
with a little band that Louis Keppard had. It was called
the Magnolia Band and we got Joe Oliver to play in it
after that.*

The rise of a professional class of jazz musicians in
New Orleans came with the second decade of the century, and
the process was a gradual one. In the beginning a man played
as an amateur, and by attaching himself to an organized
group of older and more experienced musicians, he served a
loose apprenticeship and eventually, if talented and persistent,
was taken along on a job and handed a dollar for his
services. There was no union in those days. Jobs were booked
by individual contractors who were also bandleaders;
slowly bands like Magnolia, Tuxedo, and Eagle evolved.
For a long time, music remained an avocation for most;
every musician had a day trade. He was a barber like Buddy
Bolden, a plasterer like Johnny St. Cyr, a tinsmith like
Alphonse Picou, a cigar maker like Manuel Perez, or a
longshoreman like Pops Foster. Many leading jazzmen worked
at hard manual labor; jazz drew some of its best talents
from proletarian ranks and working-class virtues rubbed off
on the music. Bolden, Keppard, Armstrong, and Bechet
owed their reputations in part to an ability to keep going, to
pile chorus upon chorus, creating a feeling of suspense
and excitement in the listener. Of course, this demanded
instrumental technique and an abundance of musical ideas;
it also demanded an uncommon amount of sheer
physical endurance. Such demands were imposed to an
even greater degree on men in the rhythm sections, especially
the drummers and bassists. Strength, endurance, and
solidity were manifest in Pops's playing from the very first;

his beat was compelling and powerful; his tone big and alive. In speaking of Lorenzo Tio and Alphonse Picou, Pops is referring to leading members of the school of master New Orleans clarinetists who descended from the old Creole class. New Orleans Creoles were of mixed European and African blood; at one time they had formed a petite bourgeoisie class. They spoke French and prided themselves on being co-heirs of French culture. The incidence of musical attainment in Creole ranks was high. All had studied with French teachers and a few aspired to jobs in the pit bands of the French theater and opera. As colonial Frenchmen, they were one with the tradition of distinguished French reed playing. In the free and easy atmosphere of prebellum New Orleans, Creoles were considered every bit as good as white folk. The Civil War and the violent upheavals of postbellum days changed all that; the Creoles were cast down as a class, stigmatized by their fractional content of African blood. The musicians among them found themselves obliged to compete for jobs with the black man. Socially the clash between *déclassé* and *parvenu* made for a certain amount of hostility and bitterness. Musically it was benign; the emerging New Orleans style, already enriched by elements from so many diverse musical cultures, further benefited from the marriage of the two schools: the clean, pure, limpid playing of the Creoles and the rough, more dynamic style of the Afro-Americans.

"The District," as Pops points out, was a wartime casualty.

It was also called Storyville, after a New Orleans alderman,
much to that gentleman's dismay; Sidney Story had been
the author of an ordinance restricting prostitution, gambling,
and other forms of vice to a specified area in the French
Quarter (1897). Tom Anderson, proprietor of Anderson's
Annex where Pops worked, was the ward's political boss and
city councilman, as well as the owner of other cabarets,
real estate, and shares in several of the most popular bagnios in
"the District," which enjoyed the reputation of being the
most extensive area in America devoted to vice. According to
social historian Herbert Asbury (*The French Quarter*), in
1910 the official count of houses of ill repute was 175 and
the total number of registered prostitutes, in excess of 800.
Of these 700 were full-time employees of houses of
prostitution, which ranged from lowly cribs to the famous and
resplendent Mahogany Hall on North Basin Street, operated
by Lulu White. About 100 part-time ladies of the night
worked in cabarets, where they danced with customers,
encouraged the purchase of liquor, especially champagne, and
escorted interested customers to nearby rooms for amorous
asides, all as described by Pops. Knifings and fights were
common and murders frequent. "The District" swarmed with
hoodlums, burglar gangs, and the Mafia, then known as the
Black Hand. The pressures that resulted in the shuttering of
Storyville originated in Washington and came shortly after
America entered World War I. When official suggestion
was not acted upon by local authorities, the latter were

put on notice that either they would close Storyville without
delay or the federal government would do it for them;
New Orleans had become the favorite duty station for tens of
thousands of service men. The actual closing date was
November 12, 1917.
The candid spirit in which the Pops Foster story is told makes
no effort to play down the licentious environment
encountered and sometimes relished by early jazz musicians.
This association of jazz with vice hung on in the minds of
most Americans for years and died hard; the notion fitted
perfectly into widespread prejudice encouraged by the
middle-class white Establishment toward Afro-American
mores and culture.
The essential point is that musicians, like other professional
workers, depended upon jobs for a livelihood. From about 1900
to 1917, the best paying and steadiest employment for
jazzmen was to be found in Storyville. It was not until the
middle thirties with their swing bands and popular ballrooms
that conditions of employment for jazz musicians underwent
any significant change.
When Pops began working in Storyville, he was a young
man of sixteen or seventeen. Magnolia was one of the leading
bands of that time. Joe (later King) Oliver was just then
attaining the peak of his powers. Oliver, Freddie Keppard, and
Bunk Johnson belonged to the second generation of New
Orleans trumpet players who followed Buddy Bolden.

3. THE MAGNOLIA BAND IN THE DISTRICT

Music was a nice sideline to make a little change back in early New Orleans, but I never thought it would be a way to make a living. I usually had a regular job longshoring or something. My job with the Magnolia Band in the District was the first music job that was a full-time job.

When I first started with the Magnolia Band, we made most of our money on Saturday, Sunday, and Wednesday. Sunday was the biggest day and we made a little money on Monday. I used to do longshore work, drive a cotton wagon or coal wagon, and a lot of other things besides play in the band. It was pretty rough playing and working a full job too; Monday was your roughest day. On Sunday you might have an afternoon job at the lake playing a picnic till six o'clock. Then you'd get on a streetcar and go way over to Gretna to play a night job at the Come Clean Hall. Back in those days when you took the string bass on the streetcar you had to have a special pass. Over in Gretna we used to play the Big Easy Hall and the Drag Nasty Hall (it's still in Gretna). The Primrose Band that was led by Hamp Benson had the Sunday job at the Come Clean Hall until we came along and took it away from them. We had a rough band.

Hamp was a trombone player, and Joe Johnson played trumpet with them. They were guys from around the Irish Channel.

You might play a dance from eight that night till four o'clock the next morning. You'd go home then, hang up your tuxedo, put on your overalls and leave about 5:00 a.m. and catch the streetcar to the stables. There you'd pick up your mule team at 6:00 a.m. and start out for the docks to pick up a load at 7:00 a.m. Once you got your team hooked up and started toward the docks, you could sleep because your mules would follow the wagon in front. Sometimes you had a helper; he'd drive the wagon where you were going and you'd sleep. He'd wake you up to load or deliver. You got off work about four o'clock in the afternoon. If you had a Monday night job you'd go home, get a little shuteye, and start playing at eight o'clock. You didn't work late on Monday night, though. After I started doing longshore work, it wasn't so rough. I'd work a couple of hours, then put somebody in my place and go on home.

When I joined the Magnolia Band in early 1908, Louis Keppard, Freddie's brother, was the leader and manager. He played guitar. They had a job playing a house party and hired me for it. They were crazy about my playing so they kept me with them. Johnny Garland was on trombone when I first started with them, but he wasn't so good so we got rid of him and got Zue Robertson for a while. Zue could play all styles real good. He was one of the best players around. Zue could play piano very good too, but he never played it with the band. He played piano before the trombone. He wasn't with us too long, and he left to go on the road with his sister and brother-in-law in a vaudeville show. They had a comedy act named McNeil and McNeil, and Zue played piano for them. After Zue left we had Eddie Atkins on trombone and sometimes Honoré Dutrey.

Harrison Goughe was our first trumpet player. He couldn't play unless he looked at the music, and he stunk. We got Joe Oliver to come with us about the middle of 1908 when he quit the Eagle Band. Arnold Dupas played drums and Dave Dupas played clarinet for us. Emille Bigard played violin; he was Barney Bigard's uncle. The Dupas brothers and Emille were close friends. After I was with the band for a while the guys wanted to get rid of Arnold Dupas because he wasn't any good on drums. They were afraid that if they fired Arnold that Dave and Emille would quit. So they fired all three of them. When you got fired in those days they'd shove a letter under your door. All it said was, "You Are Fired." We got Jean Vigne on drums after that, but he slept too much so we fired him and got a guy named Chris. After we went into the District, we had Ernest Trippania; we called him Quank. My brother Willie replaced Emille on violin. Alphonse Picou played clarinet for us sometimes, and sometimes Papa Tio did. Picou was the only guy around who played soprano saxophone. Most guys said it sounded too tinny. Papa Tio said to Picou one time, "where're you taking that tin clarinet?" Picou got mad and they didn't speak for years over it. A soprano is very hard to tune and to play in tune. Some of the notes are beautiful and some are out of tune. Years later Sidney Bechet and I used to argue about that all the time.

Papa Lorenzo Tio was a nice old guy. He was tall and drank a lot. One night he was playing for the Magnolia Band. He was drunk and sleeping through the numbers. He'd get the clarinet up to his mouth and finger the horn but nothin was coming out. I got a broomstick, picked up his clarinet, and put the broomstick on his lap. He played the whole next number on the broomstick. When Joe Oliver got ready to knock off for the next number he asked Tio, "Tea, you gonna play this next number with us?" Tio said, "I been playing all night man, don't you like my playing?" Joe said, "What are you playing with?" He said, "My clarinet," and took a look at it. Then he turned to me and said, "You did this."

Joe Oliver joined the Magnolia Band about the middle of 1908. Before that he waited tables at private parties and played with Frankie Dusen's Eagle Band on Saturday night. He met his wife, Stella, when they were working together waiting tables. Joe got mad one night and quit the Eagle Band, and came with us. I never heard anybody down there called "King." If Joe Oliver and Louis Armstrong were called "King" around New Orleans, I never heard any of it. Joe got to cutting everybody around Chicago with his horn and that's where they started calling him "King."

Long after I left New Orleans guys would come around asking me about Storyville down there. I thought it was some kind of little town we played around there that I couldn't remember. When I found out they were talking about the Red Light District, I sure was surprised. We always called it the District.

Right after Joe joined us we got the job playing in the District. When we started I was so young, I had to be careful of the cops running me in just for being there. They didn't allow no kids in the District at night. There were two cops on every corner in the District. When I'd got to work I'd be careful to stay on the side of the street where I knew the cops. Once I got to work, I stayed inside. The girls inside would be sitting with their dresses up to their knees and I'd get to see a lot of legs. That was something in those days. Before that us kids used to go downtown just to watch the girls pull up their dresses to get on the streetcars. We used to be happy when it rained because we could see more.
Things were right on top of each other in the District. Freddie Keppard was at Billy Phillips's on one corner. Manuel Perez was on the same corner at Rice's. Our band was on the next corner at Huntz and Nagels at

*Custom House and Liberty. They were two Jew guys and
were good guys to work for. In the middle of the block
was the Tuxedo Dance Hall. It was owned by Gyp the
Blood. He went to the penitentiary after he killed Billy
Phillips and his place closed. All the guys who played at
the Tuxedo Dance Hall wore tuxedos and that's where
they got the name for the band. Even after the killing
and both places closed down, the band kept the Tuxedo
name. When all of us were playing the District, we
couldn't wait for night to come so we could go to work.
Most of us loved the District and tried to stay there as
much as we could, sometimes I didn't go home for weeks.*

*We made a dollar and a half a night, or nine dollars a
week playing the District. We were the best paid band
in the District. You could live real good on it and save
money. We hired a guy for a dollar a night to pass the
hat around for us. If a good German ship came in we'd
make ten or twelve dollars apiece in tips. Those guys
would give you all their money. The German guys would
drink wine and champagne and have a good time. The
Dutch and English sailors were kind of rough. They'd
drink beer; we had Budweiser or Schlitz in those days
and it was as strong as your whiskey is today. They didn't
spend much money until they got real drunk. The French
were nowhere. We had some beautiful girls in our cabaret
and if a good ship came in we'd pass the word for all
the girls to get out that night. A lot of the girls were
white. In those days carpenters and bricklayers made
thirteen dollars a week, and guys who dug ditches and
things like that made a dollar-and-a-half a day. I thought
we had easy sitting up on that stand playing music all
night. If you were just working on night jobs you usually
got a dollar-fifty a night. On Easter Sunday and if you
got a job playing one of those swell dances downtown
you made two-fifty.*

*Liquor at the cabarets was high. They had two kinds of
whiskey. Best whiskey was I. W. Harper, Murrayhill, and*

Sunnybrook that cost ten cents in the tonks and twenty cents in the cabarets. Second best whiskey came in a barrel and was five cents in the tonks and ten cents in the cabarets. Everything in the cabarets was about double the regular price. You used to get half of a big soda pop bottle full of whiskey for a nickel. There was only one kind of champagne, and it came in a little bottle or a big bottle. You had white wine and sherry wine, and the Italians had a drink they called Angaliquor. You could get a big cup of it for ten cents. The guy wouldn't even watch you take it because he knew you couldn't drink more than a dime's worth. It tasted something like sherry wine. I think it was leftovers from all the other wines and they only sold it in the Italian barrelhouse joints. Sometimes a good party didn't come in the cabarets until 3:30 or 4:00 in the morning. We'd have our instruments half packed getting ready to go. We'd unpack and start playing. As long as they stayed, we'd play. Sometimes it lasted until 4:00 the next afternoon. Your normal playing was eight hours, but that didn't mean nothin if there were customers in the place.

In the District none of the dance halls and cabarets served food, just booze, except when Carrie Nation would come around. She was always coming around with three or four guys to check you out. She expected food to be served and all the girls to be standing on the dance floor. If she was around checking the District, the places would call each other to let you know she was headed in your direction. The owner would get some sandwiches out on the bar and the girls on the floor. If she caught you without food or with a girl sitting down drinking whiskey, she'd break up all the whiskey in the place with her ax.

A cabaret in New Orleans had the bar in the front where you walked in. All the girls stood around in the middle of the floor facing the door. The band was way at the back, at the end of the dance floor. When you came in you picked out a girl you wanted to dance with and got some

*tickets. They cost you twenty-five cents apiece and were good
for one dance. The girl took half your ticket before the
dance, then at the end of the evening she turned them
in for ten cents each. The length of the dance was
according to the crowd, but you never played a whole
number. On a good night you'd play a half of a half
chorus. You never started and played a number all the
way through and you never stopped playing for a break. If
a guy sat at a table with a girl and bought her
champagne, he still had to give her a ticket for a dance.
The girls got twenty-five or thirty cents on every bottle
of champagne a customer bought. If you wanted to go
off to bed with her, it was fifty cents to a dollar
depending on how business was — a dollar was tops. They
could take a man out and do their little business, but she
had to bring him back to buy some more drinks. If she
didn't bring him back, she didn't come back. There were
dance hall girls in a lot of places. The big places like
Huntz and Nagel's, Eddie Groshey's, Gyp the Blood's, and
Billy Phillips's, had big seven-piece bands. The small places
had piano, or piano and drums, or maybe another
instrument or two.*

*Besides the dance hall girls, there were girls who just
stuck their heads out of their cribs. There were the big
sporting houses like Lulu White's, and women down
around where Louis Armstrong lived that were only ten or
fifteen cents. They didn't look so good though. On
Monday it was your day off in the District and sometimes
you didn't go back to work until Wednesday night. You'd
get some of the girls, a picnic lunch, and go out to the
lake. Sometimes we'd hire a little band to entertain us,
and we'd eat and swim. Everybody got along real good
and had good times.*

*All the musicians back in New Orleans wanted to be
pimps. You had a lot of girls who went for you, and
you'd put your girls to work on the line. Pimping in those*

days was a lot of guys's head line and Jelly Roll Morton was one of them. He only played piano as a sideline because then you had to prove you were doing some kind of work or they'd put you in jail. Jelly was very good looking and had some good women. We'll talk about him later, I got some things to say on him. The girls back in those days liked to have a good-looking man they took care of. The girls gave you money, bought you clothes, and sent you out looking nice. If you mistreated your girl or she caught you talking to another girl, she'd get mad and call the cops and send you to jail.

The cops didn't want no man living off a woman; they wanted you to work. If you had more than one girl on the line you had to meet them at different times and be very careful. The cops would raid the District once in a while. They'd search the girls' cribs to see if there was any man's clothes in them. If a raid was coming, the cop on the beat would warn you trouble was coming. He'd just say, "Beware Man!" Sometimes you'd get the word from Henry the bartender at the Twenty-five Club; he'd say, "Pass the word there'll be a raid tomorrow morning." When you lived in the District you only kept some socks, a toothbrush and razor at your girls, in a cigar box. When the cops would get raw on the pimps, you'd see all the guys moving out carrying their cigar box.

There were some big time pimps around the District. Even the guys who worked as musicians would be lining up tricks for their girls. The really big time hustlers, like Roy Nunez's old man, worked hard at it and made a lot of money. He had a diamond stud as big around as a nickel. Jelly always had two or three girls on the line for him and that's where he got his diamond tooth. All the pimps wanted to have diamond studs, cuff links, belt buckles, and on their teeth.

Around 1909, when the Magnolia Band was playing the District, we had Big Eye Louis Nelson working with us.

Louis had a chick working out of a crib right across the street from us. Where I was standing on the bandstand, I could look out and see her. Everytime she'd turn a trick she'd clean herself with some water and throw it out the door. Then she'd come out with a broom and scrub the front with it to draw another trick. Everytime she'd scrub, I'd mark it on the wall with a piece of chalk. At 4:00 a.m. when we'd get off, Louis would ask me how she'd done. I'd call the number. Then when we'd all meet at the Twenty-five Club, Louis would ask her how it went. She'd say, "Oh babe, I didn't do so good, I just had three." He'd say "You're a damn liar, you had five." She wondered for a long time how Louis knew how many tricks she turned. Before we'd go to work at 8:00 p.m. all the guys and girls would gather at the Twenty-five Club starting about seven for some fun and talk before we went to work. Then when we'd get off, we'd all meet again at 4:00 a.m. During the day us guys used to hang out at a pool hall at Dumaine and Claiborne. After a while Henry Ponts started putting all the names of the musicians up on the wall and serving an Oyster Loaf for fifteen cents. So the musicians started to play pool and hang out there.

I had a couple of girls on the line when I was in the District. You're down there with all the pimps and hustlers and you want to be like them. One girl I had was named Edith. Joe Oliver carried me to her and introduced me. I was only sixteen or seventeen at the time, and she was way older than me. I was scared to death of her, mostly because Joker Joe was trying to go with her and I was afraid he'd fire me. When Joe came down to her place one day and found me laying up in her bed, Joe got real hot and was gonna fire me. Eddie Groshey, our boss, told Joe, "Let the boy alone, Joe, Jesus Christ, go on out and get yourself another gal." After that Joe would tell me every night, "You go out there to see her and get cut, you ain't got no job."

One evening I thought I'd been shot down. I was going into a place called Platt's to have an oyster loaf. Just as I got to the door I heard a pistol go off. Then I heard another shot go "zing." I ran inside and hit my shoulder on the door when I did. When I got inside I knew I was shot in the shoulder and nobody could tell me I hadn't been hit.

One time, Johnny St. Cyr and I were going home one Christmas morning about 3:00 a.m. We met Tom Benton on the street so drunk he couldn't find his way, so we decided to take him home first. In those days if you were drunk out on the street the cops would put you in jail until you sobered up, and if you were with a drunk they threw you in too until he sobered up. The cops got us and we all went to jail. Johnny and I had a date to make and we had to get out. Tom seemed to get drunker, and it looked like he wasn't ever gonna sober up. We asked the jailer to bring us a block of ice. When he did we took that baby and tied it up between Tom's legs. In about two minutes he was sober and they let us out.

All the girls, pimps, and other guys who worked the District and were doing illegal things used to pay a lawyer $7.00 a month to keep them out of jail. I paid him for a while. His name was Lee Peyton. You knew you were gonna get picked up sometime if you were illegal and he could get you right out. You just called him. You hardly ever went before a judge, and if you did he'd dismiss you.

In the District the guys in the band would get four or five drinks bought for them by some guy at the bar. Some of us would keep a bottle and pour the whiskey in the bottle to save for Christmas. Christmas was a big day then. New Year's Eve was nothin for parties or dances. Everybody went to church. It was a jinx to have a dance on New Year's Eve. The Mardi Gras day was something, back about 1910. Everybody started getting together about six o'clock in the morning. We'd start fooling around and having a good time. We'd have a big wagon with a five- or six-piece band, a lot of girls sitting around on it, and kegs of beer sitting on the tail of the wagon. The band would play and we'd go around to different peoples' houses. They'd have homemade donuts, hot coffee and tea, whiskey and stuff to drink. Everybody would play and dance for a while then we'd take off for another house. That would go on all day. The people from New Orleans cut up and had their own fun. The people from out-of-town went down on Canal Street and saw the parade with about twenty floats and the bands. They didn't have any colored bands playing in the parade. Some of the colored guys played in the bands but they passed for whites. During Lent everything closed down except the saloons where you could get a drink. All the guys had a trade like cigarmaker, carpenter, bricklayer, or barber, so they'd go to work for the forty days of Lent.

People go to the French Quarter now and they think the hot spots we played were along Bourbon Street. Back then Bourbon Street was just a bunch of furniture and jewelry stores. We used to have our gold belt buckles made there.

I played with the Magnolia Band from early 1908 to the middle of 1910. After that I played with them and free lanced around. I was the bass player around there and whoever had the work that's who I was with. I was with Buddy Petit, Jack Carey's band, The Silver Leaf Band, and Frankie Dusen's Eagle Band. Later I went on the boats with Fate Marable and worked Tranchina's at Spanish Fort with Picou.

In 1910 after Gyp the Blood killed Billy Phillips, they closed all the cabarets down and we were out of a job for a while. They opened them back up in early 1911 and things were good until the war came along. In 1914 they closed the District down really tight and made all the chicks go to work. I went to work in the iron foundry driving a little spring wagon. I learned all about the foundry, how to melt iron, cast iron, light cast iron and steel. After I learned, they gave me a whole gang of women from the District to work for me. I'd have them pickin' out iron for me, and I'd sleep. Closing the District hurt the women a lot more than it did the musicians because they didn't know no other work. Most of the musicians around New Orleans didn't work the District so it didn't hurt them at all. Billy Phillips's and Gyp the Blood's places were already closed from the shooting. Fewclothes's, Rice's, and Huntz and Nagel's cabarets closed, and the Tuxedo Dance Hall. The piano players in the whorehouses were all out of work. Most of the dance halls were out of the District and only opened on Friday, Saturday, Sunday, and Monday nights. None of them closed. They kept going like before and that's where most of the bands worked.

A lot of musicians left New Orleans before the District closed. Laurence Duhé was one of the first to leave about 1907. Bill Johnson went to Los Angeles and another Johnson, Nookie Johnson, I think, went to L.A. too. Sugar Johnny left early and went to Chicago. Manuel Perez and Arnold Metoyer went up. Freddie Keppard left about 1909. They left because there were more places to work or they just wanted to travel some.

When the District closed in 1914, Joe had taken the Magnolia Band over from Louis Keppard. They had to cut down in the bands, so Joe fired Louis, the bass, and trombone. I'd already left the band by then. The band went right on down after that. Louis kept all the music that belonged to the band. I always tried to get him to give it to me. Way late he told me he got tired of carrying it around and threw it away.

38

When Pops speaks of his bass playing, he does so in the spirit of the craftsman; his candor stops short of his own accomplishments. Pops Foster was one of the great bassists of jazz and the first of its bass stylists. Jazz bass playing began with Pops and, from the band affiliations cited for his early career, it is evident that his services were even then much in demand. Magnolia, Tuxedo, John Robichaux, Armand Piron, Freddie Keppard, Frankie Dusen, and Kid Ory — these were among the leading New Orleans bands of the time; moreover these affiliations reflect considerable style differences, ranging from the melodious, almost proper dance music of Robichaux to the rough, funky, blues-ey style heard in Frankie Dusen's Eagle Band. New Orleans style was taking shape in those years. The vigorous playing of uptown (black) musicians like Keppard and Dusen was gaining in popularity, all the while absorbing the useful elements of the dying Creole tradition.

The first recordings of New Orleans jazz were made in 1917 by the Victor Talking Machine Company, the principal manufacturer of phonographs and records. After surveying the talent field, Victor decided to offer its contract to Freddie Keppard. The bandleader's refusal for fear that other musicians would plagiarize his musical ideas is one of the oldest jazz legends, and is supported by Pops Foster's statements. Victor then offered the same contract to a competent but by no means outstanding white group led by Nick La Rocca

and calling itself the Original Dixieland Jazz Band. Its
style is considered derivative by most jazz writers. Thus the
first by no means definitive jazz records were made
February 24, 1917, in New York City, there being no adequate
recording facilities in New Orleans. The first Victor release,
on the old 78 rpm ten-inch discs, was *Dixie Jass Band One-Step*,
backed by *Livery Stable Blues*, not actually a blues, but a
novelty number with minstrel show overtones, spiced by
crude imitations of barnyard fauna: hen's cackle (clarinet),
mare's whinny (cornet, muted), and donkey's bray (trombone).
Thus vulgarized, New Orleans jazz was introduced to the
American public, not as serious music, but as a novelty. It
was an instant success. The Original Dixieland Jazz Band was
signed to a long-term Victor recording contract and
embarked upon a series of lucrative bookings that eventually
took ODJB to London. The exploitation of Afro-American
musical ideas by white imitators, long the complaint of black
jazzmen, may be said to date from 1917, and Keppard's
paranoiac refusal, and La Rocca's politic and timely handling
of the opportunity to make the first records. Later Keppard
had reason to regret his decision. Keppard recorded in
Chicago in 1923, but for independent record labels and as a
featured trumpeter in bands other than his own.
The question arises: what was New Orleans jazz really like?
Documentation of the real thing waited until 1923 when the
recording industry, independents as well as major labels,

suddenly awoke to the sales potential offered by the jazz and blues market. By 1923 many of the leading New Orleans bands were working in Chicago where studio facilities existed. Among those who made records at this time were Keppard, King Oliver (Oliver's Creole Jazz Band with the Dodds brothers and Louis Armstrong), Clarence Williams (with Sidney Bechet), and Jelly Roll Morton. Pops Foster first recorded in 1924, in St. Louis, with Charlie Creath's Jazzomaniacs, for Okeh. Due to the limitations of engineering techniques, bass men were not well recorded until the late thirties; several records made after World War II offer the best examples of Pops's playing.

The most representative recordings of New Orleans jazz in its purest state are the King Oliver Creole Jazz Band titles originally made for Gennett. That company went into bankruptcy during the Depression of the thirties but the titles have been reissued (see Pops Foster Discography).

New Orleans was characterized by a flowing rhythm, usually 4/4; emphasis on melody rather than harmonic embellishment; simple forms, most often twelve and sixteen bar, derived from blues, ragtime, and marching band music; and free polyphony. Polyphony was created by the constant interweaving and intermingling of melodic lines played by the instruments of the front line, cornet, clarinet, and trombone.

4. GIGGING AROUND

When I was with the Magnolia Band, sometimes they didn't
*play rough enough to suit me. So I'd lay off once in a
while on Saturday night and go play with Frankie Dusen's
Eagle Band. They were rough babies who drank a lot
and really romped. I'd try to dance the quadrilles when
they played; I'd run and jump and kick my leg out and
have a big time.*

*From about 1900 on, there were three types of bands
around New Orleans. You had bands that played ragtime,
ones that played sweet music, and the ones that played
nothin' but blues. A band like John Robichaux's played
nothin' but sweet music and played the dicty affairs. On
a Saturday night Frankie Dusen's Eagle Band would play
the Masonic Hall because he played a whole lot of blues.
A band like the Magnolia Band would play ragtime and
work the District. They'd play* Bag of Rags, Frog Leg Rag,
Maple Leaf Rag, Champagne Rag, *and ones like that;
they were all dance numbers. All the bands around New
Orleans would play quadrilles starting about midnight.
When you did that nice people would know it was time
to go home because things got rough after that. The rough
guys would come about midnight. They were pimps,
whores, hustlers, and that bunch. They'd dance with no
coats on and their suspenders down. They'd jump around*

and have a bunch of fun. They wanted you to play slow blues and dirty songs so they could dance rough and dirty. On the boats when they got to dancing that way you had to shoot a waltz in. Sometimes it was so rough you played waltzes back to back. Back in those days I thought it was rough stuff, but today I see where they were just having fun.

None of the bands around New Orleans had singers. The only singer around was Willie Jackson. He and a guy named Nookey had a black-faced comedian act. Willie could sing pretty good. Most of the guys you heard singing down there were guys who came out of the woods somewhere with a guitar playing and singing the blues.

There were three sections of New Orleans and a lot of districts. There was Uptown, Downtown, and Back of Town. The Downtown boys, the creoles, thought they were better than anybody else and wouldn't hire the Uptown boys. Most of the guys who played the District were from Downtown. Some of the Downtown bands were the Imperial Band, the Superior Band, and the Olympic Band. The Uptown musicians had the biggest names, Buddy Bolden's band and Kid Ory's Band. Bolden's band had the biggest name around there for a long time. There used to be a lot of German bands come into New Orleans on the boats, and they'd go all over town playing and serenading people. People would throw money down to them for playing. The German bands came before the war and when the war started they quit comin'. Most of them had baritone horns, trumpets, bass drums, trombone, and alto horn.

The rich people who lived in Audubon Place were always throwing affairs we'd play. Those people would never ask how much the band was, they'd just tell you to come on such and such a night. We knew when they didn't ask we'd get more than we usually made when you told them the price. In the summertime, the rich men

*would send their wives and children away for vacation
and then throw big parties all the time they were gone.
They'd have girls, party and dance all night long. Sometimes
they'd hire a barge and a tugboat for pulling it out in
the lake to party. They'd stay out there all night having
their party while we played. The drunker they got the
more they'd tip. They wouldn't know a five from a one.*

*The rich also had places especially built for their kids to
have dances. Like a big house would be on one corner,
and another on the next corner. Then in the middle of the
block there'd be a little dance hall for the kids. We
played a lot of gigs in those places. The rich also had
music at the Audubon Club, the City Golf Club, and the
West End Golf Club.*

*John Robichaux got most of the dicty jobs like that around
town. He had the rich people's jobs all sewed up for a
long time. His band played the country clubs, restaurants
like Antoine's or Gallatoire's where the rich people gave
dinners and had dancing, private clubs like Jackson Square
Gardens or the Harmony Club where they'd have parties.
John was a big shot, and hardly spoke to anybody. He
got the best jobs around and when you hired the John
Robichaux Band you had the cream of the crop.
Robichaux's band played only what was written, but they
did play some of the Scott Joplin tunes, and if you played
what he wrote you played enough. John had the best
reading band in town. He wouldn't hire anyone who
couldn't read. I played with Robichaux's band for a while.*

*Robichaux was a left-handed violin player and his band
played mostly sweet music. For a long time they had the
only piano player with a band, it was a woman who's
name I can't remember. The other guys in his band were
James Williams, cornet; Baptiste DeLisle, trombone;
Coochie Martin, guitar; Walter Brundy, drums; and George
Baquet, clarinet.*

*There were other guys who played with Robichaux, though.
Bud Scott played guitar with Robichaux's band early. He
left New Orleans around 1905 and went to New York.
He played around New York with Jim Europe and some
of those guys. For a while there he'd go back and forth
quite a bit. When I went to Los Angeles in 1922 to join
Ory he was with Ory. Bud wasn't much of a jazzman,
he played mostly pop numbers and was a good rhythm
man. Johnny St. Cyr also played guitar with Robichaux.
Johnny was a good rhythm man too and wasn't any jazz
player.*

*There were only two drummers around town who could
read music, Walter Brundy and Zutty Singleton. Walter
was the best drummer and reader. When Walter left for
Chicago about 1918 or 1919 Zutty started playing with
Robichaux.*

*For years the guys in Robichaux's band didn't speak to
each other. It's the only band I ever saw like that. Those
Frenchmen get mad at you and just quit speaking. The
guys would pass around the music to each other and play
together, but wouldn't speak. They were all mad at each
other. Ory's band was like that for a while.*

*Way late around New Orleans the dicty people got tired
of hearing that violin scratchin' all night and started to hire
some bands who'd play some rough music for them. Jack
Carey's band, the Tuxedo Band, and some others who
could read and play some sweet music too started getting
some of the jobs. The Magnolia Band and the Superior
Band could play anything, too. The bands that couldn't
read made the most money and were the biggest talk of
the town. They were gutbucket bands like Ory's band and
for a while Dusen's Eagle Band. They played hot all the
time.*

*The other best reading band around New Orleans was
Bab Frank's Peerless Band. Bab played very nice piccolo
and a little clarinet.* High Society *was a piccolo solo and*

*Bab played it very good. The only guy who could play it
on E-flat clarinet was Picou. Most of the guys played
E-flat in the bands and used a different clarinet to play
in the brass bands. Big Eye Louis played a C clarinet so
he could read the violin parts.*

*Bab was always starting trouble with the girls in the
District. When he'd see a bunch of them standing around
he'd say, "You whores ought to get yourselves an honest job,
you bunch of bitches." They'd call him all kinds of
names and one that stuck on him was "Lump of
Corruption." The guys started calling him that. The last
time I saw Bab was in 1928 in San Francisco's Third
Street Station. I was on my way to Chicago with the Elk's
Brass Band and he was working as a Red Cap. He was
gonna come around that night where we were playing, but
he didn't show up.*

*Bab had a nice band and a very good trumpet player,
Andrew Kimball. Vic Gaspard played trombone; Charlie
McCurdis, clarinet; Oke Gaspard (Vic's brother) string
bass; Coochie White, guitar; Jean Vigne, drums; and
Bab's brother Alcide played violin. Vic Gaspard was a nice
old guy and one of the best trombone players we had
around New Orleans.*

*On the stand Vic would go to sleep. The band would
knock off and he'd start right along with them, make all
the breaks and lay his horn on his lap when he finished.
If you'd wake him up he'd grab his horn and come in in
the wrong place.*

*I worked once in a while with Bab's band to take Oke's
place. This would usually happen when there were two
bands on a date. Oke would say, "Hey, Georgie, I want
you to play a couple of numbers for me, I'll be right
back." I'd get up on the stand with Bab's band. Oke
would take off and wouldn't come back. When you'd see
him next time he'd say, "You know man I didn't even
think about coming back, I just forgot." Or, "Man I*

*couldn't get away, I had a lot of business to take care of."
This happened with a lot of other guys too, and I did
it myself so nobody thought anything about it. All that had
happened was, you'd found a hot chick and you wanted
to take off with her. It was more kicks than work to
play with both bands all night.*

*Alcide and Bab played in the Edward Clem Band before
they had their own band. That was way early when I
first started in the District. In those days the violin was
usually the leader. What that meant was he called the
numbers, stomped off, and played the violin as the lead
instrument. Alcide was the leader of Clem's band. Bab
played piccolo and some clarinet in the band. Edward
Clem was a very good trumpet player and was the
manager. Miles Ross played bass; Spencer Jackson, guitar;
a guy named "Sugah" on trombone; and a drummer that
I can't remember — he drank so much they had to put
him out of the band. The band played the Funky Butt
Hall on Saturday night.*

*Frankie Dusen's Eagle Band played the Masonic Dance
Hall and the Eagle Saloon. The Saloon was at Perdido
and Rampart streets and that's where the band got its
name from. They even played there when it was Buddy
Bolden's band. We used to call them "the Boys in Brown"
because they had regular brown military uniforms with
caps that had their name on them.*

*There were a lot of different guys who played in the
Eagle Band. Dandy Lewis was the bass player until he
blew his top. Then Bob Lyons was with them. He had his
room right over the Eagle Saloon. If you picked up a
chick there, you rented Bob's room for a quarter. You'd
take her upstairs, knock out, and then go on home.
There were a gang of trumpet players in the Eagle Band.
John Penerton was the first one I remember after Bolden,
then Wild Ned was next. Both of them played what they
could see and played very good. I wouldn't call them*

*hot jazz players though. Then they got Bunk Johnson. Bunk
claims he played with Bolden, but he was in the Superior
Band when Bolden was around and I played with them.
The first time I saw Bunk was at the Fairgrounds at a
big picnic in 1908. There were three bands playing: John
Robichaux's band was in the pavilion; I was with Manuel
Perez's brass band playing dance music outside; and the
Superior Band was out on the racetrack and were playing
for people to dance on the grass. The Superior Band was
a ragtime band. They had Bunk; Buddy Johnson, trombone;
Peter Bocage, violin; Rene Baptiste, guitar; Billy Moran,
bass; Big Eye Louis, clarinet; and Walter Brundy, drums.
Bunk played a beautiful horn and nobody else around
New Orleans played the same style Bunk did. He played
the most beautiful tones. After a while Bunk got to
drinking so bad they fired him and then he went with
Frankie Dusen's band.*

*Frankie Dusen was the only guy that Bunk was afraid of
and who could make Bunk listen. Bunk would show up to
play so drunk he'd he draggin' his coat across the floor
and couldn't find the bandstand. He'd try to put his
horn up to his mouth and hit his nose or chin, and
couldn't even find his mouth. When he was like that or
just passed out, the guys would say to him, "Hey Bunk,
here comes Frankie." Bunk would straighten right up. The
reason was Frankie used to beat Bunk just like you beat
a kid. He'd get a razor strap or his belt and whip him.*

*Bunk was a very nice guy when he was in the Superior
Band, but when he went with the Eagle Band, he really
got to drinking bad. In those days the saloons never
closed and Bunk never left the Eagle Saloon. He'd drink
till he passed out and then sleep it off on a pool table,
get up, and start drinking again. If we came along and
wanted to shoot pool, we'd just lift Bunk off and lay him
on a bench. He got to drinking so bad that even the
Eagle Band fired him about 1910 and no one else would
hire him. He left town with a minstrel show and I didn't*

*see him again until 1937 when I was playing with Louis
Armstrong's band in New Iberia, Louisiana. Bunk claimed
he got Louis his first job, but Bunk wasn't even around
New Orleans when Johnny Dodds and Peter Bocage got
Louis the job with Fate Marable on the boats. Until that,
Louis just had one night gigs with different bands.*

*After the Eagle Band fired Bunk they got Joe Oliver, but
he quit and came to the Magnolia Band. Joe Johnson, who
was with us in the Rozelle Band, took Oliver's place. I
think drinking with all the heavy drinkers in the band half
killed Joe Johnson. He, John Penerton, and Wild Ned all
died young of TB after playing with the Eagle Band. Joe
left the Eagle Band too and went with Jack Carey's band
until he died in about 1914.*

*I went to Joe's funeral with the four Dutrey brothers. All
of us used to come around the church when Joe was
singing in the choir and get him out to play jobs. We'd
signal him we needed him to play; he'd drop out of the
choir and come with us. At the funeral the preacher was
really mad at us and thought we'd caused Joe to die. He
started talking about how Joe was a good church man
and how we pulled him out of church. He really started
laying it on us. I remember him yelling, "AND they're
here right now, one of them carries a string bass around
on his back and it's the devil riding his back." He was
sure talking to us. None of the guys played trumpet like
Joe. He played the middle range and played it rough
and beautiful.*

*Frankie Dusen was a slick guy with the girls. He was a
tall good looking guy with straight hair and kind of dark.
Out in the little country towns the straighter your hair was,
the more the girls went for you. Every time Frankie would
play out in the country he'd carry some girl back to
New Orleans with him or have her follow him. There was
always some country girl coming around who'd left home
and was looking for Frankie to stay with. He'd let them*

*stay with him till he got tired of them, then he'd send
them home. He wasn't married as long as I was
around there.*

*One night Frankie and I went over to Pearl River,
Mississippi, to play a date with a local band at a tenant
farm town. After we finished, we went to wait for the
ferry to carry us to the train that took us back to New
Orleans. At the ferry landing two tough guys with pistols
caught us. They wanted us to drink with them and play
the string bass and trombone. Frankie was always sick,
but he was sicker than usual and wasn't supposed to do
any drinking. I tried to talk them out of making Frankie
drink but they just said, "It won't do him no harm," and
kept telling him, "Come on and drink big boy." So we
drank and played, and they put their pistols away. It
didn't seem to do Frankie any harm. Mississippi was a
dry state, but they had the best corn whiskey in the
world there.*

*The only musician I ever had a fight with was Emille
Bigard while I was playing with Ory's band. Emille was a
nice guy and a very good violin player. We were always
friends before and after that. Ory's band had a job up
around Ory's home, and I was playing it with him. After
the job was over the band was riding back home in a
closed wagon. There was a curtain over the back. I
wanted the curtain down so I could sleep and Emille
wanted it up for fresh air. I put it down and he put it
back up. I hit him and knocked him down and that was
all of the fight. I was very sorry about it. When we were
both in the Magnolia Band, we used to rehearse at his
daddy's house. Barney Bigard was a little tiny guy then.
He used to come around and pull our music off the
stands.*

*There were a lot of players around New Orleans who
would only play with their own band. Some of the guys
were Ory, Frankie Dusen, Albert Nicholas, and George*

Brunies. Those guys couldn't read so good or couldn't read at all, and they couldn't go into other bands and start playing. Ory couldn't read too good and couldn't find a note either. If he wanted B-flat he couldn't slide up to it and blow, he'd have to slur his horn up to it. He'd stop when he got on the note. I was always able to play with any band by reading or playing by head. That's the way I played with so many bands around town. The toughest thing to play is music for toe dancing. Man, it goes so fast and has to be right on time when those toes touch the floor. They tell you you've got to hit it right with the catch. I remember once when they told Zutty Singleton to hit it on the drums when the man caught the girl. Zutty hit it, but both of them were clear off the stage when he went "bang." Very few jazz musicians can play for toe dancing.

Johnny Dodds didn't read so good and the only band he had played with was Ory's. When work got tough he was thinking about going to St. Louis or Chicago and wanted to know if I thought he could play with the other bands. I told him he should study and train himself to play with any band and not just one like he'd done. I also told him that if he could play with a band in New Orleans, he could play with the bands up there. He said, "Yeah George, that's what I did wrong, I got wrapped up around one band and I sound funny with anybody else." After that he studied and could play with all bands.

About 1914 I was playing with Ory's band doing advertising for an affair the Turtles were putting on at National Park. That was the ball park at Third and Willow. Chiff Madison was playing trumpet; he was a little bitty guy and played good trumpet. His brother Stone Madison was playing guitar, and he was a fine player. Stone was a heavy drinker and would get sloppy drunk. He was sloppy drunk that day and Ory told him to get out of the wagon and go home. Stone got out, and Chiff did too. So then we needed a trumpet player very bad. After we went a few blocks, I saw Louis Armstrong standing on a corner watching, and said, "Hey, there's little Louis over there!" We got him in the wagon and he went on to play the advertising with us, and then we carried him out to the park to play. The only thing Louis could play then was blues, so we played them all day long. Louis played them good too. As far as I know, that was the first time Louis played with a big-time band. Before that Louis just played with kid bands.

Chiff and Stone Madison never did play in Ory's band again. Stone drank himself to death right after that and Chiff didn't play too much after that. Chiff played string bass too, and when I went back to New Orleans in 1937 he was playing string bass with a little band around there. Up until Ory's band most of the bands had names like Crescent Band, Silver Leaf Band, Eagle Band, and so on. The only bands I can remember who used guys names were John Robichaux's band and Buddy Bolden's band. Ory started playing in New Orleans around 1906 and was a hot baby around town. People liked his music and it was very hot. His band could play a waltz and make it hot. He made such a big hit that all the other bands started changing the names of their band to the leaders name to copy Ory. The Crescent Band became Jack Carey's Band, the Silver Leaf Band started being called Albert Baptiste's Band, the Young Olympia Band became Ernest Johnson's Young Olympia (there were four or five Olympia bands around there). Ory's band would have still been going strong today if he hadn't let his wife run his band.

Eddie Garland, we always called him Montudie, was always fighting with Ory so I'd go play with Ory's band and Montudie would play with the Magnolia Band until they started getting along again. A lot of us guys would trade off among bands to take out of town jobs. Whoever didn't have a day job, or could make it, would go.

Montudie started with Ory about 1908, and those guys played and fought together nearly all their lives.

I got Johnny Dodds his first job around New Orleans with Ory about 1909. Johnny was working at the rice mill and at noon they'd stop for lunch. He would come out on the road to sit and eat his lunch, and practice blowing his clarinet. I'd be driving by on a wagon and I'd stop to listen to him play. After I heard him several times out on the road, I asked him if he wanted a job playing in a band. He said he did, so I met him that night and carried him down to Globe's Hall where Ory was playing. He played with the band and Ory liked the way he did, so he hired him. Ory's band was the only one Johnny played with until he left New Orleans.

Not too long after Johnny got the job with Ory, he got salty with me because I wouldn't go with Ory's band and went with Joe Oliver instead. Johnny wanted to get rid of Montudie and wanted me to take the job. But Montudie and I were great friends, and I wouldn't take a job from him. We are still great friends, and he's one of the last of the New Orleans guys. The only time we'd take each other's jobs was when we were having rough times with our own band and wanted to get out for a while. I've heard people say Johnny was mean but he wasn't. Sidney Bechet and Leadbelly are a couple of mean babies, but not Johnny. I used to visit him and his wife in Chicago years later. I knew her before he did and used to try to check in on her.

The guys around New Orleans used to call Johnny "Toilet." The guys in Ory's band started it but all of us picked it up. The whole Dodds family was short and they all had bad hearts. It seems like the whole family died of heart trouble.

Before Johnny Dodds went with Ory, their clarinet player was Johnny Brown. He also played violin. Once he got started playing his clarinet, he couldn't stop, he just couldn't make no ending. When you got to the end of a number, you'd reach over and pull the clarinet out of his mouth so he'd stop. After I carried Johnny Dodds to Ory, Johnny Brown went to violin. Him and Dodds sat beside each other in Ory's band for years and never spoke to each other.

William Ridgley was the leader of the Tuxedo Band. I got Papa Celestin his first real job playing with them before they left the Tuxedo Dance Hall. That was back about 1909 or 1910. Back in those days we called him Sonny, and that's what I still call him; way late they started calling him Papa. Sonny was working for the Texas and Pacific Railroad making $1.25 a day and gigging around with different bands. I used to go over to his house and hang around waiting for him to come home. I'd cut wood so his wife could fix his dinner. One day they needed a trumpet player in the Tuxedo Band and I came to tell him to go down. He didn't want to go; he was afraid that he'd lose his job on the railroad. Finally, he decided to take it. The last time I saw him around New York we were talking about it, and he said he wished he'd quit and gone to work in the District a long time before he did.

The Tuxedo Band had William Ridgley, we called him Bebe, playing trombone; Sam Dutrey, clarinet; Sonny, cornet; Ernest "Quank" Trippania, drums. Johnny Lindsay played bass; later he took up trombone and turned out to be a real nice trombone player. His brother Herbert played violin in the band. Herb played a whole lot of jazz like Stuff Smith and he was very good. Herb was a mean guy who was always getting into some kind of trouble and he looked just like me. The cops were always picking me up for his trouble, but I knew the station cops and they knew him, so they'd let me go. He had a beautiful wife and sometimes she'd come to dances we were playing. If she danced twice with the same guy, Herb would get off the stand and take her home. My brother used to do the same thing. They were a couple of jealous babies.

It was a rule in New Orleans if you didn't play any blues you didn't get any colored jobs, and if you didn't play lancers you didn't get Cajun jobs. White jobs didn't care what you played. The Tuxedo Band didn't play any blues; they were a ragtime band and didn't get colored jobs. They got a lot of show jobs and later on some of the dicty affairs.

I played some with Freddie Keppard before he left New Orleans. Freddie played what I called a walking trumpet. It was TaTa-Ta-Ta-Ta. They were straight clear notes. When Freddie left in 1909 he took five guys with him: Eddie Vinson, trombone; Big Eye Louis Nelson, clarinet; a guy named Clerk on piano; Jimmie Palao on violin; Dink Johnson was their first drummer, then they had a guy named Mac. Up North all the bands had to use piano. Clerk got sick and died. They needed another piano player so they sent for Fess Manetta to go up and join them. Freddie was the first guy to go North with a whole band and play. They played at the Palace Theatre first, and they had that job booked before they left. When they got up there they found the field was so big, they started booking three or four jobs a night. They'd play two hours one place, then go on to another and play two hours. Chicago paid more than New Orleans and those guys were doing great. It wasn't long before the New Orleans guys were taking all the work away from the Chicago musicians. They were so popular the union had to give them a card. Freddie and his Creole Band really opened up Chicago for the rest of the guys to go.

Freddie also had the first chance to record, but passed it up because he was afraid other guys would steal his stuff. Instead the Dixieland Band did and that's how ragtime music got the Dixieland name. The guys called Dixieland players today think the loudor you play, the better you are. Most of them are just loud. Back in the early days we used to play soft and hot. Most of the time it was so quiet you could hear the people's feet shufflin' on the floor.

Freddie was a big guy when he was in New Orleans, but he wasn't fat. After he went North he started drinking a lot and put on whiskey fat. Freddie left when I was playing the District. One of the last jobs we played was a banquet at Perseverance Hall on Berry Street. The societies would have them on Mondays to get new members. They would lay out a big table a block long full of meat and all kinds of food, and they'd have a barrel of wine and a couple kegs of beer. There was no whiskey unless you brought it yourself and everybody waited on themselves. You only got a dollar for playing one but you got all you could eat. Freddie, George Baquet, and I were in the band that played that banquet.

The last job I played with Freddie was a Labor Day parade. The parade was put on by the longshoreman's union. They had white unions and colored unions; each one had their own parade and picnic. For the parade all of you just got out in the street and played and marched. The union followed along behind you and up front the grand marshal led you. Freddie and I were playing in Jack Carey's Brass Band. Freddie was on trumpet and I was on bass drum. The old guys in the brass bands would make the new players play the bass drum to get their rhythm and most of the drummers around New Orleans started on bass drum in a brass band. The only drummer out of New Orleans that never had much rhythm was Zutty Singleton. Zutty was a hardheaded guy who was headstrong and would never listen. He was always wanting to fight about something but he never did, he just wanted to make a big disturbance.

Back in those early days we used to do a lot of funny things like when one of the bands would be playing and

a good looking chick would come in the place, one of
the guys would say "Gee, I know she's got good bread."
Then someone else would sing it and pretty soon the
whole band would be romping along playing and singing,
"Gee, I know she's got good bread." It meant she's got
good pussy. We used to do a lot of things like that.
Another one was, when you'd leave the stand you'd say,
"Don't kill me when I'm out." Sometimes they'd pick up on
that and sing it. It meant don't drink the bottle up while
I'm gone.

There was so much work around New Orleans, it's tough
to remember it all. It seems like there was always some
new kind of job we were goin' on. One of the darndest
was on a boat going to British Honduras around 1914 to
play for the passengers. We took a five-piece band of
the four Dutrey brothers and myself. Honoré was on
trombone; Jimmy, drums; Pete, violin; Sam, clarinet; and
me on bass. We only got as far as Spanish Honduras
and they turned us around and ran us back to the
States. They wouldn't even let us off the boat; we unloaded
our cargo, loaded up with rock ballast, and started back.
We didn't have any idea why we were sent back until
we got to the jetty in New Orleans. Then the river pilot
got on and told us it was because Germany was blowing
up all the boats coming out of New Orleans. We were
scared then. During the rest of the war we'd load up
boats with mules, horses, and things, then the Germans
would sink them right out of New Orleans; it was
something brutal.

Another kind of job we used to get was on train excursions
on Sundays. They were run by the Southern Pacific and
the New Orleans and Great Northern railroads. It cost a
dollar for the trip. You'd load up about nine in the morning
and ride until eleven in the morning when you'd be at
Homer, Breakaway, Thibodaux, or White Castle, Louisiana.
The train would pull off on a siding there, and you'd stay

*there the rest of the day. The band would play, the
people would picnic and dance under the trees, and
everybody would have a lot of good times. At six in the
evening the train would start blowing its whistle. Everybody
would load back in the train and head back for New
Orleans. It took a long time to get everybody out of the
woods, then we'd make a lot of little stops so you'd get in
about eleven at night. The band would play going out and
until six in the evening, but we'd sleep or party after that.*

*We used to have a club of musicians at the Twenty-five
Saloon before we'd go to work and after we'd get off.
There was Freddie Keppard, Jimmie Palao, Eddie Vinson,
myself, and a couple of other guys. When we'd get off
work, we'd buy six drinks all at once for each of us. We'd
drink them and then go leapin' off home. Only sometimes
we'd have to help each other out of the place. Most of the
time after everyone met at the Twenty-five Club, we'd start
home. Usually we'd stop off at whoever's house we came
to first and stay there till 6:00 a.m., when the saloons opened.
At six we'd cut out for the saloon to have one last taste
before bed. Sometimes we'd end up staying together until
6:00 p.m. that evening, when we had to start getting ready
to go to work. One of the things we used to do for each
other was go around to your house and serenade you if it
was your birthday. We'd go over after work at 3:00 a.m.
or 4:00 a.m. and play numbers we knew you liked. The
neighbors liked it too. A lot of times we'd go serenade
good customers, or people we just liked. If a guy was
building a house, we'd show up and play and help him
build it. When we were playing, we were having fun, the
pay sometimes just made it a little bit sweeter.*

*Easter Sunday was the biggest day of the year. You'd be
hired from one year to the next to play it, and you made
more money than any other day. In the day you'd play a
picnic and at night you'd have another job playing a dance.
New Year's Eve was nothing. Everybody was Catholic and*

all the saloons were closed, so you went to sleep. Out in the Garden District there was a bunch of Irish guys who called themselves the Buzzards who used to give lawn parties. They used to wear blackface and dress up like buzzards on Mardi Gras day. The Odd Fellows had a parade they held on the tenth of May we used to play. That was Odd Fellows Day.

No matter what dance hall or affair you were playing in New Orleans you stopped for an hour at midnight and had dinner. Whoever was having the dance fed the musicians. Usually you'd have a big plate of gumbo, rice, and French bread. Gumbo was just a pot of water with okra, onions, and celery that you boiled. Then you'd put in the meaty parts of crab all cracked up and add cut-up chicken, ham, sausage, oysters, shrimp, or any other kind of meat you wanted to. You let that baby boil down till it's thick, then serve it with salt and pepper on it. Then you eat. At the dances they'd usually have a whole washtub of gumbo, a huge pile of rice, and all the French bread you could eat. When you ate your midnight dinner you'd usually go down the street or around the corner and find musicians in another band to talk to. Back then you never talked about music when you were away from it. Most of the time you talked about parties, booze, and chicks.

All the musicians ate good at rehearsals too. Everybody wanted you to rehearse at their house so they could have some fun. It would be just like a lawn party. They'd have beans and rice, gumbo, a keg of beer, or a half keg of claret wine. We'd start rehearsing about eight o'clock in the evening and play till eleven or midnight, according to when the juice ran out. You'd be rehearsing inside and people would be dancing outside. After we'd play a number three or four times we didn't need the music anymore. Everybody who played in New Orleans had to memorize. I can still remember a lot of numbers we played back in 1909. I hear one bar of it and I'm ready to romp.

59

Continuing with his story, Pops describes the everyday events that were accompanied by live music in New Orleans. In those years there were no media; no radio, no sound movies, no TV, no phonograph records, indeed, no sound amplifying equipment. Music was the product of flesh-and-blood musicians. Bands were hired for informal affairs as casually as one engages a caterer today. As an omnipresent part of life in New Orleans, music was fittingly present at wakes and funerals. The city contained a number of fraternal organizations that functioned as burial societies, taking care of the final expenses of their members and seeing to the proper interment of the deceased. Musically these were impressive affairs. The coffin was carried to the cemetery followed by one or more bands moving with slow step and playing a dead march. At the burying ground, the band played a hymn or gospel song while the coffin was being lowered into the ground or, as was more often the case in the marshy terrain of the Delta, being placed in the family vault. Immediately following the interment, the band struck up the most lively of tunes, *Didn't He Ramble* ("Oh, he rambled all around, all around the town, 'till the butchers cut him down . . .") and, with this as the theme, marched in quick-step time back to town where, as often as not, drinking, feasting, and revelry followed ("as the deceased would have wanted it").

That great raconteur of New Orleans mores, Ferdinand Jelly Roll Morton, has discoursed at length on the New Orleans funeral (Library of Congress recordings). The music of dead march and the playing of such hymns as *Nearer My God To Thee*, and *Didn't He Ramble* have been re-created successfully on phonograph recordings (see Pops Foster Discography). In a little known interview, Louis

Armstrong described the excitement of New Orleans funeral music:

McDonald Cemetery was just about a mile away from where the Black Diamonds (MY TEAM) was playing the Algiers team. When ever a funeral from New Orleans had a body to be buried in the McDonald Cemetery they would have to cross the Canal Street ferry boat, and march down the same road right near our ball game. Of course when they passed us playing a slow funeral march, we only paused with the game and tipped our hats as to pay respect. When the last of the funeral passed, we would continue the game. The game was in full force when the Onward Band was returning from the cemetery, after they had put the body in the ground, they were swingin' It's a Long Way to Tipperary. They were swinging so good until Joe Oliver reached into the high register beating out those high notes in very fine fashion. And broke our ball (game). Yea! the players commenced to dropping bats and balls, etc., and we all followed them. All the way back to the New Orleans side and to their Destination. . . . [Louis Armstrong, interview, "Scanning The History of Jazz," Jazz Review (July, 1960)]

Brass bands were also in great demand at street parades and carnivals. By the turn of the century, New Orleans parade music had broken away from its formal 6/8 meters, inherited from the old French and German marching bands of colonial days, and become a jazzed music. New time signatures, cross-riffing, countermelodies, and the inevitable polyphony had transformed the old styles into a new kind of music that was unique in America, or for that matter, the world. When a number of bands participated in parades on more important holidays, these affairs became a kind of musical tournament in which the merits of the rival organizations were judged by the crowds.

5. LAWN PARTIES AND FUNERALS

Joe Sullivan was the union leader for the longshoremen,
and he had all the best musicians working on longshore work.
That's what I did most of the time I wasn't playing. Joe
lived out in the Irish Channel and would throw lawn
parties on Monday nights. He'd ask the guys who worked
for him to come out and play. He always had the best
band and would draw a big crowd. Joe took care of us
and if a good boat was coming in, he'd send word around
to the guys to come to work. If a ship needed tying up,
it took about ten minutes and you got paid for a half a
day at forty cents an hour. Joe tried to play string bass,
but he wasn't any good.

The colored musicians in New Orleans didn't have no
union but man we stuck together. Like if we had a job
playing the St. Charles Hotel alternating with Bab Frank's
band and it was Babs time to go on and Oke Gaspard his
bass player hadn't shown up, I'd go right over and start
playing with them until he showed up. He'd do the same
thing for me. The guys never tried to cut each other's
throat; it was better in those days without no union. In New
Orleans the colored bands had most of the work.

The whites had a musicians' union and my cousin Dave
Perkins was president of it. They didn't know he was

colored. He played tuba and trombone, taught music, and lent out instruments. He played with all of the white bands. The white union would book colored bands on a job with a white band if someone wanted one. A lot of times the white bandleader would be the man who booked you. Many times the Brunies Band would have a job for another band and they would call us. They'd also use Jack Carey's band, Amos Riley's band, or someone else. The Dixieland band in those days was a mixed band and nobody paid any attention. The leader was Larry Shields and you had Achille Baquet, George Baquet's brother, playing with them. He was colored and went all over with them. Shields, Brown, Fisher, and the band went on to New York and made some records and were the first New Orleans musicians to do that. That's how everyone got to calling our music Dixieland because of the name of their band. Their band was one of the hottest white bands around New Orleans. Leon Rappolo lived about a block from me and I knew him and Shields, Fisher, and Tom Brown. They used to play with eight pieces sometimes and had a baritone horn then.

Out at the Halfway House they had white bands. After a while the Brunies Band got that job. They played for a lot of dances all around New Orleans where I'd be on the same bill with them. The last time I played on a bill with them I was with Amos Riley's band and we were playing a country picnic out of Bay St. Louis, Mississippi. I missed the train with the other guys and had to get a later one. When I got to Bay St. Louis I hired a wagon for fifty cents to carry me out to the picnic. When I arrived they weren't there and I started eating sandwiches, having some drinks, and having a good time. When Amos's and Brunies's bands arrived they were sure surprised to see me. They'd gotten lost and couldn't find the place. The Brunies and their band played very good.

Johnny Lala had a white band around New Orleans. His daddy owned the French Market. He played trumpet in the band and was very good. Tony Parenti was another Frenchman, a cajun guy that had a band. It was one of the best white bands. Tony could read very good and I was on some of his records way late. He left New Orleans and went to Chicago. He loved to gamble and got in trouble with the big gamblers in Chicago, so he skipped to New York. After awhile he got in trouble in New York and left for Florida. He got too slick there too and came back to New York. Tony will see you walkin' down the street and bet you you can't walk. If you play cards or dice with him you've got to keep your eyes on him or he'll slick you.

In New Orleans the colored had Lincoln Park and the whites had White City Park where a big brass band played. The band had two drums — a snare drum and a big bass drum. They played marches and things like that.

None of the white bands had any violin, guitar, mandolin, or string bass. Only the colored played them. Lately a guy down there named Souchon has been saying he played guitar with white bands down there. I never heard of him and I never heard of any white guitar players around New Orleans. The first white guitar players I saw were Eddie Lang and Dick McDonough way late when I was in New York. The white and colored musicians around New Orleans all knew each other and there wasn't any Jim Crow between them. They really didn't much care what color you were, and I played with a lot of them around New Orleans.

Every saloon in New Orleans had a shed on the front and a bench under it. There was a board nailed up out there where they hung coffee cans up. If you wanted a drink you'd pull one down and rinse it out, then go in and get it filled with beer. That was a "can of beer" in those days, and it cost you ten cents. When you got through drinking it, you'd hang it up. At lunch time, three or four guys would buy a can of beer and pass it around. In those days the Italians owned nearly all the grocery stores and

*saloons. When I worked doing longshore work we used to
hang out at Tony's Saloon at Celeste and Chapatula. It was
strictly for colored. Most saloons had two sides, one for
whites and one for colored. The colored had so much fun
on their side dancing, singing, and guitar playing, that you
couldn't get in for the whites. It was the same way at
Lincoln Park for the colored; you couldn't tell who it was
for, there were so many whites there.*

*There were a lot of dance halls around New Orleans. The
Love and Charity Hall was way up on Carlton near Eagle
and Poplar. St. Dominic's Hall was on Maple, two blocks
from Carlton Street. Elizabeth's Hall was at Camp and
Fallon Streets; it wasn't a very big hall and we'd play it
on Monday nights. All over town they had lawn parties.
There were a lot of them in Niggertown; that didn't mean
what it does today. A lot of colored lived there but most
of the people weren't colored. It was just a place to us
and I lived there for awhile and so did Brock Mumphrey,
Henry Zeno, and Joe Johnson. In the Greenville District out
on Carlton there were a lot of lawn parties, and in
Pensiontown too, that's on Oak at the Protection Levee.
Pensiontown was mostly colored. We played the Irish
Channel and there were a lot of Irishmen out there. Frankie
Dusen lived in the Twelfth Ward which was another section
of town. On Tuesday nights we used to play for the Bulls
Club in the Garden District; they'd have two bands playing.
If you joined their club you had your own key, and the
club was for gambling and carrying on. The Turtles was a
big club and they used to put on dances at the ball park
at Third and Willow. Back of the District was called the
Battlefield. When we were kids we used to go back there
and pick palms to sell for Easter Sunday. We'd also go
there to catch crayfish and pick blackberries.*

*I met my first wife playing a lawn party out in the Irish
Channel and married her in 1912. Her name was Bertha
and her folks couldn't stand me. Her folks were poor and
hated me playin music for a livin'; they didn't think it*

*was enough for anybody to do. Back then everybody
classified musicians as bums, which they were — a musician
was just no good. If a girl was with you at a dance
nobody would talk to her, she was a bad woman. It was
very rough to find a room to rent if you were a musician.
I stayed with Bertha about ten years. After we got married,
I sent her to school. She got so smart she didn't want to
do nothin'. In 1922 I left her for a short trip to Los
Angeles to play with Kid Ory and haven't seen her since.*

*The worst Jim Crow around New Orleans was what the
colored did to themselves. The uptown clubs and societies
were the strictest. You had to be a doctor or a lawyer or
some kind of big shot to get in. The lighter you were the
better they thought you were. The Francs Amis Hall was
like that. That place was so dicty they wouldn't let us come
off the bandstand because we were too dark. They would
let the lightest guy in the band go downstairs and get
drinks for all of us. They hired one guy they called Foster
who entertained them all the time. He was as black as the
ace of spades, and he was very smart and spoke eight
different languages. When he finished entertaining he had to
go into a little room and stay there. Some of the societies
were so bad they wouldn't even let black people go in.
There was a colored church in town that had seating by
color. The lightest ones down in front and darker and
darker as you went back. There was a place over in Biloxi,
Mississippi, where they had albinos. They had white kinky
hair and couldn't see good during the day. We used to
play dances for them, but they wouldn't let you into the
dance unless you were an albino. The Negro race has
always been crazy. They're the most mixed-up race of
people you ever saw. You get every color in the Negro
race, the skin is different, the eyes, the hair is different
color and kinky or not so kinky.*

*In Washington, D.C., way late I was playing a dance for
the colored mint workers and the colored mail carriers. The
mint workers were lighter than the mail carriers. They had*

themselves roped off and wouldn't allow the carriers on their side. We moved the whole band over to the mail carriers' side and told them this was our kind of people over here. That was the only dance I ever played where the colored people came on time. Usually colored don't show up at a dance until eleven or twelve and the band starts at eight or nine. You've played your brains out by the time anyone gets there. That's why by the time the people show up the guys are all drunked up sometimes. The colored usually stay until three or four in the morning.

A lot of people have talked about the funerals the colored used to have in New Orleans, but they don't mention the wakes. I guess that's because they only saw the funeral going by in the streets. The wakes for the dead were the big thing. They also called the wakes "Coffee Boats" or just "Boats." They'd lay the dead man out in the parlor on what was called a "coolin' board," and everyone would sing hymns over him. You'd drink coffee, beer, wine, and whiskey, and they had sandwiches to eat. Guys who could sing and knew all the hymns were in demand and got invited to all the Boats. There were always a couple of guys who hung out with us who could sing the hymns. They'd invite us to the Boat to sing or we'd go and stand outside the window and they'd pass sandwiches out to us. They didn't play any instruments at the wakes, just sing and get drunk. People would get carried away shouting and clapping; the girls would faint because some guy could sing so good. They were just as happy a time as the march home from the burying. If you went to a wake you couldn't make it to work the next day.

One night we went to a Boat for a small guy who'd died. Everybody went to the back of the house to drink and eat, and left him alone in the parlor. This woman named Charlotte snuck in the parlor, took the dead man and propped him up in the corner. When we all came back in the parlor he wasn't on the "coolin board." Everybody started looking around for him and then we saw him in the corner. Everybody headed for the door and a lot of people got hurt getting out of there. Charlotte was sitting across the street watching everything and laughing. The judge gave her thirty days in jail for hurting the people.

A whole lot has been written about colored funerals in New Orleans. We used to play a funeral two or three times a month. They always buried on Sunday for a long time, then they started burying on Mondays. No matter how much of a bum a guy was his friends would pass a cup to get money for a funeral when he quit the scene. If there was any money after paying for the funeral the widow would get it. The guys would rent a set of tails for the grand marshal, hire a brass band, and buy some flowers. Going out to the cemetery the band would play hymns like Nearer My God To Thee *and* When The Saints Go Marching In *very slow. These are hymns and you never played them fast or jazzed them up. You also only played hymns at church services, never in the District. In the thirties when I was in Louis Armstrong's band we nearly got run out of a little town in Texas for playing* When The Saints Go Marching In *at a dance. As soon as they put the guy in the ground, the trumpeter would hit a couple of high notes. When the trumpet hit the last note the bass drum would start off. Boom boom, boom-boom-boom, boom-boom-boom-boom, and then everybody would take off on something like* Didn't He Ramble. *We'd play jazz music all the way back. I played the string bass in the bands.*

Today guys are always asking me about the funerals and brass bands back then so they can play like them. Up here when they try they always have a guy with cymbals, or a stick, lead the band. In New Orleans the trumpet player led the band. He hit a couple of notes and you started. Up here someone has to blow a whistle to get them started. All the guys in New Orleans used to wear band uniforms and they looked very nice. I used to put it on and carry my bass by a strange girl I wanted to meet. That would start her talkin'.

Out on the beaches the colored had their side and the whites theirs. On the train out to West End the train would stop and the colored would get off on one side and the whites on the other. The colored side was Milneburg. At West End and Spanish Fort, which was an amusement park for whites, they hired colored bands.

We'd get a lot of jobs to go out to those little towns in the country. Sometimes they'd hire one or two New Orleans musicians to play with a local band, and sometimes they'd hire our whole band. At the dances in the country or over in Mississippi, white people would come to the colored dances. The whites would sit on the bandstand or in front of it and listen to the music and watch the colored people dance. Sometimes they would have a roped-off section for white spectators, and sometimes we'd play two nights; one for the whites and one for the colored. At colored dances there'd usually be as many whites as colored. Over at Bay St. Louis in Mississippi, we had a sheriff who wanted to go to one of the dances so bad he opened the jail and brought all the prisoners with him. He'd buy the boys beer and gumbo. He said it was one time he could get out and have some fun. The next day going home we saw the sheriff and the prisoners out workin on the road.

The first time I ever saw a barbecue was at one of those country dances. They dug a hole in the ground just like a grave, and put some kind of bark in it that they'd burn down to coals. Then they'd put some metal rods across the top and lay a half a hog on to barbecue. You could smell the meat cooking for miles and miles. You'd get hungry the minute you smelled it. I didn't know what to call it at first so I called it "hog on the ground."

We used to play over in Algiers at the Perseverance Park and the Perseverance Dance Hall. When I was still a kid I had a little thing going in Algiers with an older woman for a long time. I wanted to fool around with older women then. She was a friend of George Hooker's wife. George was a baritone horn player with the Onward Brass Band

*and he had a nice little wife. I used to go to his house
a lot when he wasn't home to see his wife's friend. Her
husband was a bad man who was a barber. I'd meet her
at George's house, then we'd go in the bedroom and do our
little business. Then one of us would take off, then the
other would take off. I went with her for years. I played
a dance at the Perseverance Park every Sunday. Man,
they sure had some beautiful women around Algiers.*

*Once I was playing Magnolia, Louisiana, and I was walking
a local chick home after the dance. We were walking
behind these two old hens and all they could talk about
was those bad old musicians and what they did. It gave
me fits. Musicians were nowhere in the South. If you'd play
a dance in the country, you'd carry a few girls along to
entertain at the dance. If any of the local guys would
talk to the show girls, the local girls wouldn't have anymore
to do with them because they'd been out with those bad
old show girls. Show people were classified as nothin' and
musicians were rotten. They weren't no good either. We did
a lot of funny things in those days. We were always being
put out of hotels for the stuff we did. All of us made a
lot of noise and had a lot of pleasure. We thought it was
funny to get put out of a hotel.*

*In Baton Rouge, Louisiana, there was the Toots Johnson
Band. It was very good and Guy Kelly played trumpet with
them. They wanted me to go to Montana with them, but
I found out it was very cold there and it was wintertime.
I told them I wouldn't go because it was too cold, so they
wrote a letter to find out. When they got the answer they
found out it was, so they didn't go either.*

*Over in Bay St. Louis, Mississippi, one time, we were
playing advertising for a dance that night. I was on the
back of the wagon playing bass and we went under a low
tree. The neck of the bass caught on a limb and we both
went swinging out. Then the limb broke. I landed on the
bottom and the bass landed on top of me, so neither of
us got hurt. Everybody but me laughed their heads off.*

"In those days it was called *Rag Time Music*," recalls
Louis Armstrong, "and when ever there was a dance or
Lawn Party the Band of six men, would stand in front of the
place in the sidewalk and play a half hour of good ragtime
music." [Louis Armstrong, "Scanning the History of Jazz,"
Jazz Review (July, 1960)]
Pops expands on Armstrong's idea — piano ragtime composers
like Scott Joplin and James Scott wrote it down and the
New Orleans musicians were first to play the music on other
instruments. Certainly ragtime was one of the main
ingredients of the New Orleans musical broth. Ragtime made
its first appearance at the Chicago World's Fair of 1893.
Along with a dancer called Little Egypt and an authentic
troupe of musicians from Dahomey, a piano-playing contest
was one of the many exotic features of the fair. The
piano-playing contest went on for days, attracting a great
deal of attention from the public and the press. Several of the
contestants played a novel, peppy, rhythmic style that a
writer in one of the Chicago newspapers described as "ragged."
Somehow the name caught on and the emerging style came
to be known as ragtime. This was in the day when every
respectable American home had its own upright piano.
Ragtime caught on rapidly. Simplified versions of the
complicated virtuoso pieces played by ragtime specialists
enjoyed a large sale, and a publishing industry devoted
exclusively to ragtime piano compositions appeared in most

cities of the East and Middle West.
The centers for serious ragtime playing (and composing)
were in Missouri. By 1900 schools of ragtime, led by brilliant
performers and supported by composers and publishing houses,
were located in Kansas City, St. Louis, and Sedalia. Most
of the leading composers and players were black. Ragtime
was a written rather than an improvised music, requiring
composers with training in harmony and performers with a
sound foundation in piano technique, for rags were difficult
to play well. Ragtime forms themselves appear to have been
derived from brass band music, the most common being
AA BB A CC DD, with a modulation at the halfway point.
The harmonies were those heard in the brass band compositions
of John Philip Sousa and Arthur Pryor, to which the
public ear had been conditioned by these and like
organizations during several decades of popularity.
This sort of material had a strong appeal to musicians in the
evolving jazz bands of New Orleans. To the precise format,
simple key modulation, familiar harmonies, and strict (2/2) time,
jazzmen made their inescapable modifications. As had
happened with brass band music, time became free and
more flowing, and also more complex; harmonies were blued
by flatting the third, seventh, and sometimes the fifth; and the
New Orleans spirit of improvisation soon saw to the
creation of polyphonic textures. Among the most popular
titles, first appearing in the form of piano ragtime music,

to be taken up by New Orleans bands were *Maple Leaf Rag*, *The Entertainer* (Scott Joplin), *Climax Rag* (James Scott), *Sensation Rag* (Joseph Lamb), *Bugle Call Rag* (Eubie Blake), *Twelfth Street Rag* (Euday Bowman), *Harlem Rag* and *Buffalo Rag* (Tom Turpin).

Pops's discussion of individual jazz style in New Orleans, in the chapter that follows, is extensive and detailed. The musicians named were founding fathers of style on cornet, clarinet, trombone, and the instruments of the rhythm section.

Louis Armstrong and many others have testified to Joe Oliver's position as the dean of New Orleans cornetists. Sidney Bechet's discography is one of the largest in jazz; Bechet first recorded in 1923 and continued to make records until 1959, the year of his death, in France. In the present chronicle Jelly Roll Morton appears as a controversial character, which is the way most jazzmen saw Morton: a man with great talent, but a still greater ego, given to endless conversation and boasting. Morton's memoirs, recorded for the Library of Congress by musicologist Alan Lomax, remain a prime document of jazz history.

Morton's playing, both as a solo pianist and a bandleader, may be heard on several reissues available today. Tony Jackson did not record. Where available, listening references are furnished in the Pops Foster Discography.

6. JAZZMEN

When people ask me about who started jazz I tell them I
give the guys in New Orleans the credit for playing it, but
the ragtime composers most credit for writing the music.
None of the guys who wrote ragtime came from New
Orleans. Ragtime music is different from other music because
it's a happier kick, and Dixieland is an even happier kick
than ragtime. Ragtime is regular 2/4 time and Dixieland
is fast 2/4 time, between 2/4 and 3/4 time. What's
called jazz today was called ragtime back then,
and the blues back then was called honky-tonk music.
Bands that played ragtime usually didn't play nothin' else.
Some bands you played with you had to play waltzes,
schottisches, and polkas, but these were too dicty for the
ragtime bands. If you danced to ragtime you could grab
the chick and squeeze her anyway you wanted to. We
played a lot of blues too. Blues were rough and dirty. The
blue notes are the strongest notes you can play.

The guys who wrote ragtime for us were Scott Joplin, Tom
Turpin, and Walter Jacobs. We should give a lot of credit
to St. Louis and Kansas City for those guys. I never met
Walter Jacobs; he was in Kansas City and I never was
around there much. Tom Turpin was around St. Louis when
I was. I was around St. Louis so long a lot of the guys

will tell you I'm from there. Tom and his family ran the Jazzland Dance Hall there. I played there a few times with Charley Creath and Dewey Jackson.

I remember one time Charlie Creath's band played there at a promotion for Jack Johnson the boxer. Jack, his manager, and his sparring partner were big crooks. They'd put on a thing, collect all the money, and catch the train before they'd pay anybody. I heard about this and told Charlie to get his money early if he wanted to get it. Charlie stayed at the box office and got it as it came in.

Tom Turpin was a cracker, that's what we called a very light-colored person back then. He was thin and about my height. Every once in a while he'd come around where the band was playing with a new number and say, "I'd like you boys to try this." We'd play the tune and he'd get an orchestration of it. He'd thank us and take off. I never knew him to talk much to anyone, but Tom sure wrote some good numbers.

Scott Joplin and Tom Turpin both came from Texas then worked around Kansas City and St. Louis. Joplin went on to Chicago and then New York. He left St. Louis before I got there.

In order to play Scott Joplin numbers right, you've got to be able to read. A whole lot of the guys back there couldn't read and didn't want to learn. They'd call the guys who could read "cute guys." The bands that couldn't read could play nothing but choruses. They'd play nothing but chorus after chorus.

Jazz is happier music than any other, the beat and the tempo make it. When the white boys started playing it they thought it had to be played fast and loud. Joe Oliver and Manuel Perez used to play together with the Magnolia Band in a little small room and didn't blast anybody out. Nowadays you've got to stand back from the band or get your ears blown out.

*For a long time the violin was the top instrument around
New Orleans, and then for a while it was the clarinet. Most
of the time it was the trumpet. The violin and clarinet could
play a whole lot of melody that the trumpet couldn't play.
If they don't announce a number that the trumpet plays,
you can't tell what it's playing. In all your ragtime bands
your trumpet, trombone, and clarinet were your brass, then
you had your guitars, drums, and bass for rhythm. The
fiddler usually could read and taught the rest of the band
the numbers, and played a whole lot of everything. That
was for a full seven-piece band, and that was a big band.
Your brass bands were usually around ten pieces and didn't
go over twelve. They played all kinds of dance music.
When you got a job with any band around New Orleans,
the first thing they put you on was the bass drum for your
rhythm. You'd beat that drum, boom, boom, boom, boom;
boom boom boom boom. It was straight marching band
rhythm. Later it changed. The first snare drums I saw in
the bands were the bodies of five string banjos. The guys
would cut the neck of a banjo, lay it down on a chair,
and beat it. They didn't have no stands. The guys liked
them because they had a tinny sound. The bass drum had
a cymball on the side to play with the sticks. After a while
they had a sock cymbal on the floor that you patted with
your foot. Finally, they hooked up a hammer to the foot
pedal that worked the mall on the bass drum, when you
hit the foot pedal the hammer hit the cymbal and the
mall would beat the bass drum.*

*In the early days when you had a solo, the other
instruments were always doing something behind the solo.
None of the guys took their horns down for a chorus to let
another guy play a solo. When the band knocked off, the
whole band romped on a tune from your left hand to
your right corner. The music was written so you couldn't
take down your horn. You could take your horn down to
dry your lip, but you took it right up again. If any of the
instruments would quit playing, the manager or whoever*

hired you would come right over and say, "What's the matter with that guy, is he tired?" or, "Your lip sore, man?" In those days we all sat on stools or chairs so we didn't get so tired of standing like you do today. About 1920 or 21 guys started taking down their horns after they'd blown a chorus. Now the rhythm guys are the only ones who work hard. They play all the way through and the bass player stands up all the time.

The instrument I've played most is string bass. I also play tuba and a little guitar, I have played cello but I wasn't so good. The string bass is part of the foundation of a jazz band. It's like a leg on a table. The bass and the drums are the foundation that the rest of the band works on. I don't think the bass or the drums are solo instruments, they're the rhythm, and I don't like to play solos. What I like to do is get to romping on a fast number and slap out a good rhythm.

The bass isn't a loud instrument, but it cuts through the band. It goes zing, zing and just keeps cutting through, you can feel it. When I start playing a number I don't tune up before a number, I wait till the number gets started then I play while I tune what I need.

I don't know who started the pizzicato bass. It was always in music and I don't think anyone around New Orleans invented it. When we used to pick the bass we'd hold onto the bow at the same time, now they have little things called bowcaddies you put the bow in while you pick. I still usually hold onto the bow while I pick unless I'm going to slap the strings too. In New Orleans we'd have two pick notes in one bar, then you'd go six bars of bowing, and maybe have one note to pick. You can't put your bow down and play that way. In New Orleans we picked two beats to the bar and in New York we started picking four to a bar. Now we pick four or eight beats to a bar or full note.

I first learned to bow the bass, then I started doing a lot of picking. Pretty soon everybody else was picking too, so

*then I went back to bowing. Before long everybody would
be bowing again. It seems like I've been switching like that
all my life. I always thought Henry Kimball was the
greatest bass player around New Orleans and he never
picked. When he went to work on the boats for the
Streckfus people, they told him to go around to me and
get some ideas from me. Ever since I'd watched him at
Lincoln Park as a kid he was my idol, and I was very
embarrassed. My brother Willie told me to go ahead and
show him how to pick up on the bass, so I did.*

*Drummers are the biggest problem bass players have. It
seems like they're always trying to drown out the bass by
hitting the cymbals. Sometimes they play so loud you can't
even hear the trumpet player. In my life I've played with
a whole lot of bad drummers and a lot of good ones. Baby
Dodds and Tommy Benton are a couple of good ones.*

*There were two different types of trumpet players in New
Orleans. The jazz type played hot and made the band
swing. Most of them played like Armstrong, only they
started way before him. They had a nice peppery style.
They were guys like Joe Oliver, Wild Ned, Buddy Bolden,
John Penerton, Buddy Petit, Freddie Keppard, and Louis
Armstrong. Their styles were pretty much alike. Then you
had the guys that played straight and played more for tone.
They were your sweet trumpet players and played real
well in a band. The guys in their bands had to put their
own swing in the music and make their own feelings.
These guys were Bunk Johnson, Papa Celestin, Arnold
Metoyer, and Manuel Perez. They really played beautiful
tones, but they wouldn't make their own breaks off the
melody like the hot trumpet players would. If they had to
play a break, it had to be written for them. Bunk would
make his own breaks though, even though he was a sweet
player.*

*After the guys from New Orleans got around, guys from
the East and West, all of them, tried to play like the guys*

from New Orleans. A lot of the guys around New Orleans were just loud trumpet players. I think Wild Ned was better than Bolden. Bolden was just a chorus man, he wouldn't play a whole number. Most of the New Orleans bands of the day, you didn't hear them play a full number. The Ory Band and the Eagle Band never played a whole number. If they played Sweet Georgia Brown, *they'd just play the chorus and none of the other part. They never did make no coda, they'd end on the coda and make their own ending.*

My favorite trumpet player was Joe Oliver. He played a whole lot of horn. Joe had all kinds of things he put on his horn. He used to shove a kazoo in the bell to give it a different effect. A guy named Tony who played with us in Cairo, Illinois, got a guy to make a thing you put in your horn with two kazoos in it. He had another thing that had about four kazoos welded together that really gave the horn a funny sound. Those babies sold like a house on fire all over the country and Joe didn't get nothin for it.

Freddie Keppard and Joe Oliver both used to play with a handkerchief over their fingers. Both of them did it for kicks to bug other guys and didn't do it very much. Sometimes Joe would do it to keep guys from learning a new number we had. We used to have musicians clubs where you paid fifty cents dues. We'd write away for numbers by Scott Joplin, Tom Turpin, or Walter Jacobs. For a dollar you got four numbers. When we got a number nobody had, we'd cut the title off the sheet and write "Some Stuff" up there and put a number on it to keep track of them. If a guy would ask what it was, we'd say "Some Stuff" and that way he couldn't order a copy of it.

Joe Oliver didn't drink hardly at all; he just chewed a lot of tobacco. He used to get a big pack of stuff they called "King Bee Tobacco." He'd hook one finger in the pouch and pull tobacco out, that was one chew. He'd chew it and blow his horn. At the place we were playing there was a hole in the floor where Joe used to spit. He spit there so much it rotted the wood out. He had real bad teeth and pyorrhea that bothered him a lot. Joe was still chewing tobacco when he died. I tried it a few times, but it made me sick.

When we were working the District, Joe and I used to have dinner together almost every night before we went to work. One night I'd buy and next night Joe'd buy. I'd have one hamburger and a glass of milk. Joe would have six hamburgers and a quart of milk, so I always got stung. Back then I had a girl who'd send me some lunch to eat at midnight. Joe and my brother started telling me, "Man don't eat that stuff, it's poison. Somebody's trying to knock you off and that food just ain't good for you." Then they'd say it was OK if they ate it because the poison wasn't meant for them. Then Joe and Willie would sit and eat my lunch. I fell for that for a long time.

We had a couple of nicknames for Joe, one was "Tenderfoot." He had corns all over his feet and they were always sore. Sometimes they'd get so bad he could hardly walk. He'd buy real big shoes so he'd have lots of room in them. He had a bad temper and if we wanted to make him mad we'd throw a book down by his feet. He'd jump and really get hot. One night we were playing the Big Easy Hall and Joe got mad at some gal. He threw his trumpet case at her and knocked a big hole in the wall. She said she was gonna go get her gang and clean us out, but she never came back.

Another name we had for Joe was "chalk" because of his eye. He had a big white spot or growth on his eye, and we called them chalk eyes. Joe and I were both pool friends. We used to play a lot to see who could take the money from who. Willie played a lot with us. We'd play straight pool or what you call rotation. The guy who broke usually got all the balls in and the others guys wouldn't even *get a chance to shoot. I was very good until I started wearing glasses way late. Joe didn't talk very much.*

Joe and I were always booking dates for each other when we'd play a dance. Up on the stand you were always trying to get dates with the girls for after the dance. Sometimes you'd book three or four girls to wait, and sometimes all of them would wait. Then you'd have to make it out the back window of the dance hall. We'd be up on the stand and Joe would say, "I've got a couple over here." and I'd say, "Man, I've already got two for us over there." It was tough when both of them wanted me or both wanted Joe, we'd have to split them off easy. Back in those days people didn't want their girls hanging out with musicians. They thought we were dirty rats and tramps. Anytime you played music you had a bad mark against you. Back then the slick guys would wait til you were making time with some chick, then they'd roll up and say, "Hey man, how about loaning me a deuce?" They're too embarrassed not to give it to you. It always works. After Joe left New Orleans he started running around with those funny little chicks and spending all his money. When he didn't have no money left, them funny chicks kicked him out.

In New Orleans if you got thrown in jail and you worked you got two days for one. In about 1911 I got sent to jail for thirty days. They claimed I was shooting dice on the street, but I wasn't. I stayed in for two weeks working and having fun. We swept the yard and cleaned up. The guys would sing the blues and keep rhythm with their brooms. The sounds were beautiful. Joe nearly went to jail when we were in the Magnolia Band. All the bands used to wear uniforms. The caps had the name of the band and "Leader" or "Manager" on those guys hats. The first uniforms we had were green and we wanted some blue ones too. Joe was our treasurer and he was supposed to order them from Western Uniform Company in Chicago. They cost $12.00 apiece which was a whole lot of money then. For about a month there Joe and I went around playing pool, drinking

*all day, going to baseball games, and having a good time
on Joe's money. I didn't know it, but then Joe wrote a letter
to the band and had someone mail it from Chicago. It
said that the Western Uniform Company had burned down
and we couldn't get our uniforms or our money back. The
other guys got wise to it and wanted to throw Joe in jail.
The Western Uniform Company wanted to furnish the
lawyers to get Joe. On one side was Sam Dutrey, Arnold
Dupas, Dave Dupas, and Emille Bigard, and on the other
was Louis Keppard and I. We said, "We don't want to
put Joe in jail and we won't stand for it." We promised to
pay the money back. So I worked driving a cotton wagon
for about two months to help Joe pay the money back.
Everybody got their money except me. Joe never did pay
me and died owing me money. That's why I'd never make
records with him.*

*Buddy Petit was another one of my favorites. He didn't
hit a lot of high notes like Armstrong did, he played down
in his horn, in the low range. Everything he played was
low, nothing way up there and he wasn't any loud trumpet
player. He was strictly a jazz player and was very pleasin'
to listen to. Buddy couldn't read. A lot of the young guys
were like that — they just wouldn't learn. I played with
Buddy's band at Spanish Fort in about 1915. Bechet played
clarinet with Buddy for a while and then we had George
Boyd; a kid named George Washington played trombone;
another kid named Chester played bass for him before I
did; Fasco played drums, and then Chinee Foster did.*

*Chinee and Buddy used to both stammer. When Chinee
would start to say something Buddy would break in and
say, "'aaaaw sssshut up aaaaand let a mmmman what can
ttttalk, talk." Chinee also played with Papa Celestin and
Jack Carey. George Washington was a little bitty guy, he
was shorter than Jimmy Archey. He was in reform school
the same time Armstrong was and he played tuba in the
reform school band with Louis. One night we were playing
and this real ugly guy with one eye and big red lips came*

up to George Boyd and said, "My word and honor George, you're an ugly man." The whole band cracked up and we couldn't play for laughin'. George was ugly but the guy who told him was twice as ugly.

Buddy and I used to get limber drunk on the bandstand. We couldn't even stand up. Buddy drank more than I did, and he'd get so drunk we'd have to tie him down to keep him from knockin himself out. I don't remember him getting into any trouble except for hurtin' himself. Buddy was drunk all the time and he finally drank himself to death.

Buddy's father or stepfather, I don't know what he really was, was Joe Petit. Joe only had one tooth in his mouth but he played the loudest valve trombone you wanted to hear. I don't know how he did it. Joe had a horse that got sick and laid down next to their house. The horse started kicking around and got under the house, then he died and after a few hours started to swell up. He raised the whole house up and they couldn't get him out. Finally they called the aggravatin' wagon to come and pull him out. You had to pay $2.00 to have them come and haul a horse or mule away. Big Eye Louis was Buddy's cousin.

Two other jazz trumpet players I liked were Joe Johnson and Louis Armstrong. Louis and I used to drive coal wagons around New Orleans. I worked for Pittsburgh Coal and he worked for Tennessee Coal. Every morning we used to meet at a joint and have some whiskey. One morning I'd buy and the next he'd buy. When Louis was playing at Tom Anderson's with my brother, Willie would play the tunes on the violin so Louis and Albert Nicholas could get them down. In all Louis's books and things he never mentions Willie. Willie could read very good and play any stringed instrument. He taught me more about playing the bass than anybody, and he played with most of the good bands around New Orleans. Louis should've given him credit for the things he taught him. Kid Shots Madison and Kid Rena were high range jazz trumpet players like Louis was.

Manuel Perez was a wonderful trumpet player and a nice guy. He was one of the best. Manuel and Joe Oliver were working in a thirteen-piece brass band for a while and you could hear those two trumpets over all that other noise. Both of them were very powerful guys. Manuel and all those Creole guys were carpenters and cigar makers. If you needed a house built a gang of them would get together and build you a nice four room house in a day. They'd play music, drink wine and beer, have gumbo and sandwiches, and have a picnic building a house for you.

Louis DuMaine fooled around with the trumpet a long time before anyone would hire him. He played sweet and could read more than most young trumpet players we had down there. He was good and wasn't no loud trumpet player. I got him to come on the boats with us. He made one trip and got sick. He stayed sick for a long time. People loved his playing but he was too sickly to stay. Years ago the doctors never knew what you had, they just took your money and that was it. Sometimes you'd get well and sometimes you'd go the way of Fat Henry. That means you quit the scene or died.

Frank Keely was a very good trumpet player. He was one of the first guys to leave for Chicago. That was about 1907 before Sugar Johnny who went in about 1908 and Freddie Keppard who went in 1909. Frank would come to New Orleans and stay a while after that and then go to Chicago for a while. When Freddie left he had a lot of jobs lined up and somebody would get a group to play them. The last job I played with Frank was a pick-up group we'd gotten together to handle a job Freddie had gotten playing a picnic at the lake. Frank was a bad kind of guy, rough and hard to get along with. He used to make all kinds of funny sounds on his horn, one was making it sound like a chicken. Joe Johnson used to do that too. The last time I saw Frank was in Henry Martin's barber shop in New Orleans about 1926 or 1927. Henry was a drummer. His shop was on Custom House between Franklin and Basin.

*That's where the sporting house cribs were and after they
ran the girls out the cribs made nice barber shops.*

*Amos Riley was a violin player first, then he started playing
trumpet. He had his own little band. It was one of the
uptown bands. Amos was a nice little trumpet player but
not too good. My brother was with them for a while. Alec
Smith played string bass. He also played some guitar and
he was one of the guys who taught me some things about
string bass. Amos also played with the Silver Leaf Band
and the Gold Leaf Band around the Irish Channel. Albert
Baptiste was leader of the Silver Leaf Band. I played with
both of these bands around 1910, 1911, and 1912, but
they didn't get much work. Another trumpet player who
used to play the big dances with the Silver and Gold Leaf
bands was George McCullen. He was a nice trumpet
player and worked as a cotton grader. He also played with
Robichaux's band. His son was named George, and he
played trumpet and was a cotton grader too.*

*Another Uptown band was the Primrose Band that was led
by Hamp Benson, the trombone player. Joe Johnson was
their trumpet player when he first started out. It was a
reading band. One night Hamp collected the money that
was due the band and they never saw him again. About
fifteen years later, about 1925, I saw him in St. Louis.
That was the only trouble I knew of around New Orleans
of the leader paying you off. You sure had trouble with
the guy who put on the dance or party, but you never had
any trouble with the bandleader.*

*Willie Hightower was a trumpet player who had a little
band that played St. Catherine's Hall on Saturday nights.
Willie was a real nice guy but he didn't play enough horn
for me. There were quite a few nice guys around New
Orleans who didn't play much horn. I had worked with
Joe Oliver, Freddie Keppard, Manuel Perez, John Penerton,
and guys like Hightower weren't high-powered like they were.
Willie had Baby Dodds on drums, and Roy Palmer on*

*trombone, and I can't remember the rest of the guys
names. Roy went from guitar to trumpet to trombone to
baritone horn. He was playing the baritone the last time I
saw him in Chicago. Hightower was a carpenter for his
regular job. Dave Perkins taught him the trumpet and Dave
taught most of the guys around there. Willie left New
Orleans about 1914 or 1915 for Chicago.*

*Tig Chambers was a cornet player and a barber that had
a little band. Little James Williams was his clarinet player.
His father, James Williams, played trumpet with Robichaux's
band for a long time. Little James came out here to
California and died out here. Yank Johnson played valve
trombone (his brother Buddy played trombone in the
Superior Band); a guy named Nini was on drums; Pete
Dutrey, on violin; Emmett Johns was the guitar player. Johns
went to Chicago and quit music to run a kotch game. He
played string bass too. Another guy we got was Willie
Humphrey on clarinet after Little James left for California.
I played with Tig's band in about 1919 and was with them
for a pretty good while. We used to work the Willow
Lawn every Monday night; it was at Josephine and Willow.
One night Tig made me mad and I walked off the job on
them and never came back.*

*There was one guy named Thornton Blue who played real
good trumpet, and I played in his band around 1912 or
1913. We mostly rehearsed and didn't have no job. I also
worked with him driving cotton wagons for Grants. Blue
used to play very loud and at a funeral one day he was
blowin' so hard, he just dropped dead. He lived out in the
Irish Channel and had his own little band. Kaiser Josephs
played clarinet, Fasco was the drummer, and Oscar
Kendalls the bass player. Their trombone player was named
Black Joe. He hit those screaming notes like Armstrong did
on trumpet. For awhile he had New Orleans all sewed up,
no one could hit those notes but him. That's all he could
play though, he didn't know nothing about music. He had to
slur his horn up to a note like Ory, but he could play with*

*any band that way. He also played with Kid Rena, Tig
Chambers, and some of the other small groups around
town.*

*One of the reasons it's hard to remember a lot of the guys
who played is there aren't too many pictures of them. A lot
of the guys didn't want any pictures of them made. They
said it was a jinx.*

*Jack Carey played trombone and got the Jack Carey
Crescent Band together. Jack was a guy who had kids
all around New Orleans. We'd be playing a place and
someone would come around saying one of Jack's kids had
died. Sometimes we'd play two or three funerals and find
out they were all for Jack's kids. I played with Jack's band
in about 1914 and 1915. In Jack's band we had an old guy
named George Caldwell who played clarinet. He used to
carry three clarinets on a job with him, a C, B, and A.
Some nights I'd unscrew all the clarinet parts and put them
back together wrong. He'd spend the whole night trying to
get them together right and he'd be a hot baby. Another
clarinet player we had was Willie Humphrey. His father,
Jim Humphrey, played trumpet and couldn't stand me. He
was always saying, "You'll never be a musician," and "You'll
never play nothin'." We'd be playing some place and he'd
start worryin' me with, "You'd better learn how to read." I'd
say, "Oh man, go hide yourself," or "Don't rush yourself, go
ahead and play." Those old guys wanted to read and play
different than we did. Jim Humphrey and John Robichaux
wanted to play one way, and Freddie Keppard and us
wanted to play ragtime. Old man Humphrey didn't like
anybody who couldn't read, and he didn't like the way I
picked the bass; he wanted me to bow it. His son Willie
came to L.A. and played tenor sax around L.A. with Mutt
Carey for twenty years. Willie had a son named Little
Willie Humphrey that played clarinet too. I played with
him on the boats with Dewey Jackson. Jack Carey's band
was out at the lake playing a picnic one Sunday. Everybody*

had brought a big picnic basket and put them up on the bandstand then went to stroll around. Jack started snooping around through the baskets tasting the wine. He reached over a mud puddle to get one bottle and fell in with his white suit on. After we quit laughing, we went off and stole a tablecloth and wrapped him up in it. He played all afternoon standing up there wrapped in that tablecloth.

George Filhe was the best trombone player around New Orleans. He worked in the early Imperial Band. George was great, very musical. He knew his horn and could hit a note; he didn't have to look around for it. Another very good trombone player was a guy we called Sugah. He played with Edward Clem's band, and they mostly played the Funky Butt Hall at Liberty and Franklin.

Willie Santiago was a good guitar player, when he wasn't sleeping. He'd sleep on the bandstand all night long, then when we got off he'd want to shadowbox and horse around. There was a beer and wine place called the Alley that Willie hung out at. If we needed him for a job we'd go there and get him. He played with a lot of different bands and was with the Olympia Band for awhile.

Big Eye Louis Nelson was the best ragtime clarinet player we had down there. He was strictly a jazz clarinet player. He didn't know as much music as the other guys like Picou, George Baquet, Charley McCurdis, Sam Dutrey, and those guys who were straight clarinet players. Louis always played a "C" clarinet and played the violin parts. Albert Nicholas was almost as good as Louis, but he wasn't as fast and he never could read too good. Albert was very hard to get along with, he had his own ways and he didn't want nobody to tell him nothing. His uncle, Wooden Joe, played a beautiful trumpet. Johnny Dodds was very good on the stuff he knew. But Big Eye Louis played hot and played more clarinet than anybody in those days. I really liked to play with him because he had such a nice style. Big Eye Louis was the greatest clarinet player I ever played with.

Next to Big Eye Louis, Sidney Bechet played the most jazz clarinet around New Orleans. I started playing with Sidney when we were both kids and both of us played in the Jack Carey Band for a long time. I'm six years older than him. Sidney played the District with Jack Carey. He was an ear musician and a wonderful jazzman. One night we ended up in jail together. He was fooling around with a chick at a dance out at the lake. She pulled a knife and stabbed him. I grabbed a stick and started after her. When the cops came we told them we were playing. They took us to jail and then let us go. When we got back to the dance, she thanked us for not getting her in trouble. Sidney was always wanting to fight but they never did come off. Sidney is all for himself and jealous of everyone. He and Louis Armstrong were two of a kind, you didn't make any showing when you played with them. I played with Sidney all of my life and I used to tell him, "Your name is in the lights, man, nobody can hurt you. If you've got a good band with you, it makes you better." But he wouldn't listen. Sidney could play a little on almost any instrument and could pick some guitar.

Sidney wasn't the only guy who got into trouble. Black Benny, the drummer, was always in trouble and lived in jail most of the time. He was a very good bass drummer and when we had a funeral to play, we'd go down to the captain and get him to let Benny out of jail to play. Then after we'd take him back to jail. His house was only about four blocks from the jail. When he did something wrong, the police would send some kid down to tell him to come in, and he'd come. Once Benny got a new serge suit and was wearin' it when a policeman picked him up and handcuffed him. He told the cop he was gonna wear the suit that day and he'd go to jail the next day. The cop wouldn't let him go, so he got mad and started runnin' while he was still handcuffed. He drug the policeman through the mud in the streets and tore his new serge suit. Afterward he said he was sorry. Benny was a mean ignorant guy — he'd hit a woman with a piece of wood or a bat or anything and knock her down. That's how he got killed. He hit this woman and then turned his back on her and she cut him down.

Jean Vigne the drummer had kids all over the country. Wherever we'd land, he'd have a kid there. We couldn't go anyplace he didn't have a kid. Jean had a funny color, you couldn't tell what he was. He was light brown with straight hair. His wife was very light too. One night we were playing the Come Clean Hall over in Gretna and before we started I asked Jean, "Hey, you got any kids over here?"

He said, "No man, it's not like that."

Afterwhile the doorman come up to him and said, "Mr. Vigne, somebody wants to see you at the door. He says he's your kid."

Jean jumped off the stand, went and got him, and introduced him around. Afterward I said, "How many more you got over here Jean?" He said, "Oh, man, I don't know," in that fine voice of his.

Jean had a business in the District selling bundles of wood and little buckets of coal to the girls so they could keep warm while they stood in their doorways and hustled tricks. He was partners with MacMurray who was another good drummer. He could read like Cottrell and was more of a show drummer. Jean must have had a million kids, it seems like everywhere we played a funeral some kid was coming up calling him "daddy." One of his boys, Sidney Vigne, was a wonderful saxophone player and he had a band on the boats for a while. Another of his kids I got to know was "Babe." He was a sweetback boy who hung around with all the musicians a lot, but never played nothing.

Lorenzo Stall the guitar player was another guy like Jean. When us musicians would go out in the country towns we'd always make out. Lorenzo was so popular he'd have girls

*waiting outside his room for their turn to go in. He was
very good looking. Lorenzo played mostly guitar and was
good; he played some banjo later on. He was with the
Jack Carey Band and Ory's band. He ran a little pressing
shop and had a couple of girls on the line for him all the
time. When he died I was with the Gold Whispering Band.
Our whole band went and marched behind him.*

*The first slide trombone I ever saw was brought down to
New Orleans by a cousin of mine, George Williams. That
was right around the time we left the Plantation. George had
gone up to Memphis and gotten a job with W. C. Handy's
band. He got the slide trombone there and brought it
back with him on a visit. Up until then there were nothing
but valve trombones The whole town was excited about
them and guys started buying them. There were a whole
bunch of numbers you could play on them. The minstrel
shows started using them a whole lot too. At first the guys
who bought slide trombones would bring the valve and slide
trombone on jobs. They'd use the slide on numbers like
Slidin Jim. Now you hardly see anything but slide trombones.*

*Before W. C. Handy went to Chicago, and then New York,
where I got to know him, he had a band in Memphis.
It traveled all down through the South and it played mostly
society dates. The band was called a blues band, but they
didn't really play any blues. They just played everything
straight. It sure wasn't a jazz band. In a jazz band you
play a chorus as an introduction so you'll know what they're
playing, then they take off. With him it all came out like
it was written in the book. His band was a society band
like Robichaux's.*

*I got to know Handy pretty well up around New York. He
had a store that was just one big room where you could
sit around. He sold copies of his tunes there and he
published a couple of numbers for other guys. I made some
records with him around 1938 or 1939 and I used to go
down to his store sometimes to try and teach his son to*

play the vibraphones. His son had a very fine set of vibraphones but he never did learn to play them.

Old man Handy was a nice old guy and he got all his fame from writing the St. Louis Blues. *He actually stole it from a guy named Frank Butts who was a honky-tonk player around Memphis. Butts called it, "I Got the Mojo Blues."*

Handy was supposed to get the tune copyrighted for Butts, but he changed the name to St. Louis Blues *and copyrighted it for himself. Jelly knew all about the deal and every time Jelly would see Handy talking on a corner to some guys, he would get on the other corner and start telling guys all about Butts and Handy as loud as he could so Handy could hear. I never knew Butts, but Jelly claimed he knew all about what happened and he used to cuss Handy out and call him a "horse thief."*

Those tonks like Butts played in were really something to see. Most of them were for the roustabouts who worked on tho lcvces. They had them In St. Louis, Kansas City, Memphis, New Orleans, and a lot of other places. Tonks had piano playing, drinking, and gambling. There was always a pool table or two in a tonk but the guys never played no pool. They'd block the pockets up and use it for shootin' craps. When the cops would come around to check you out, everybody would throw the balls on the table, unstop the pockets and get the cues sticks down. The cops would come in, look around, and see a nice little pool game goin. As soon as they'd take off the crap game would get goin' again. Those guys were so well organized it was really something funny to see.

The Boston Symphony made the St. Louis Blues *for Handy by playing it and making it popular. The rich people around New York knew about it and Handy, and they used to hire him for society dates. Once you've heard the* St. Louis Blues *you've also heard the* Memphis Blues *and the* Beale Street Blues, *they're all the same. If you're playing any of those tunes you've really got to watch yourself that you don't play the wrong tune, they're so close. Handy never claimed he was any "Father of the Blues" around me or any of the colored — we knew he wasn't.*

All around the New Orleans area we had street corner players. They used guitar and mandolin and played for coins on the corners. If they did pretty good they'd enlarge and add a string bass. Those guys would walk down the street and if they'd see a gang of people they'd stop and play them a number. Then they'd pass the hat around. Guys would put a coin in. Lonnie Johnson and his daddy and his brother used to go all over New Orleans playing on street corners. Lonnie played guitar, and his daddy and brother played violin. Lonnie was the only guy we had around New Orleans who could play jazz guitar. He was great on guitar. Django Reinhardt was a great jazz player like Johnson. They'd really take off on a number. Lonnie was tough to follow.

There were a lot of blind and crippled street musicians in the South, but the only one I remember around New Orleans was Blind Freddie. He was born blind and played a whole lot of harmonica in the streets. One day he put down his harmonica and the next day he was playing clarinet. For a while there he played with a lot of bands. Then he got some kind of religion and quit playing. After that he told fortunes for a long time. He could tell your voice and name you no matter how long it had been since he saw you last.

Most of the street corner players came out of the woods or some little town someplace.

A lot of times in New Orleans I used to take my bass and walk down the streets of the District in the daytime looking for someone to invite me to play. I'd pass a whorehouse or a tonk and one of the piano players would yell, "Hey George, come on in and play something." We'd play a few numbers, have a couple of drinks, and I'd move on. I never played with a band in a whorehouse because they didn't hire bands. All the piano players played in theaters, tonks, or whorehouses. The only bands who had piano players were Robichaux and the Tuxedo Band.

Every whorehouse had piano players, but Lulu White's had the most. If you needed an extra piano player, you called Lulu's and they'd send you one. Lulu's place was the biggest and highest class sporting house in New Orleans. Today they call Lulu White's place Mahogany Hall but we never did. You went in there and she asked you what you wanted. She had any color, nationality, kinky hair, straight hair, blond, or almost anything you wanted. Lulu had different prices for different girls and different rooms, and according to how long you wanted to stay and what you wanted to do. She had beds where the headboards and footboards were mirrors and you could watch yourself while you were doing it. There weren't any 50¢ or $1.00 girls at Lulu's; they were $25.00 or $50.00 depending on what you wanted. Lulu White herself could handle three men at once — one in every hole. She called that her around the world trip. That was very expensive. Lulu herself liked women for sex.

I never played with Jelly Roll Morton around New Orleans and didn't get to know him real well until we were in New York. Around New Orleans sometimes I used to let him take me to some of the whorehouses with him. He'd take me in, talk big, and show me some of his chicks. He was very flashy; he'd get four or five one dollar bills and wrap them around a roll of silk paper to make it look like he had a roll. A lot of the guys used to do that. Jelly worked mostly at Lulu White's place, and back then was just another piano player who worked the District.

The Twenty-five Club was open twenty-four hours, and most of the piano players who played the District used to come there before and after work. Jelly never did come around the Twenty-five Club or hang out with the musicians around New Orleans. Jelly knew more of the guys after he left New Orleans than he did when he was there, and he never played in a band until he went to Chicago. Jelly actually was from around Biloxi or Bay St. Louis, Mississippi. That's where his mother and her people are from. He talked a lot about fighters and cabarets and all that stuff that none of the guys knew anything about. All the young kids up in New York used to listen to Jelly talk and they believed him. He just blasted away and they got a lot of publicity for him he really didn't deserve. I knew Jack the Bear he talked about. She was a bad woman and lived on Julia Drive. She wasn't as bad as some of the guys. Aaron and Boar Hog were the two baddest guys down there. They weren't bad to everybody, just to little weak and lame guys. They'd catch a lame guy and beat him up. Musicians always thought they were tough and could fight, but they couldn't. Guys like Aaron and Boar Hog would beat them up when they caught them.

Jelly was what we called a big-time pimp around New Orleans. He had that gold on his teeth and a diamond in one. If you wanted to find Jelly you had to go to the whorehouses because that's where he'd be pimpin'. Music was just a sideline for him to prove he had something to work at in the District. If Jelly wasn't in a whorehouse he was trying to be a slick pool shooter or a card shark. He wanted everybody to think he was a big-time gambler, but he couldn't shoot pool and wasn't a very good gambler. If you listened to Jelly talk about gambling, you'd think he was the greatest gambler in the world, but if you played with him you'd know different. Just like he did a lot of lying on his Congress records. He claimed he invented a lot of things he didn't. If you'd listen to him talk long enough, he'd claim he invented the piano or anything else that came to his mind. When he'd get through talking, he'd make you believe anything he told you; he was a very good talker. Jelly was always talking himself into something. I'm only speaking facts about Jelly, because he's still a friend of mine.

One piano player Jelly talked about that was a great piano player was Tony Jackson. He wrote some good music too. He didn't play flashy like Jelly, but what he did, he did nice. His stuff had more swing than Jelly, but even Clarence Williams had more swing than Jelly. Tony and Clarence wrote down a lot of tunes for Jelly, and Clarence might have stolen some from Jelly; Clarence was a horse thief.

Tony was one of the first guys to leave for Chicago. He left about the time Frank Keely did. All of those guys took the train. A lot of little trumpet players went up. Sugar Johnny went up. He had a trumpet style like Armstrong and Oliver. He was a huge guy. Bigger than Keppard or Oliver. I think he was from around Breakaway, Louisiana. He played at Pete Lalas for a long time before he left. Another guy who left early was a guy named "Pork." He played for awhile and finally got on the Chicago police force. He was a chief detective and played in the policemen's band. When Joe Oliver went up, he made it bigger than any of them because he started to make records.

Jelly had a nice style of playing the backward bass. A whole lot of guys play that style now. He had a lot of numbers he could play like The Pearls. *He worked both of his hands together; he couldn't work one separate from the other. He had a good right hand but his left hand was no good. If you listen to* The Pearls *and* King Porter Stomp, *you can tell how them hands worked together.* King Porter Stomp *is strictly a bass number and Jelly had to get someone else to play it right for him. I don't know this first hand, but some of the guys said that he had to get high-powered guys like Tony Jackson, Albert Calb, or Eudell Wilson to go and cut the bass parts of a record for him. Jelly would play the melody with his right hand and the other guy would play the bass behind what he did. It was like Pete Johnson, Meade Lux Lewis, and Albert Ammons. Pete played more blues than any of them, and Meade Lux Lewis played a lot of blues, but they didn't have no left hand and could only play in one key. Albert Ammons was a musician who could play with both hands in any key. Albert would play the bass parts for them on records. Pete and Meade Lux Lewis could never play in any band because of just playing in one key. Jelly is what we called a honky-tonk piano player.*

Jelly was the best entertaining piano player by himself in the sporting houses. He knew all the dirty songs and that's where he was great. When a customer would come in the door, Jelly would make up a dirty rhyme on your name and play it to his piano playing. Even if you'd walk by the place, he'd get off a rhyme and start vamping on the piano. They didn't play or sing no pop numbers. We had another guy around New Orleans named Black Pete that was great at that too. A bass player named George Jones was the best at rhymes. He made more money than any musician around New Orleans and couldn't play a nickel's worth of bass. He worked the whorehouses, banquets, and parties. Everybody would hire him. If you were giving a party, you'd hire him and give him a list of the names of the people who were coming. When they'd walk in, he'd saw on his bass and make up a funny rhyme on their name. After the guests were there, he'd stand up sawing the bass and talking funny. He even had a special pocket he kept most of his tips in. Sometime during the party he'd turn his pockets out to show how little money he'd made, and people would give him more. Jelly did rhyming like George except Jelly put more music to it.

Jelly was right that the piano players in those days made more money than other musicians. They got a lot of tips because they were playing the whorehouses. Jelly also got in ASCAP before any of the other musicians from New Orleans and claimed all kinds of blues numbers. Before that they were anybody's numbers. They were just blues in B-flat or some other key. He used to play the numbers and have a writer there to write the notes down. Then they'd make up a lead sheet, send it in, and get it copyrighted.

*Up in New York I used to play with Jelly. I never used to
sit around and listen to him play and talk though. He was
always talking one thing and doing another. He said that
jazz music should be played softly with plenty of swing.
But Jelly didn't play what he talked; he talked sweet jazz
and played a juggy style. It didn't swing like most jazz and
wasn't up to date like James P. Johnson's.*

*Around New York Jelly would always be saying he had
a job and start getting a band together for rehearsal. He'd
hire a rehearsal hall and we'd rehearse with him for two
or three weeks, then nothing would happen. What would
happen was Jelly had a job all right. He'd talk himself on
a job, but he'd just keep talking to the guy who was
going to hire him, and before he'd get to play, he'd talk
himself right out. The guy would fire Jelly just so he
wouldn't have to listen to him talk. He got a job playing
the World's Fair in 1932, that I was gonna be on. We
got fired before we opened up, but we got a week's pay
and didn't do no work. Jelly told us the guy was scared
for his money and got salty. Most of the time we didn't
get any pay, but we'd be glad to come to rehearsal
because we didn't have no job anyhow. I don't think Jelly
really cared whether he got the job or not because he had
plenty of money coming in from song royalties.*

*Jelly couldn't play good behind someone's singing. There's a
whole lot of piano players who can't do that. Earl Hines,
as great as he is, can't play with a singer. Guys like Jelly
and Hines are too much for themselves, they're so busy
playing for themselves, you can't hear the singer for what
the piano player's doing. Jelly was a good man by himself
or in one of those whorehouses.*

*One time in New York we made some records with Wilton
Crawley. Crawley hired Jelly to get a group together for
the date, then he forgot about it. He hired Luis Russell to
get another group together for the same date. Both groups
showed up for the date. Jelly was really hot, him and*

Crawley spent the whole two hours for the date arguing. We had to come back for the next day to make the records. Jelly and the Victor people told Crawley he had to pay all the musicians. So Crawley had to pay for three groups. Two the first day and one the second. Jelly came back and played the piano with us.

The most harm Jelly ever did was to himself. He just talked too much. Musicians called him "Loudmouth" or "Run at the Mouth." He'd stand on a corner and talk very loud and get himself in trouble. He used to always tell me that New Orleans had the best musicians. I'd argue with him and say, "No man, New Orleans had the luckiest musicians. You take Johnny Dodds, Sidney Bechet, and those guys, they just lucked up on making some early records. Guys like Manuel Perez, Arnold Metoyer, Frank Keeley, and Tig Chambers, they could play, but where are they?" I think there were a lot of guys around New Orleans and New York like James P. Johnson who played better than Jelly.

There were a lot of piano players around New Orleans besides Jelly. Some of them were Alfred Wilson, Sore Dick, Albert Calb, Drag Nasty, Eudell Wilson, Clarence Williams, Black Pete, and a whole bunch of guys. Eudell Wilson was from Kansas City, and a lot of the guys came from places like that to get jobs working the District. Black Pete played at a small house on Gasper Street. Albert Calb used to play out at the theatre in Lincoln Park.

The piano players waited for their tricks just like the girls did. If a trick was good for the girls, it was good for the piano player too. Most of the guys who went in the whorehouses were half stewed and the drunker they were, the more money they'd tip. The customer picked out the girl and piano player he wanted, and they'd go off to a room. The customer and the girl would drink and make love while the piano player would play some slow blues. The piano players only made 50¢ or $1.00 a night from

the house, but sometimes they'd made $50.00 or $60.00 a
night in tips. They never wanted to see a guy come in
with a tuxedo on because they knew they didn't have
nothin in their pockets and they wouldn't get a good tip.

Most of the guys who played piano around New Orleans
wouldn't play with a band. We'd call them "Sissies" or
say "look at that faggot up there." The band musicians
thought piano was for women. The guys who played piano
would learn another instrument like guitar or violin to get
with a band. The guitar was the piano for the bands.
There were other reasons we didn't use a piano. The band
had to bring the instruments and you can't carry no piano
around with you, and none of the places had pianos in
them. Another reason was most of the piano players couldn't
read and could only play in one key like F-sharp. Most of
the bands couldn't transpose the music to play with them.

A couple of guys I remember who switched instruments to
play in a band were Tommy Benton and a guy named
Cato. Cato had a stiff leg so we called him "Pineleg." He
learned to play string bass; Tommy learned to play guitar.
He said he didn't want no one calling him a sissy and
all that. If we were at a place where they had a piano,
Tommy would play it sometimes. He couldn't read music
but could play in all the keys.

The Tuxedo Band was the first band after Robichaux's to
use piano. They had to rent their own piano and put it in
the dance hall. A guy named My Knee Jones played the
piano for them. I called him "Pineleg" and for a long
time I thought he had a wooden leg, but it was just stiff
and didn't have any feeling in it. When I played with the
band I used to hit his leg with my bow and say, "I just
wanted to see if you're in tune with us." He published a
couple of numbers around New Orleans.

Steve Lewis, the piano player who played with Piron,
lived next door to me when we were kids. He lived with
his aunt and she didn't want him to play piano. When

*she'd go off she'd lock him out of the house so he couldn't
play the piano. He'd wait until she was gone then climb in
a window to practice. I'd watch for him and if she'd come
back too soon, I'd throw some rocks at the house so he
could get out before she caught him. Steve couldn't read
but Piron taught him to play in all the keys.*

*Clarence Williams was a friend of mine in New Orleans.
He worked some in the sporting houses, but not as much
as the other guys. Clarence knew Jelly in New Orleans, but
I don't think Jelly taught him any piano. Clarence knew how
to play piano before he left Plaquemine, Louisiana. I don't
think Jelly could teach anybody anything because he was
too busy talking.*

*Clarence wasn't down there too long when he and Armand
Piron opened a little music store and music publishing house.
I think that was around 1910 or 1912. We used to rehearse
there sometimes. If you had written a number, you'd go
to Clarence to write it down. He could write very fast; as
fast as you could do the number, he could write it down.
After he'd write it down, he'd arrange it and send it to
have it copyrighted and published. Clarence always managed
to cut himself in on a number. When a number was
published, it would have four or five names on it.
Clarence would get as much of it as he could. His name
would be in two or three places and the guy who really
wrote it was usually way down the line. After he got
through, he had more of your number than you did. Louis
Armstrong wrote Sister Kate and had Clarence put it down,
copyrighted and published it, and Louis never did get
nothin' for it. Clarence was a real horse thief. We called
him "Spool Head." He didn't have that little old sharp head
for nothin. None of us ever called him "Spool Head" to his
face though. Around New Orleans I didn't know Clarence
was my cousin. I found that out way late in New York.*

*Clarence was the first guy from New Orleans to go up
North and start making records. He played piano on a*

whole lot of them. It was really something to make records in those days. They had a megaphone for everyone to play in and they couldn't record certain instruments, like the string bass. If you cut a hog in a record in those days, you had to stop and start over on a whole new wax. Sometimes you even had to come back later and do it all over. Nowadays if you cut a hog, they have you play a couple of bars over and splice it in.

The shuttering of Storyville put more prostitutes than
jazz musicians on the rolls of the unemployed, but for the
latter there was sufficient belt tightening. Some of the
steadiest jobs had gone, and New Orleans musicians began to
pay attention to reports filtering back from Chicago about
high wages there and the brisk demand for those who could
play in the authentic style that seemed a New Orleans
monopoly. Public interest in the new musical style had been
whetted by appearances of the Original Dixieland Jazz Band
and by their fast selling records on the Victor label. By 1920
Freddie Keppard, King Oliver, Johnny and Baby Dodds, Sidney
Bechet, Honoré Dutrey, and Emanuel Perez
were in Chicago. Others, like Jelly Roll Morton, Papa Mutt
Carey, and Kid Ory, went to California. Still others, Pops
among them, took employment on the riverboats; they too
were headed north, though at a more leisurely pace.
Pops Foster began his travels in 1917 when he joined the Fate
Marable Jazz Syncopators on the S.S. *Belle of the Bend*.
Marable was a leading contractor of bands for riverboats. A
pianist (and steam calliope virtuoso), Marable was a native of
Paducah, Kentucky, and had been employed on riverboats
almost continuously after 1907. Alumni of Fate Marable
bands would eventually include Pops, Louis Armstrong, Red
Allen, the Dodds brothers, Emanuel Perez, Johnny St. Cyr and,
later, Al Morgan, Earl Bostic, Gene Sedric, and Jimmy
Blanton, Duke Ellington's great bass player. Marable

remained on the riverboats until they stopped using bands in the thirties and then worked ashore in St. Louis, where he died in 1947.

The riverboats were floating dance halls, the natural successors to the romantic sidewheelers eulogized by Mark Twain in *Life on the Mississippi*, and to the showboats that brought opera and minstrelry to the river towns at the turn of the century. Few towns boasted ballrooms; what could have been more convenient than to bring both dance hall and an authentic New Orleans orchestra to the town dock for an afternoon or evening of fun? The *Belle of the Bend* belonged to a fleet of riverboats operated by the Streckfus family of New Orleans, pioneers of the floating dance hall idea. Aboard ship musicians ate, slept, lived, and played together for weeks or months at a stretch. Bandleaders, usually older than the sidemen, acted as heads of their musical families. Discipline was strict; drunkards and agitators were weeded out and discharged along the way. Most veterans of the riverboats have described the food and accommodations as good; in addition to one's keep, the salaries paid, although not princely, afforded the more provident an opportunity to accumulate a stake.

The riverboats ran as far north as St. Paul; occasionally they found their way up the Missouri and Ohio rivers. In this fashion New Orleans jazz spread through the cultural corpus of middle America. Without exception the towns where

the boats stopped and their bands played made significant
contributions to jazz style in the following generation.
Bix Beiderbecke lost no opportunity to hear the floating
orchestras when they played his home town of Davenport.
St. Louis was much impressed by the New Orleans trumpet
stars, Keppard, Armstrong, and Oliver, and ended up becoming
a trumpet player's town and the center of a school of brilliant
brass style beginning with Dewey Jackson and ending with
the contemporary Miles Davis.
Two photographs of Pops Foster taken during his riverboat
period can be seen in the illustrations. One shows the
Fate Marable band on the S.S. *Sidney* with Baby Dodds,
drums; Bebe Ridgley, trombone; Joe Howard and Louis
Armstrong, cornets; Fate Marable, piano; David Jones, alto horn;
Johnny Dodds, clarinet; Johnny St. Cyr, banjo; and Pops
Foster, string bass. The photograph is dated 1918. The other
"taken in the early 20's," shows Eddie Allen's Gold Whispering
Orchestra aboard the S.S. *Capitol*, another Streckfus boat,
with Johnny St. Cyr, banjo, and Pops, tuba, doubling bass.
As Pops has told us, he played both instruments and from
his account and that of other jazzmen, it is evident that a
great deal of doubling took place. The role of the contrabass
as the essential string instrument of the jazz rhythm
section was not firmly established until the late twenties.

7. ON THE BOATS

From about 1915 to 1917, I was with Armand Piron's
orchestra at Tranchina's. At first we had Arthur Campbell
on piano, Peter Bocage on trumpet, Tom Benton on guitar,
me on bass, and Piron, violin. Arthur Campbell left after
a while and Tom Benton took over on piano, and then
Johnny St. Cyr took his place on guitar. About this time
piano started being used in some places. Usually we didn't
have a trombone but once in a while we did. Spanish Fort
was like Coney Island; it was on the lake. They had a
mean chef out at Tranchina's, a real nasty guy. He was
supposed to feed us a steak dinner one night and he
wouldn't so Johnny St. Cyr and me quit. When they got
it straightened out, I had gone to longshore work that
paid more money.

About a week after I quit at Tranchina's, Captain Johnny
Streckfus and Peter Bocage came for me to go on the
boats. They had Frankie Dusen's Eagle Band out there for
awhile, but they couldn't make it because they had to
read music and they couldn't. Most of the big stars around
New Orleans couldn't read. It was the first time colored
musicians had ever worked on the boats. For about two
months we rounded up musicians for the Streckfus people.
We couldn't get Baby Dodds right away, so we got another
guy named Alexander Lewis. He was a nice little drummer.

He didn't think the job was gonna last, so he quit and went with one of them little touring shows. We had Louis Cottrell for awhile. He was one of the best drummers we had around New Orleans both for a show drummer and an all around drummer. Any music you gave him he could play. We ended up having three or four drummers before we finally got Baby Dodds who could read good enough. I went down to St. Catherine's Hall where he was playing every Sunday night with Willie Hightower's band and finally got him to come with us. Everybody was crazy about him.

Joe Howard and Peter Bocage played trumpets in the band. Peter could also play violin and trombone; he was good. We got Sam Dutrey on clarinet; Dave Jones on mellophone; Johnny St. Cyr, banjo; Frankie Dusen, trombone; Fate Marable on piano; Baby Dodds on drums, and me on bass. When the picture was taken on the boat Sam Dutrey was drunk that day so Johnny Dodds came and sat in for him. Frankie Dusen was on and off the boats twice; he just couldn't read, and we got Bebe Ridgley. Fate had been on the boat a long time playing at the piano bar at the back of the boat. A lot of guys who came on the boat didn't make it because they said it was too strict. You had to go to rehearsals on Tuesday and Friday mornings and you got fined more for missing a rehearsal than you did for missing a night's work. You also had to play the music you had and a lot of guys couldn't do it. I couldn't read so good in those days, but once I heard a number that was all I needed. I stood by the piano at rehearsals so I could dig the chords from it.

The Streckfus people were funny to work for. You played music to suit them, not the public. As long as they were happy you had the job. You had fourteen numbers to play in an evening and you changed numbers every two weeks. The numbers were long. You'd play the whole number and maybe two or three encores, and sometimes two choruses. A lot of guys didn't like that and quit. The Streckfus people made musicians out of a whole lot of guys that way. Louis Armstrong, Johnny St. Cyr, and I didn't know nothin' about readin' when we went on the boats, but we did when we came off. That's what started us off.

As long as I can remember, the Streckfus's had an excursion boat with a five-piece white band playing around New Orleans. It was called the Belle of the Bend. *It went out every night and played a dance. They also had showboats that played the little towns around Louisiana.*

Captain Johnny Streckfus came up with a name for us — the Jazz Syncopators. That's the first time I heard the name jazz. Later on in 1919 we changed the name to Fate Marable and His Jazz Maniacs. After that everybody started being jazz this and jazz that — Papa Celestin and His Jazz Band, and like that. Before it was like Ory and His Ragtime Band. The Streckfus people always wanted us to play music at a tempo of sixty beats or up. When you got down around forty or forty-five guys would be out on the floor doing nothing but shaking their butts very slow and dirty. The boats had floorwalkers looking for guys who were twisting themselves all up like that.

Arnold Metoyer played trumpet for awhile on the boat when we were around New Orleans. He'd show up for the dance and say, "Man, my kid was sick so I had to hock my horn." Captain Johnny Streckfus would loan him the horn they kept on the boat and give him money to get his out. It kept happening all the time, so they finally made him leave his horn on the boat. Arnold loved to play "Kotch" and would lose all his money trying to play it. When we were playing at Jim Tom's Road House in 1920, he'd always come out there saying he'd lost his horn. So we had to fire him.

Most of the times I worked on the boats in New Orleans, I also worked at longshore work during the week. The boats only worked on Friday night, two dances on Saturday, and at least one on Sunday. If there was a special party or something we'd play all day and then at night on Sunday. Sometimes you'd play special dates during the week. All the dances on the riverboats were for the whites except when we went to St. Louis where we had ones for the colored on Monday nights. You'd pay fifty cents to get on and be given a little book for the fourteen dances. You'd make notes in the book about who the dance was with and where you'd meet. Like by the left side of the pilothouse, or by the candy wheel, or downstairs at the bar. Most everybody came alone, but left with someone on their arm. It was a pleasure to see them having such a good time. Man, everybody was having fun in those days. The boat left at 9:00 p.m. and went downstream quite a ways, then started back to get in at 11:30 p.m. We started played at 8:00 p.m. and played for an hour tied up at the dock. If I wasn't doing longshore work, we'd go to baseball games, the racetrack, or shoot pool during the day.

We got started playing on the boats just before the influenza epidemic of 1917. It hit and we had to lay off for a couple of months. We finished out that season and then I did longshore work until 1918, when I went back on the boats. In 1918 we played the boats in New Orleans and got the band together to go to St. Louis in 1919.

Fate Marable was on the boats for the Streckfus people a long time before anybody else. He was practically raised on the boats because his mother worked on the boats when he was born. She was a maid on one of the boats they had to tow barges up and down the river. She would take care of the rooms for the crew. I never met Fate's mother but I met his brother and sister. His brother worked at the soda fountain on the boats for awhile and he was around New York for awhile. Fate was from Paducah, Kentucky, and in the summer he would go up the river on the steamer Washington *on a tramp trip. They'd go all the way up the Mississippi to Dubuque, Iowa. They'd stay up the river for four months during summer then come back to New Orleans for eight months. The river really froze up in winter. Fate played the piano and the steam calliope before any of the colored musicians went on the boats.*

On May 3, 1919, I left New Orleans with Fate's band. We left on the train and got off at Paducah, Kentucky, to join the union because they didn't have any colored union in New Orleans. We stayed in the union one night and transferred to Local 44 in St. Louis. The next morning we caught the train to Rock Island, Illinois, to pick up the steamer St. Paul. We got to Rock Island May 5, 1919, and opened May 10, 1919, at Rock Island on the boat. While we were there they cut enough ice out of the river to last a month. They had a big saw and guys would get out there and cut big blocks out for the freezer. Some of the guys like Peter Bocage didn't want to go to St. Louis, so they quit.

The boat carried no passengers or cargo; it was strictly for entertainment and for us to sleep on. Our pay was $35.00 a week with room and board on the boat. In St. Louis it was $65.00 a week and no room and board. When we first went on the boat with Fate it was $37.50 a week with no room and board. Our schedule was to Alton, Illinois, where we played a couple of nights, then there was a little town before Keokuk, Iowa, we played, then we played a couple of nights at Keokuk. We were the first big boat to go through the locks at Keokuk. We stopped at a little town called Louisiana, Missouri, and then went to Ft. Madison, Des Moines, and Dubuque, Iowa. Later on we used to go up the Mississippi as far as St. Paul, Minnesota. We started back from Dubuque, and it sure was cold there. The boat had to hurry to be in St. Louis on May 30, which was Decoration Day. That was a big day. We stayed in St. Louis a while before taking off again.

When we went on the boats in 1919, we had the greatest band from Dubuque, Iowa, to New Orleans. Even around St. Louis we were the best. They had some good musicians in St. Louis but no good bands. The Streckfus people had

*four bands on two boats running out of St. Louis and none
of them were from St. Louis. They had to send away to
New Orleans, Chicago, Iowa, and Paducah, Kentucky, to get
them.*

*The two bands from Chicago were Louis Panico and Ralph
Benson. The one from Paducah, Kentucky, was Percy Suggs,
and from Iowa there was Tony and His Iowaians. Suggs
and Tony played mostly on the steamer* Sydney. *Percy
Suggs would get the boat in New Orleans and take it to
Iowa, then Tony and his boys would take it on up the
Ohio River to Pittsburgh, Pennsylvania. All the bands were
white except us and Suggs; we were the only colored. The
white bands all had violins and played real sweet music.
All the music I ever heard when we traveled was very
tame. We hardly played any pop numbers after Louis
Armstrong came on the boat. We started romping and
played mostly ragtime like* Maple Leaf Rag, Bag of Rags,
Champagne Rag. *In St. Louis we could get all the ragtime
music and we played more of it than we did around New
Orleans. They didn't seem to play rags anyplace else.*

*The Streckfus people had different boats and did quite a
bit of shuffling of the bands on the boats. There was the*
Capitol, *the* Sidney, *the* JS, *and the* St. Paul. *They tore up
the* JS *after they got the* Capitol. *I played mostly on the
steamer* St. Paul. *The* St. Paul *and the* Capitol *would
play out of St. Louis and make trips up and down the
Mississippi from St. Louis. One would go up the river and
the other would go down. On the two boats playing around
St. Louis, they had two bands. Benson's band and Tony
and His Iowaians would leave on their boat about 8:00 p.m.
and get back about 11:00 p.m. Our boat would leave about
11:30 p.m. The white guys came around to hear our music
and they liked it. They'd all come over and get on our
boat and have a good time.*

Fate's band was called the night band on the streamer
St. Paul. *It was a tough band and we had people lined up*

to get on the boat. When we first started playing in St. Louis, we had some guys always standing around the bandstand. We didn't know who they were but later on we found out they were guards. The Streckfus people thought we might have trouble from the white musicians and the gangsters. But we didn't have any. The Streckfus people wouldn't let us play any other jobs around St. Louis because they claimed the gangsters were after us. The gangsters weren't even thinking about us. The Streckfus people just didn't want us to get crowds anyplace but on the boats, and they thought we might quit and go someplace else. When we went to work for them, they had a little one room shack down on the waterfront. After we went on the boats they moved downtown and took a whole floor of offices — we made them so much money. In the four months of summer in 1919, most of the time we worked from eight in the morning until eleven-thirty at night. That was long playing.

Besides the dances at night, they ran excursions during the day. For the dances at night one of the boats would go up the river and one down. The one going up the river would go as far as Alton, Illinois, and would take six hours to get there. Then they'd turn the boat around, start back; it took two hours to come down. The one going down the river would go as far as the army barracks, I think it was the Jefferson Barracks, and then come back. The St. Paul was known as the rough boat where they played jazz. The Capitol was known as a clean boat where they played sweet music. Each one had their own special crowd.

The Streckfus people liked to have a guy who fronted his own band. They had Fate, Charley Creath, Dewey Jackson, Eddie Allen, and a guy named Floyd Campbell; he only lasted about a year. We all got paid by the Streckfus people, not by Fate or the other guys, and they did the hiring and firing. Fate got more than us because he was hired as leader. He would call the numbers and start them off, and conduct rehearsals. You had a book of numbers and you played them for a month. Then you got another set. We played the numbers different lengths, sometimes we'd play one chorus, sometimes three, and then we'd make different endings. Fate used to trick the band on new numbers. He'd get a new number and wouldn't show it to the band for a couple of days. He'd read it over and practice it on his lap every evening. Then on Friday rehearsal he'd show it to us, then sit down and play it like he could play it straight from the music.

I didn't learn how to read music good until I went to New York in 1929. Johnny St. Cyr and I used to have to really work on the numbers we played in Fate's band. On the boat they had a cashier who had a good ear for music. She used to keep a lead sheet and when we hit a clinker she'd mark it down. Then the Streckfus people would make us do it right. We'd call the clinkers "Blue Notes." I got fired a whole lot of times off the boats and hired a lot of times. They didn't want Captain Johnny Streckfus to drink and I'd sneak whiskey to him. I'd tie a string on a bottle and throw it over the back of the boat or hide it somewhere else. When Captain Johnny would get drunk he'd run around the boat and fire everybody but me. That made Captain Joe suspicious of me. One day in Dubuque, Iowa, he caught me and Captain Johnny with the whiskey hid under the seats. He was a hot baby, but he didn't fire me that time.

When we played little towns along the river, they'd advertise ahead of time what night we were stopping. We'd come in at about three in the afternoon and Fate would be on top of the boat playing the steam calliope and everyone would be down at the river to see the boat come in. Then about 7:00 p.m. at night Fate would play the calliope again to let everyone know the boat's in town. There were two calliopes on the boat. The steam one on top and the electric one by the bandstand. Sometimes Fate would play the electric one with the band but most times he'd play the piano. If you were standing next to those things you

*couldn't hear people talking for fifteen or twenty minutes
afterwards. Fate was a fair piano player who could read
pretty good.*

*The riverboats had to lower their stacks when they went
under a bridge. They'd lay the stacks right down on top of
the boat. After they got under they'd raise them again.
When you went to work on the boats you had to walk a
little narrow plank to get aboard. If you wobbled or looked
like you were drunk, they wouldn't let you come on the
boat. Sometimes we'd be drunk and would fall off in the
water.*

*At Ft. Madison, Iowa, Johnny St. Cyr was going to have
some teeth pulled and I decided to have a couple pulled
because Johnny was. The dentist said some of my back
teeth needed pulling too. He pulled about seven of mine
and a bunch of Johnny's. Neither one of us could eat for
a week after that.*

*On July 4, 1919, Louis Armstrong, Johnny Dodds, and me
got off the boat and went up a hill in St. Louis to Boots
Saloon to get a half pint of whiskey each until Prohibition
blew over. We didn't think it was going to last. On the
boats they sold ice cream and soda pop and they had a
big freezer to keep it in. After Prohibition came, the
bootleggers would keep their whiskey in the freezer and sell
it on the boat.*

*The dances on the riverboats were segregated. Monday night
out of St. Louis was for the colored. There were as many
whites as colored on Monday nights and you could hardly
get on the boats that night. In New Orleans no colored were
allowed on the boats. In Memphis and Pittsburgh sometimes
they had colored on Monday nights. We called Mondays
"Getaway Night" because you could get away with anything.
The guys in the band would walk around smoking cigarettes
and drinking, and come down off the stand. On "Getaway
Night" we used to nearly wreck the boat when we got to
fighting. If a big fight breaks out in any dance hall, it's*

important you keep playing so the crowd won't panic. On the boats it's very important that the people keep dancing. If they all run to one side of the boat, the boat'll tip over. It seems like most fights break out around the bandstand and a lot of them want to get right up on the bandstand and fight. Usually you have three or four guys around the bandstand just to keep people from getting up on it. When the shootin' starts it gets rough. The first shootin' I was in was at McCall Plantation. Willie had just laid the bass down and started outside. One bullet went right through the string bass. I was outside and jumped in a barrel. The guy that did the shootin' ran past me and took off over a barbed wire fence. He left about half his pants on the fence. On the boats the guys who acted up got put in the freezer with the ice cream and soda pop. One guy started trouble when we were just gettin goin'. He spent the whole evening there and was blue and stiff when he got out. Red McKenzie, the guy who blew the comb, used to be one of those little tough guys and was always standing at the bandstand getting in trouble. One night the bouncer hit him on top of the head and he bounced right up into the bouncers hand. I used to tell him later, "you got a very tough head."

Ernest Johnson was a bass player in one of the bands on the river. One day we were talking and he said he had some chafing between his legs and wanted to know what to do about it. I told him to put some Sloane's Liniment on it and rub it in, and that would cure it right. I never thought a guy would be crazy enough to do it. The poor boy did it and then jumped in the river to keep from burning up. He couldn't walk for a week. He was gonna shoot me over it. There were four colored bass players on the boats. I was the first, then Jim Johnson, Henry Kimball who I admired so much, and then Al Morgan, Sam's brother who got a job way late. Isaac Jefferson was a piano player who worked the boats with us and was very good. Burroughs Lovingood was another guy that played piano very good. The last time I saw Isaac he had a good job in Detroit in the thirties. With Fate we had a very good trombone player named U. S. Grant Cooper. He was about the size of Jimmy Archey and looked like him. We needed a guy who could read music good and he could. Before him we had Bebe Ridgley for about a month. But he quit and went back to New Orleans. Grant Cooper wasn't any fly trombone player, but he could play what he saw. Later on he was with Charlie Creath. We got Louis Armstrong out of the Ory Band to work with us. Louis was the only one out of Ory's band who could read at all, and Louis couldn't read so good. Joe Howard, one of the old trumpet players in Fate's band gave Louis a lot of help. Louis should give Joe a whole lot of credit. Dave Jones the mellophone player in the band helped Louis too. Dave played as much music on mellophone as Louis did on trumpet. He wanted to play sax though, just like I wanted to play tuba and no one could tell me anything. Another guy who helped Louis was Sam Dutrey. Later on Lil Armstrong helped Louis a lot. Lil played a whole lot of piano. Louis can read very good now.

Some of those old records just don't move me at all. Like the one my brother's on with Fate — it stinks. If you try to play like those guys did back then, you're dead. After we got back to New Orleans in 1919 the Streckfus people hired another bunch of guys for Fate's band. I think the only guys that were left were Louis Armstrong and Baby Dodds. Baby left soon after that.

The opening paragraphs of the next chapter furnish the
jazz historian with valuable information. The enlargement
of the small jazz band into the ten- or twelve-piece dance
orchestra was part of the inevitable commercialization of
New Orleans music. Pops places the date as early as 1921.
Brass and reed sections were doubled or even tripled, and
saxophones were introduced to smooth out the overall sound
of the band. The old New Orleans front line with its functional
cornet-trombone-clarinet instrumentation would eventually
disappear; the saxophone would overpower and eventually
doom the clarinet. The greater instrumentation created
difficulties for contrabassists; as Pops relates, he bought and
began playing his first tuba in 1921. Only the brass bass
possessed sufficient power to drive the rhythm sections of the
new dance orchestras, or so the leaders and music contractors
thought. It would be several years before Pops stopped
doubling and convinced bandleaders that the string bass
was indeed the most suitable instrument for the rhythm
section.

No trace of the glass recordings made by the Gold
Whispering Band has ever been found but Pops's disclosure
will undoubtedly set collectors on the shadowy trail. Pops's
tenure with the inflated Eddie Allen Orchestra, apparently not
much to his liking, marked the end of his first riverboat
period. Several New Orleans jazzmen who had gone to the
West Coast reported good jobs to be had in that part of
the country and Pops accepted trombonist Kid Ory's
invitation to join a band working at the "One Eleven" in
Los Angeles. The place of employment proved to be a taxi
dance hall (most likely at 111 West Third Street, since
Main and Spring are parallel; the area was then known for
its dime-a-dance parlors, rather sedate versions of the
New Orleans cabaret). Customers paid ten cents for the
privilege of dancing with glamorous hostesses; the dances
lasted about sixty seconds each, requiring constant changes of

tunes and tempi. After the job with Kid Ory at the One Eleven,
Pops worked with Papa Mutt Carey, a fine New Orleans
trumpeter, at the Liberty, on Third Street east of Main.
Los Angeles proved to be a dull place. Although Ory and
Carey stayed on, Pops returned in 1923 to St. Louis, which
had become a familiar secondary base of operations during his
riverboat period. Musical activity was on a level only below
that in Chicago and New York. Charlie Creath and
Dewey Jackson were booking Negro orchestras; Frankie
Trumbauer had a dazzling band at the Arcadia Ballroom
with Bix Beiderbecke, Pee Wee Russell and, briefly, Jack
Teagarden and Peck Kelley. The only untoward aspect of
working in St. Louis was that jazz bands were really dance
orchestras, cut in the new style and tailored to the requirements
of ballroom audiences. The pure New Orleans style
was being submerged. Pops began playing tuba again.
In 1924 Pops made his first phonograph records for Okeh, as a
member of the Charlie Creath Jazz-o-maniacs. A man
named Ralph Peer headed the artists and repertoire department
of the Okeh concern and was in charge of building a jazz
and blues catalog to exploit the "race" market. Okeh had
established studio facilities in a building in downtown
St. Louis, augmenting its main studios in Chicago. The label
and Peer were responsible for much of the best jazz recorded
in the early years; in addition to recording Charlie Creath
and Dewey Jackson, Okeh achieved an important first with the
Bennie Moten Orchestra from Kansas City, all of these
sessions being conducted in St. Louis. Among the important
artists to visit Okeh's Chicago facilities were New Orleans
jazzmen King Oliver, Louis Armstrong, Johnny Dodds,
Freddie Keppard, Clarence Williams, and Sidney Bechet.
In later years original Okeh 78 rpm recordings became prime
objects of searches by jazz collectors. The label stayed in
business until forced into bankruptcy during the Depression
years.

Pops Foster made a total of fifteen titles in St. Louis. In
December, 1924, and March, 1925, he was a member of
Creath's eight-piece band (see discography). In November, 1925,
the Creath Jazz-o-maniacs had been increased to ten pieces
with the welcome addition of Lonnie Johnson, violin, and
New Orleans percussionist Zutty Singleton, drums. In 1926
Pops was anchorman in the rhythm section of the Dewey
Jackson Peacock Orchestra, which cut three titles for Vocalion
in June, 1926, and an additional two titles for Okeh, in
May, 1927. The May engagement benefited from the addition
of trombonist Albert Wynn, reedman Horace Eubanks, and
Burroughs Lovingood, a veteran pianist (and calliope player)
from the riverboats. Pops played tuba on all fifteen sides.
The music recorded was of good quality but lacked the brilliant
solo work heard on performances by King Oliver and other
more definitive authentic New Orleans bands, playing in
Chicago.
Reading between the lines, one gathers that life in St. Louis
was pleasant for Pops, although the musical associations left
something to be desired. One day at the Okeh recording
studios Clarence Williams told Pops, "You ain't got no
business here," suggesting that he seek faster company and
perhaps try New York. Pops did not go East, but his travels
began once more. After a six-month stint on the riverboats,
Pops returned to New Orleans for a job with Sidney Desvignes.
A footloose period followed: there were jobs with Creath
in St. Louis; Mutt Carey, Lips Page, and the Elks Brass Band in
Los Angeles; Desvignes again in New Orleans and on the
boats, and finally with Dewey Jackson in St. Louis. Such
frequent changes of bands and locales were very much a part
of the life of the jazzman in those days. Not until 1929 did
Pops finally take Clarence Williams's advice and push on to
New York, for the longest and most important affiliation
of his career, with the Luis Russell Orchestra.

8. PROHIBITION

In 1920 I fooled around with Ory's band, Bab Frank's band
at Jim Tom's Road House, and the Tuxedo Band. Then in
1921, before the season opened, Charlie Creath sent for me
and Johnny St. Cyr to go to work on the steamer St. Paul.
We gave the Tuxedo Band a two month, two week notice.
Then when we left Bebe Ridgley said, "Hate to see you go
man, you coulda stayed with us, you guys are dirty."
Everybody liked Papa Celestin but the guys didn't like
Ridgley and he had the band. They finally split off. Ridgley
had the Original Tuxedo Band and Papa Celestin had
Celestin's Original Tuxedo Band. Papa Celestin hired Emma
Barrett as his piano player and she was the only woman
I knew who played in a band. Then the bass player left
Ridgley and started the Young Tuxedo Band. For a while
there were a gang of Tuxedo bands around New Orleans.

I worked a month with Charlie and the Streckfus people
put me with Eddie Allen's band. That was the year I first
started playing tuba. I bought my own in 1921. They built
the band around Eddie Allen and called it the Gold
Whispering Band. That was the first time they started using
soprano, tenor, and alto saxophones. Before that they were
all C-melody horns. We had Harry Lankford, trombone;
Sidney Desvignes, trumpet; Floyd Casey, drums; Eddie Allen,
trumpet; Johnny St. Cyr, banjo; Isaac Jefferson, piano; Walter

*Thomas, alto; Norman Mason, alto; me on tuba; and Gene
Sedric, tenor. We called the band Eddie Allen's Gold
Whispering Band. Part of that year I worked in Eddie
Allen's band on days and Fate's band at night.*

*When I got back to New Orleans with the Gold Whispering
Band, we cut some cylinders at somebody's house on
Perdido Street. It was one of those old windup things. They
were glass records. Two of the tunes we made were* Hot
Lips *and* When Hearts Were Young. *We made a bunch
of tunes that day. I never heard them. Darnell Howard did
and he said they came out good. Johnny St. Cyr had
the cylinders.*

*I played with the Gold Whispering Band around New Orleans
for a while and I jobbed around with other bands. It was
around that time that Johnny Dunn came down to New
Orleans and got stranded there. I played with him a
few times while he was there. Dunn came from Memphis
and I didn't think much of his style. Just a wa-wa-wa style.
There were some blues singers from Memphis too. But
the good ones came out of those little backwood places
like the plantations and cottonfields of Mississippi and from
the railroads. Guys working on the railroad sang some
good blues. Around New Orleans women sang the blues
and no men sang them.*

*Kid Ory had taken part of his band to Los Angeles by
then. Mutt Carey, Eddie Garland, and Ory had gone.
They hired Dink Johnson who was already out here and a
couple of other guys. Montudie and Ory got in a fight like
they always did. Montudie went to work for the Black and
Tan Band, and Ory didn't have a bass player. He wrote
to me to come out. I wanted to get away from my first
wife, Bertha, so I went. Back then if a bandleader wanted
you to play with him, he'd write and send you money for
the trip. After you started working you had to pay it back.*

*When I got out to California Montudie saw me and said,
"What are you doin out here George, this ain't no place*

for you." He didn't want me out here and wanted me to go back to New Orleans. He and Ory fought so much I think Ory's band was without a bass player most of the time. Those two guys would fight about anything. Stuff was always flyin around like, "Man, why don't you cut it out and learn how to play." "Hey, Montudie, where'd you get that silly hat?" "Why don't you learn how to blow that horn." "You're jealous of me man, you're too cheap to even buy a hat." "Straighten up your cap, man." Stuff like that would go on all the time. The last fight they had when I was with them, was at the Club Hangover in San Francisco. We were up on a raised bandstand. They got to arguing and Montudie pushed Ory off the back of the bandstand where they stored the empty bottles. Ory nearly got killed. He cracked some ribs and got cut up. They've always been the best of friends.

While I was with Ory we played the One-Eleven Dance Hall near Main and Spring. We played at night from 8:00 p.m. to 11:30 p.m. during the week. Saturday night it was from 8:00 p.m. to 1:00 a.m. On Sunday's L.A. really closed up. The only things on the streets were police, ambulance, and fire trucks. If you wanted to go out of town you had to get a permit. On Sunday nights the dance hall didn't open until midnight. In the band we had Ory; Papa Mutt, trumpet; Fred Washington, piano; Bud Scott, banjo; Bonner, saxophone; Billy Butler, saxophone, and me on string bass and tuba.

We always called Ory "Dut." Nobody I remember from those days called him Ory or Kid. Bonner the saxaphone player and me decided to buy a car and put up $75.00 apiece. I couldn't drive but I was supposed to have the car on Saturday and him on Sunday. He had a family and wanted to take them riding on Sunday. I never did learn how to drive so he used to drive me. On Saturdays we'd drive someplace like down to Watts and buy some bootleg whiskey from the cops. In those days Watts was known as Leake's Lake.

*Frankie Dusen and his band came out to L.A. in 1922.
They had Buddy Petit on trumpet, Elzy Cooper on piano,
and a little guy named Pills Coycault on clarinet. Pills was
Ernest "Nenny" Coycault's brother. Nenny had come out
to California way early and had started playing with the
Black and Tan Band. They were the only band who
played ragtime for a long time out here. Frankie's band was
playing in a theater. The first week they played their music
and the people raved over them. The next week the
vaudeville acts came in and they had to play music for
the acts. None of them could read and that was it. Frank
told me later he went back to the place where he was
living with some people. They were cooking some beans
with a big hamhock in it. He said he went in and it sure
smelled good. He couldn't wait for the beans so he stole
the hamhock, wrapped it up in a paper, went on, and
caught the train back to New Orleans with the hamhock.*

*I got tired of playing with a band that couldn't read so I
left Ory in the fall of 1923 and went back to St. Louis to
play with Charley Creath. Charley had several bands going.
He had all of Missouri and southern Illinois sewed up. We
even went up to Chicago and played a few gigs. One of
his bands was still playing the boats. The boats were so
crowded on Saturdays, the crew and the band would go
on the back of the boat so the insurance man wouldn't
count us in the limit of 500 people. Sometimes they'd get
700 or 800 people on the boat. It would be so loaded the
least little wave would wash over on the deck. One time in
Davenport, Iowa, one guy bet another guy $10.00 he
wouldn't jump overboard. He did and everybody ran to that
side of the boat. The band was on a break and we started
playing right away to get the people dancing. One of the
guards pulled out his pistol and shot it a couple of times
to scare the people into moving. They put the guy that
jumped in jail.*

*Every band Charlie sent out wanted a bass player and
I was the only bass player around St. Louis. He'd get extra*

money when he sent me but he didn't tell me. I found
out about it one night when I didn't want to go on a job.
He kept beggin' me so hard I knew somethin' was up, so
when I played the place I asked the guy what he paid
Charlie and he told me he had to pay quite a bit more
for the bass. I went to Charlie and told him I wasn't goin'
out no more unless he paid me extra. He did.

The only other band around St. Louis was Willie Austin,
until Dewey Jackson took off on his own. There were a few
little bands that just had violin, guitar, and one or two other
instruments. Charlie had the area all sewed up. At one
time he had about ten bands all pulling the dough in for
him. He was so busy he only made appearances at the
biggest jobs. He had a big Marmon car he drove around
from job to job. He'd stop at the job, play a number with
the band and leave. A lot of people thought Dewey Jackson
was Charlie because he played a lot more jobs than
Charlie did. Bob Schoffner did a lot of playing for him
too. Charlie could play very good. He's the only trumpet
player I ever saw that never pulled out the tuning shank
on the trumpet. He never even tested it. If he wanted a
sharp or a flat he just licked it on the mouthpiece and
blew. He had a strong lip and a nice reputation. He
played straight and powerful. He ruined himself though.

The first time I met Coleman Hawkins was in St. Louis
about 1923. He was with Fletcher Henderson's band at the
Coliseum. We liked to run them out of gas with Dewey on
trumpet. Dewey is very fast at fingering and plays long
straight powerful notes like Charlie. Dewey played with a
mute most of the time. Whenever a rough new trumpet
player would come to St. Louis on a traveling show and
wanted to cut the guys, we'd send for Dewey. He was a
rough baby. The guys from Fletch's band came around to
see us; I was slapping the bass real hard and looked up.
Hawk and a lot of other guys were watching me. After I
got down they started saying, "Man, that's great, you should

*come to New York and play with us." I told them I was
doing all right in St. Louis.*

*I met Bix when he was playing the Arcadia Ballroom with
Trumbauer, Rod Cless, Pee Wee Russell, and those guys
about 1923. Bix and Pee Wee lived over in Granite City,
Illinois. On Monday's all the musicians had the day off
and we used to all go over there to see who could burn
up the most barbecue. They didn't have a regular barbecue,
we just dug a hole in the ground, put rocks in, then
some wood and got a fire going. We'd cook the barbecue,
eat it, and drink a lot of corn whiskey. We never played
or jammed together in those days, that all started in New
York. We just got together for kicks. The colored and white
musicians were just one. We'd stay out all night, drink out
of the same bottle, and go out with the same girls. We
used to all pile in Bix's car and go over to Kattie Red's in
East St. Louis and drink a lot of bad whiskey. It was green
whiskey, man, they sure had bad stuff, but none of us
ever got sick on it. I heard Bix play trumpet and piano
and he was good. Trumbauer was a nice guy and a
wonderful saxophone player. Him and Trumbauer never
came around to sit in with us even in New York. One of
the few white guys who used to sit in with us in New
York was Jack Teagarden.*

*Around 1923 the delegate of Local 44 got a one night job
over at Beardstown, Illinois, for a little pickup band. It was
a little coal mining town where the miners come in and
bring a jug to drink on all night. This one big tough guy
with a long mustache came carrying a crock jug over his
shoulder. He was unshaven, dirty, and chewed tobacco,
and sat in a chair he'd pulled right in front of the
bandstand. He laid a big pistol in his lap and told us to
play nothin but* Yes We Got No Bananas. *We started
playing it and the guy who put on the dance came up
and told us to do what the guy wanted or he'd break the
dance up. All night long we played* Yes We Got No
Bananas *and the people there danced to it. Sometimes*

during the evening he'd want us to drink with him and would pass the jug up. None of us wanted to drink behind him, but we did. He'd sit there and sing to the music, twirl the pistol on his finger and point it at us. Once in a while he'd get up to go to the bathroom. He'd stand up and tell us to stop playing and not to hit a lick until he got back. We didn't care how long he stayed, we waited until he got back. When he came back he'd say, "Alright fellas, let's go," and we'd start playing. After all the people left he asked us if we had a good time. We all said "yes." I never will forget that guy and fifty years later I still can't play Yes We Got No Bananas *without nearly getting sick.*

Some of the other trumpet players around St. Louis were Big Bob, a guy named Crackter, and Benny Washington. Wellman Braud carried Crackter to New York after Braud left Duke. They were all good. Bob Schoffner was one of the best trumpet players besides Charlie and Dewey. I remember when he was playing around with us in Charlie's band. He came up to Johnny St. Cyr and me and said he knew we were from New Orleans and wondered if he could get some charm for luck to gamble with. A lot of the guys in those days thought anybody from New Orleans knew voodoo, magic, and all that junk. Johnny told him, "Yeah man, George here can fix you up." I told him, "Yeah man, I'll fix you up." I got my landlady to cut up a nice square piece of red flannel from some old underwear and sew it into a pouch. Inside I put a lump of coal and rosin. I told Bob I had to have $9.15 for it and the money had to be nine silver dollars and three nickels, and I wouldn't take it any other way. When he got the charm I told him not to look at it for nine days or it would break the spell. He went right out and started gambling and lost all of his money. He looked at the charm and the next night he came up on the bandstand with a shotgun wrapped in a tablecloth wanting his money back. He was really hot. I gave him the money back and told him he must've crabbed his luck

by looking at the charm. He said he had looked and then
he wanted me to make him another one. I told him, "No
man, I don't think your hand is right. Let me look at it."
I looked at it and told him, "No man, it's impossible, you
already broke your luck charm."

When we used to make records in St. Louis, they'd hire a
loft in one of the downtown store buildings. The band would
practice without the bass and drums. We'd sit over to one
side having some fun until they were ready for us. Then
we'd play with the rest of the band and cut the records.
They had big megaphones going into the wall. We'd stand
up to the megaphone and play. The wax was cut on the
other side of the wall. If you cut a hog you had to start
all over and cut the wax again. Clarence Williams got to
be in charge of the colored music for the Okeh Company,
and he used to go all over the country hunting for blues
singers. He's the one that carried Lonnie Johnson to New
York. Clarence came down to St. Louis one time we were
cutting records with Charlie Creath's band. When he saw
me he said, "You ain't got no business here, you should
come to New York where you can do better." I said I
might do that someday. The other guys said, "We're doing
all right here with Foster."

Those days with Charlie Creath were really good ones. I
lived at Charlie's house with him, his wife Pauline, and
his sister Marge. When Charlie would get paid off from
jobs he'd pay me and the other guys off, then he'd go
lose his money gambling. Then he'd send Pauline around to
ask me for a loan for the rent money. I'd say, "Charlie's
mad at me and not even talking to me. I can't be loaning
money to no one that's not talking to me." He'd pop up
and say, "What do you mean not talking to you, you'd
better pay the rent." I'd go on outside in the street for
awhile and then I'd give Pauline the money and tell her
not to let Charlie know. When we were on the road playing
a date, the band would usually get together and gamble.
I'd get lucky sometimes and win all the money. Charlie

*would get mad. I'd tell him that I was gonna take Marge
and ride the train home and he could go in the car. They'd
be so broke they didn't even have gas money. He'd come
around before Marge and I left saying, "Hey George, we
haven't got any gas for the car." I'd say, "Man, I don't
need any gas, Marge and I are taking the train back."
He'd start being sweet and saying, "Aw don't be like that."
I'd loan him five until we got back.*

*Charlie was a good guy, he just did himself a whole lot
of harm. He loved to gamble more than anything. Mostly
he played stud poker and dice. He never knew when to
quit. He'd only quit when he was broke. Then he'd get all
clean and brush himself off. Chasing women was another
one of Charlie's problems. He left a good wife for a tramp.
Then he got caught white slaving girls from St. Louis to
Chicago. Charlie just kept going down. He got so bad he
was living around there with a queer so he could eat and
had a job sweeping the decks of the riverboats. In 1938
when I was with Louis Armstrong in Chicago, I got a note
from him saying he was in the Bridewell (that's the jailhouse
in Chicago) and for me to send him all the money I
could because he needed plenty of it. I wrote him back
telling him I could use all the money I could get too.*

*About 1925 I got a job with Dewey Jackson's band on the
boats. We played around St. Louis and went up the river.
Dewey is about as old a guy as I am and I'd been
playing with him since 1919. Dewey was very fast at
fingering and had good syncopation, but didn't have much
tone. His band was a good romping band. I played with
Dewey's band for about six months and then the Streckfus
people fired me. Charlie Creath wouldn't hire me after that
because I'd gone with Dewey. My brother told me to come home
and I could work in Sidney Desvignes's band, so I did.*

*I worked with Sidney's band until 1927. On Tuesday and
Friday we played a club, Wednesday and Thursday we
played Uptown, and Sunday we played at the lake. We*

also traveled around the country a lot playing in Mississippi and Alabama. We played a lot of school dates over there. New Orleans bands had been traveling since way early. I remember around 1914 or 1915 I played Dallas, Texas, with the Original Tuxedo Band. The New Orleans Pelicans were in the Southern Baseball League and we went over to play for the team. Both teams were white. It was around 1926 that Sidney's band got an offer to go to Miami, Florida, to play a job. That was just after Jack Carter's band had been down there and one of his guys got killed from being tarred and feathered. Jack's band was from around Chicago and he'd played drums in Noble Sissle's band. Some of the guys in Jack's band tried to teach some white girls to dance at the place they were playing. This gang of white guys didn't like it so they played like they wanted to hire them for an extra date later that night. When they got out there they really got it. Somebody in Sidney's band knew the chief of police in Miami and they called down there to see if he would give us protection. He said he couldn't because down there they didn't want colored playing for whites and we didn't go.

Later on when I went back to Los Angeles I found out Jack Carter had taken a band to Shanghai, China. He took Darnell Howard and Albert Nicholas with him. A lot of guys would get jobs on boats from the West Coast and when they got to China they'd jump the boat and get a job playing.

We had Sidney Desvignes and Gene Ware on trumpet, Eddie Cherie on tenor and clarinet, Ory Umphrey on trombone, Tuton on alto, Louis Barbarin on drums, me on bass, and my brother on banjo and violin. In early 1927 Willie left for New York to join Joe Oliver and we got John Marrero on banjo and violin. Sidney was a straight trumpet player and could read very good. His tone was green and was hardly no tone at all. He wasn't a very good trumpet player.

The whole band went to Mobile, Alabama, to play a job about 1927. When we got there they sent me over to a very nice room, but Louis Barbarin heard about it and took off to get there before I did. Louis rented it out from under me and when I got there he was out in front telling the guys how good the room was and how soft the bed was. I skipped around back and loaded his bed up with fire wood and coal. He brought the guys in to see it and ran over and jumped on the bed. After he hit it he sure was hot. He said he was gonna kill the guy who did it if he found him.

On the way back to New Orleans that time we met Sam Morgan's band. They had hit a detour in the road they were on and had gotten lost. Isaiah Morgan, who couldn't talk so plain, hollored at us that they would be a lot further if there hadn't been a "Detroit" in the road. We got him to say it several times and then we all cracked up laughing; we thought it was very funny.

A lot of the time I was with Sidney we worked on the Island Queen. *It was owned by a Captain Scholtz out of Philadelphia. In the summer of 1926 we went up the river on the boat. We got up there and fooled around so long the river got low and we couldn't get out. If the river was too high you couldn't get under the bridges and if it got too low you hit bottom. We came back down to New Orleans on the train until the boat could get out, when we went back and got it and came down the river. In 1927 Sidney's band was playing at the Peaceman's Temple and Papa Mutt came to New Orleans to visit and asked me to go back to L.A. and play with him. I went.*

Papa Mutt had taken over Ory's band and changed the name to the Liberty Syncopators. We played the Liberty Dance Hall on Third Street between Los Angeles and Main Streets. We had Minor Hall on drums, we called him "Ram," Joe Darensbourg played clarinet, and Leon White, who played drums way early with the Black and Tan Band, on trombone. I was on bass and Papa Mutt was on trumpet.

Ram was a funny guy that I had some fun with one time. He came around telling us he was getting a hardon every night on the bandstand. I told him to tie a string around it just before he went on the stand. He really tied it around and then went on. Pretty soon the whole thing started tightening up on him and in a few minutes he ran screaming off the stand. He couldn't get the string untied and had one hellava time getting it loose. When he got back all the guys really kidded him.

While I was playing with Papa Mutt I got to the dance hall early one night. I decided I would go down and play the Chinese lottery. The Chinamen had a restaurant with a back room and a counter where you went to play the lottery. As I was going in a couple of guys were coming out. They said, "Going to try your luck, man?" And I said, "Yeah." When I got to the back room there wasn't anybody there. I stood around and called for a minute before I heard somebody knocking in a closet. I opened the closet and out fell Ram and two great big Chinamen all tied together. I started laughing and Ram started yelling to untie him or he was gonna punch me in the mouth. I laughed some more and finally untied them. The place had been robbed by the guys I'd met on the way in.

Papa Mutt and Jimmy Archey were the two funniest guys I knew. When they lived with Alma and me in New York, Alma lost about 25 pounds laughing at their jokes. She'd be laughing so hard she'd forget to eat. Mutt loved to tell about a drummer and an alto player he had. They both stammered. When they met for the first time the drummer said, "wh, wh, ah, ah, when ev ev ever ya ya you're ready ta, ta, ta, to sss start." The alto player said, "Ya, ya, ya you mmmmmockin mmmme," and they started fighting.

The Black and Tan Band in Los Angeles was the only band around there playing ragtime for a long time. I never

William Bebe Ridgeley, trombonist and leader of the Tuxedo Orchestra. (Courtesy of Karl Gert zur Heide.)

Fate Marable Band, on the S.S. Sidney of the Streckfus lines out of New Orleans, about 1918. From left: Baby Dodds, drums; Bebe Ridgeley, trombone; Joe Howard, trumpet; Louis Armstrong, trumpet; Fate Marable, piano; Dave Jones, French horn; Johnny Dodds, clarinet; Johnny St. Cyr, banjo; Pops Foster, string bass. (Courtesy Archives of New Orleans Jazz, Tulane University Library.)

Eddie Allen's Gold Whispering Band playing on the S.S. Capitol, about 1921. From left: Harry Lankford, trombone; Sidney Desvignes, trumpet; Floyd Casey, drums; Eddie Allen, trumpet; Johnny St. Cyr, banjo; Isaac Jefferson, piano; Walter Thomas, saxophone; Pops Foster, tuba and string bass; Norman Mason, saxophone; Gene Cedric, clarinet. (Courtesy Archives of New Orleans Jazz, Tulane University Library.)

Advertising card for W. C. Handy, about 1910. In 1910 Handy had just resigned from Mahara's Minstrels and again settled down in Memphis as a bandleader and teacher.

W. C. Handy, about 1940. Handy was then head of his own publishing firm in New York.

W. C HANDY,

Teacher of Band, Orchestra,

AND

Vocal Music.

Kid Ory's Band, Los Angeles, 1922. From left: Kid Ory, trombone; Papa Mutt Thomas Carey, trumpet; unknown, piano; Fred Washington, banjo; Boner, saxophone; Billy Butler, saxophone; Pops Foster, tuba and string bass.

Advertising card for the Black and Tan Orchestra, Los Angeles, about 1915.
From left: Paul Howard, saxophone; Ernest "Nenny" Coycault, trumpet;
Leon Herriford, clarinet; James H. Jackson, piano; H. A. Southard, trombone;
Leon White, drums.

Curtis Mosby's Dixieland Blue Blowers. Band is playing from a truck-driven float advertising Charleston contest, presumably August 6, 1923, at Solomon's Penny Dance Hall in downtown Los Angeles. From left: Henry Starr, piano: unknown with toy trombone; Bob Brassfleld, saxophone; Freddie Vaughn, banjo; Harry Barker, trumpet; Lloyd Country Allen, trombone; Curtis Mosby, drums.

Musicians' get-together, Los Angeles, 1925. From left: Marcellus Levy, drums, Peacock Melody Strutters; Harry Barker, cornet, Lloyd Allen, trombone, Curtis Mosby, drums, Curtis Mosby's Dixieland Blue Blowers; Myers, cornet, Sonny Clay's Jazz Band; Willie Porter, cornet, Sunnyland Band; Alex Levy, reeds, Peacock Melody Strutters.

Eddie Montudie Garland, Oakland, California, about 1928, in Elks Marching Band uniform similar to one worn by Foster in 1927.

Lionel Hampton, about 1932.

Don Redman Orchestra, early 1930s. From left: Sidney de Paris, trumpet; Bennie Morton, trombone; Shirley Clay, trumpet; Claude Jones, trombone; Manzie Johnson, drums; Langston Curl, trumpet; Fred Robinson (?), trombone; Horace Henderson, piano; Don Redman, saxophone; Edward Inge, reeds; Talcott Reeves (?), guitar; Bob Carrol, reeds; Bob Ysaquire, bass; Rupert Cole, reeds.

Louis Bacon, about 1930.

Theodore Teddy Hill, about 1930.

Johnny Dodds, about 1928.

Henry Red Allen, Jr., about 1930.

Luis Russell, about 1930.

Luis Russell and His Famous Orchestra, about 1932. From left: Pops Foster, string bass; Luis Russell, piano and leader; Sonny Woods, vocals; Paul Barbarin, drums; Henry Moon Jones, reeds; Lee Blair, guitar; Charlie Holmes, reeds; George Washington or Jimmie Archey (?), trombone; Gus Aiken, trumpet; Bingie Madison, reeds; Leonard Ham Davis or J. C. Higginbotham (?), trombone.

The Duke Ellington Orchestra at the Oriental Theatre, Chicago, about 1930. From left: Bubber Miley, trumpet; Tricky Sam Nanton, trombone; Rex Stewart (?), trumpet; Juan Tizel, trombone; Arthur Chief Whetzel, trumpet; Duke Ellington, piano and leader; Sonny Greer, drums; Harry Carney, reeds; Fred Guy, guitar; Johnny Hodges, reeds; Wellman Braud, string bass; Barney Bigard, reeds.

Earl Hines, about 1930.

Horace Henderson, about 1935.

Fletcher Henderson, about 1933.

James P. Johnson, about 1930.

Thomas "Fats" Waller, about 1935.

Alma Foster, about 1930, New York City.

worked with them but I knew them all. Ernest Nenny Coycault played trumpet with them and came from Breakaway, Louisiana. He played around New Orleans and then came out here way early. Later on he was with Sonny Clay's band. Way late he changed his name to Ernest Johnson. Their drummer was Leon White who played trombone with us in Papa Mutt's band. He was a nice trombone player, very good. Jim Jackson was their piano player, but later he switched to tuba because he couldn't play enough piano. Paul Howard and Leon Herriford played saxes and clarinet. I worked some jobs with them, and they were with Reb Spikes for a while. Harry Southard was the leader and played trombone. He was a good trombone player and owned a barbershop in L.A. He was also the Conn instrument dealer around there.

I think the Black and Tan Band made some records around L.A. before Ory did and I think Curtis Mosby played drums on the records. Curtis had a band around L.A. for a long time. I played some of the big parties with them when I was there in 1922. Fatty Arbuckle used to give a bunch of wild parties we played. Curtis was more of a promoter than a musician and wasn't too good on drums. When the band had to play the big shows, Curtis hired Lionel Hampton to play drums. Leon Herriford played first alto and Les Hite played second alto. Paul Howard played first tenor. All the saxes doubled on clarinet. They had Parker Berry who was an outstanding trombone player from Cincinnati. There was another trombone player named Tin Can Henry Allen. Willie Porter and a guy named Meyers were on trumpets. Meyers was a light guy from Kansas City. Henry Starr was the piano player and did the vocals in the band.

Henry Starr was a very good-looking guy with straight blond hair and grey eyes. You didn't know whether he was white or colored. He had several girls on the line for him and considered himself a pimp and hustler. Music was just a sideline for him and the band couldn't keep up with him.

Henry would be with some chick and wouldn't show up or say he didn't feel good and couldn't make it. He was a cute guy and they could never find him, so they sent to New Orleans for Walter Jacobs to come out and play with them. One night Starr walked in the theater and found Jacobs playing the piano. He straightened out after that and stayed with Mosby. Both Starr and Jacobs could play the piano and sing, so they traded off. I used to do a lot of party jobs around town with Walter and Henry. There would be piano and bass music, and one of the guys would sing. Henry was originally from San Francisco and was a very good piano player.

Curtis had a very nice band. They played the Lincoln Theatre and other places for the little TOBA shows. In 1927 Les Hite formed a band to go into Frank Sebastion's Cotton Club and wanted me to go with them. I told them I wouldn't go unless they took our whole band, so we didn't get the job. I think Les Hite had a better band than Mosby's. Curtis ended up in San Francisco and in the 1950s he had a little club on Eddy Street where I used to go see him sometimes. He died in the fifties.

When I was in California I was supposed to go to Australia with Sonny Clay's band for ten months. I didn't go and they ended up staying only ten days. Australia is the worst Jim Crow country in the world and the musicians over there didn't want them to play. Over there colored weren't supposed to have any white girls in their rooms. The white musicians hired some white girls to get friendly with Sonny Clay's boys and get in their rooms. When the party got going good one of the girls pulled a window shade down and that was the sign for the cops to come in. They knocked on the door "to let them in in the name of the King." The cops took them all to the stockade and then shipped each guy out on a separate boat. Some went to Bogalusa, some went to Texas, and about everywhere but where they started from. That was around 1922 and after that

*Sonny came back to California and started another band.
He was playing there in 1927.*

*Lips Page came out to California way early and made
some records. They had an old bus that had wheels like
a covered wagon. I made the records with him. They used
the name Papa Midnight and His Band. Lips couldn't use
his name because he worked for another record company.*

*In September, 1928, I left Los Angeles with the Elks Brass
Band playing tuba. We had Teddy Hill on piano and tenor
sax. We needed him to play piano at night at dances so
we got him a job playing the sax in the band during the
day. He marched in the band and held the horn up like
he was playing it. We played San Francisco, Oakland, Salt
Lake City, Kansas City, St. Louis, and went on to Chicago.
In Chicago I stayed with Johnny St. Cyr and all his babies.
He wanted me to stay and play around Chicago. I looked
into it but I would've had to wait until all the other bass
players in town got a job before I'd get one. I went on
back to St. Louis and joined Dewey Jackson all over again.*

*I stayed with Dewey Jackson until 1929. I lived with Jesse
Johnson while I was there. Louis Metcalf had seen me in
St. Louis and told Luis Russell about me. Luis Russell sent
me a telegram wanting me to join him in New York. Jesse
Johnson got the telegram and kept it for three weeks before
he gave it to me. Jesse did all the booking for bands and
entertainments around St. Louis and was a good friend of
Dewey's and didn't want to see me go. Jesse and his wife
Edith had a fight and she told me to make Jesse give me
my telegram. I used to fool around with Edith before Jesse
married her, and he was always accusing me of fooling
with her. He used to carry a pistol and say he was gonna
shoot me for fooling with her. I'd tell him, "When you catch
me right you can shoot."*

*After I got the telegram and found out Luis Russell wanted
me, I sent myself a telegram saying "Come Home At
Once," and left for New York on February 11, 1929.*

After I got to New York I used to send extra sheet music to Dewey and the guys around St. Louis. Dewey wrote me some years ago saying he'd got religious and joined the Sanctified Church. He said he was only playing for the Lord.

The Luis Russell Orchestra was one of the quality jazz
bands. That it did not attain the eminence of Fletcher
Henderson or Duke Ellington was perhaps as much a matter of
luck as anything else. The band swung well and did not
lack for solo talent. Henry Red Allen, Louis Metcalf,
Rex Stewart, trumpets; J. C. Higginbotham, trombone;
Albert Nicholas, Teddy Hill, Omer Simeon, Barney Bigard, and
Charlie Holmes, reeds, were among its solo stars. Luis Russell
was a Panamanian with an interesting history. The son of a
church choir director and piano teacher, he had won $3,000
in a lottery when he was seventeen, using the money to migrate
in 1919 with part of his family to New Orleans where he
fitted quickly into the musical scene. Luis Russell had
joined the exodus of New Orleans musicians to Chicago in the
early twenties and, after various affiliations with name bands
there and in St. Louis, had arrived in New York where
he launched a band of his own.

Luis Russell did not ask Pops to play tuba; he was too
sound a New Orleans musician for that. Pops abandoned the
brass bass instruments for good and concentrated on the
string bass. By this time he had developed three main
techniques on the instrument: the conventional *arco* and
pizzicato methods, plus a unique slapped technique, whereby
the fretboard was struck simultaneously with the strings,

creating a strong tone with great carrying power. It was just
the effect needed to install the contrabass once and for all as a
respected member of the large orchestra rhythm section. Its
advantages over the tuba and sousaphone in handling all
manner of tempi, the faster ones in particular, had always
been evident; the thing lacking was the sonority and now
that was achieved by Pops's innovative slapping technique. The
combination of Pops's bass, the driving percussion style of
New Orleans drummer Paul Barbarin, and Luis Russell's
solid, full-chord comping on piano created an impressive
sound and beat.

Unfortunately for Luis Russell, no sooner was the band's
personnel solidly established than the Depression began to
have serious effects on the music business. Nightclubs
folded, dance hall and theater budgets were cut to the bone,
and even recording activity ceased for a time. The period
from 1930 to 1935 was the "panic" years in the music business,
and many musicians were obliged to fall back on vocations
not followed for a decade. As the leading jazz bassist in
New York, Pops was able to keep going. He was in demand
for a variety of engagements: casual gigs around New York,
one nighters with pickup bands, short tours with the
standby and readily-assembled Luis Russell Orchestra, plus

the odd record date. Jazz discography makes no mention of a
session with Bessie Smith, but the dates with Jelly Roll
Morton and Fats Waller are there; both produced excellent
performances and the four Morton titles have recently
been reissued by RCA Victor (see discography). The one-shot
session (March, 1929) with Louis Armstrong produced two
titles, including *Mahogany Hall Stomp*, Pops's own favorite
recording. Several fine sides were made under the nominal
leadership of Henry Red Allen, including *Swing Out*
and *Feeling Drowsy*, which give the measure of the 1929
Luis Russell Orchestra just after Pops had joined. The Jelly
Roll Morton session was actually a Luis Russell group
with Morton replacing the leader on piano. *Hello, Lola* and
One Hour, with Coleman Hawkins and Pee Wee Russell, were
made in 1929 with the Mound City Blue Blowers, and
these recordings have long enjoyed a reputation among
collectors as outstanding small band jazz performances.
The Fats Waller session, also in 1929, brought together a
diverse and exciting group of jazz talents: Pops; Fats;
Kaiser Marshall, dynamic Fletcher Henderson drummer; Red
Allen, Albert Nicholas, and J. C. Higginbotham from the
Luis Russell ranks; and Jack Teagarden, the distinguished
white trombonist from Texas.

9. NEW YORK

I left for New York on February 11, 1929, and arrived
there February 12, 1929. That night I played a dance with
Luis Russell's band at the Savoy Ballroom. Benny Carter's
band was at the Savoy too. We'd play a half hour and
they'd play a half hour. Louis Armstrong was next door
with Cal Dixon's band, but we drew all the crowd. We
really had a romping band. The union let me in right away
because I was the only one around playing my style of
string bass and a lot of guys wanted me. Luis Russell's
theme was Call of The Freaks. We called Luis Russell by
his nickname "Fess," for professor. Most of the guys in all
the bands called their leader "Fess." I used to call Luis
"Toilet" but he'd get salty about it and I cut it out. That's
the same name the Ory Band had for Johnny Dodds in
New Orleans.

The big music field was Chicago from 1920 to 1925. From
1925, it was in New York. In New York you had a whole
bunch of dance halls that had fifteen- to eighteen-piece
bands. Then all the dancing schools would have six- or
seven-piece bands. There were a million nickel dance halls
that all had bands. When you'd go to work on the train, it
would be loaded with people and when you'd come back
in the morning, there'd be nothing but musicians on it. With
all that music and dancing, it seems like I would have

learned to dance. I never did, all I do is get on the floor
and wiggle, or run and jump.

Fess Williams was the regular house band at the Savoy
Ballroom. After Benny Carter finished, Fess came back in
as the other band alternating with our band. We were
romping so good that Fess used to come over and ask us
to play a waltz so his band wouldn't look so bad. Fess
wore a high hat with rhinestones and diamonds all over it.
He also wore a white tuxedo and the other guys in his
band wore black ones. His playing reminds me of
Mezzrow's — just toot-toot-toot. I didn't like his band or his
clarinet playing. He tried to be funny but he sure wasn't
funny to me.

We played the Savoy Ballroom from February, 1929, into
the summer. Then we went to the Roseland Ballroom and
took Fletcher Henderson's job away from him. We were
really romping then, really bouncing. The rhythm was playing
great together and the trumpet players were screaming soft
so you could hear the people's feet scraping on the floor.
You could stand right in front of the band and they weren't
blasting you out. We had Red Allen, J. C. Higginbotham,
Paul Barbarin, Albert Nicholas, Charlie Holmes, Teddy Hill,
and a whole bunch of great guys. We worked seven days
a week and we loved it. We'd rather be working than be
at home. It was like it was back in New Orleans. Back
then I used to sit around wishing I could go to work. It
was a pleasure to work in those days. Russell's band was
romping so good in twenty-nine we had everything sewed up
around New York. We were playing the same style we
played back in early New Orleans.

Some of the guys in New York used to call us the rehearsal
band because we rehearsed a lot. But you've got to
rehearse to get things together no matter what kind of band
you've got. We used to have separate rehearsals for the
saxes, the trumpets, the brass, the reeds, and the rhythm.
I had to make them all to pick out the rhythm. By the
time we played a show, I knew the music so good I never

looked at it. Even when you rehearse, you've still got to play with guys a while before you know what they're going to do. A lot of the bands were just screaming bands; they're not really doing nothin' but screaming. Most of the white bands think if you're not blowing loud, you're not playing nothing. None of them want to study tonation, they just want to blow.

While we were at the Roseland Ballroom we split the bill with Milt Shaw's band out of Detroit. They played half an hour then we played half an hour. George Raft used to come down there and dance the tango. He was the chauffeur for Arnie Madden, the gangster. We were at the Roseland for about three or four months and then we went to the Saratoga Club.

Wilbur De Paris was in The Saratoga Club when we went there and we took his job. We stayed there from late 1929 to about the end of 1931 when the Depression set in. Rex Stewart was with us a while after he left Fletcher Henderson. Rex was a very good musician and a good guy but he used to drink a lot of liquor. Another guy who used to play with us was a white kid named Jack Purvis who came around to sit in. He wanted to play with colored bands so bad he stayed out in the sun for hours getting tanned and then he'd black his face. During those days from 1929 to 1933 we made a lot of records. I think we recorded under everybody in the band's name except mine.

I met my second wife, Alma, when we both lived in the same apartment house in Harlem on 137th Street in 1931. Her real name is Annie Alma and before she married me her name was Gayle. During the Depression there was a lot of robbing and murdering going on, so Alma used to get to the apartment house five or ten minutes before I got home from work at the Arcadia Ballroom with Russell's band. She'd wait until she saw me at the corner then she'd start in because she figured I'd save her if anything happened.

This waitin' for me and then goin' in went on for a few weeks and I began to wonder what was up. One night I decided to wait until she went in the door and then I'd run after her. I really took off and she thought it was a robber after her so she took off. When I caught her she was nearly scared to death. We talked a lot after that. I'd borrow clothespins and recipes. Finally in 1936 after I was on the road with Armstrong, we decided to get married. We got married at City Hall with Louis and Alpha as our witnesses and the next day I took off on the road again.

After we were married Alma turned Catholic, and we were married in the Catholic church. Now she's a lot stricter about religion than I am. At Lent she gives up something she likes. I give up what I can't get. If people ask me at Lent what I've given up, I tell them, "all the things I can't get." Alma and me never had any kids, but we really love them. I don't think there's anything kids can do to worry us. We love to be with them. Talk to them and play with them.

When we left the Saratoga Club, Luis decided to change his style. We started fooling around with big arrangements and quit romping or playing what you call Dixieland. While we were playing Dixieland we were great. When we started playing like all the other bands, finding work got rough. Why should they hire you when they've already got the same thing?

We had a lot of funny arrangers and song writers around New York. One white cat that used to write a lot of numbers for McKinney's Cotton Pickers used to get drunk and go sit in the middle of the pond in Central Park on a box to write numbers and arrange tunes. He was very good and came up with some nice numbers. He was a piano player out of Philly. When he'd have a number to sell he'd come around to where the band was rehearsing with his good-looking girl friend. She'd sit so Luis could see

*a lot of leg up her dress while the guy would sell Luis
the tune. Then they'd leave. This guy had hair so long you
couldn't see his face and he lived down in the Village. He
made a very nice arrangement for Armstrong on* Shoe Shine
Boy.

*Arrangers are really funny guys. Some of them write music
you can't read or play. They put notes so you can't tell
whether it's on the line or under the line. You've got to
guess what the notes are from the first to the last. Some
guys write music so hard, the musicians can't play it, then
they laugh at them. I remember when Bingie Madison wrote
some music for Russell's band nobody in the band could
play. Someone got an idea of how to fix him. When Bingie
came around next time, the guys asked him to come up
and play the tenor sax parts he wrote so we could see
how they go. He got up and tried, but they were so hard
he couldn't play them himself.*

*There was a band around New York called the Savoy
Sultans and they got a job playing the whole summer in
Atlantic City. They wanted to get some numbers to play so
they got Claude Harper to arrange some music for them.
Claude arranged the music so hard for them they couldn't
play it, and they lost the job. Then Claude stepped in
and took the job for the summer. There was a white boy
named Bob Sylvester we used to hire to copy arrangements
of other bands down. He could copy down any arrangement
he heard once. You had to be careful with him though; if
you were rehearsing a number he'd come around and hear
it. Then you'd hear someone else play it before you did.
Bob was a kick. He played nice saxophone too. Red Nichols
used to come into places where you were playing and sit
there all night picking up ideas. You'd hear him later doing
the same thing you did.*

*Another thing that's a kick is to play with a band you're
not used to. After 1931 things were rough and we only
played with Luis Russell when he had work. Otherwise we*

jobbed around. I played with Duke sometimes this way.
The first time I played with him, Duke's boys started
pulling out the hard stuff to play. I was wise to it and said,
"No man, let's play some of this stuff," and I reached way
down at the bottom of the music and pulled out stuff I
knew they never played either. The guys who were trying
to kid me started saying, "No man, we never played that
stuff." Duke, Cootie, and some of the guys started laughing
at the guys who were making the joke. Duke's band could
play real good, but they couldn't read very fast.
Every day they'd go to rehearsals and rehearsed just like
Russell's band in different sections, then all together. If you
work with Duke's band you've got to memorize. They don't
hardly play from music at all. Sometimes they just write a
few notes down that are hard to remember. Guys like
Hodges and Carney don't use any music at all, they got
memories like elephants. Most of the gigs I worked with
Duke were around Philadelphia.

Joe Oliver is the one who made Duke so big. After Joe
went to Chicago, he got too big and started wanting too
much money for himself. When they opened the Cotton
Club in New York, they sent for Joe. Joe was working for
the gangsters at the Plantation in Chicago and he wanted
so much money to go, the New York boys wouldn't hire
him. They put Duke in there instead and that made him.
After that Joe had a lot of trouble getting jobs because of
the money he wanted.

I gigged some with Fletcher and Horace Henderson's band
then. Usually it was with Joe Steele, Horace, and Joe Smith.
Joe Smith was one of the best trumpet players around New
York; he had a good style. Horace was a very good piano
player, I think he plays more piano than Fletcher.

After we left the Saratoga Club we played a lot of different
gigs. One of the first jobs was backing Armstrong for two
weeks. After that we turned the band over to Cab Calloway
for ten weeks. We played three weeks in Philly, two

*weeks in Washington, D.C., and two weeks in Baltimore.
Then we played two weeks at the Apollo Theatre for Cab,
and then two weeks as the Luis Russell Band. Cab's
regular band, the Missourians, were playing the Cotton Club
and he had two sets of dates. After that we did about a
three-month run at the Arcadia Ballroom.*

*When Prohibition came in the gangsters kept getting more
and more powerful. Around New York and Chicago "The
Boys" pretty much told you where you were gonna work.
The union didn't say nothin'. There were a lot of punks
around too, we called them the "rat gangsters." We played
a dance for them in the early thirties and when we finished
they didn't want to pay us. We all got mad and started
fighting them. It turned into a battle royal. I got knocked
on the head with a chain and got all bloodied up. They
took me to the hospital and fixed me. When they finished
I tried to get charity treatment, but they saw a diamond
ring I had on and made me pay.*

*There was a guy who lived in Asbury Park named Dupree
that booked bands all through the South. We started going
on the road more and more in those days. Dupree had an
act of his own, singing chickens. When he'd give different
signals they would make a noise for him, it was pretty
good and it took a long time to train the chickens. When
he was on the road with us once, a guy around the corner
from where he was staying stole his chickens. He caught
the guy and got him and the chickens before the judge.
The judge asked him how he could tell his chickens. He
said, "They'll sing when I tell them to." Then he had them
sing. The guy who stole them had already eaten one of
them. The judge sent him to jail for awhile.*

*One night when we were down South the bus broke down
in a swampy area. Otis Johnson, the trumpet player, and
I took off out in the swamp looking for a snake while they
fixed the bus. We found one and killed it, then we walked
about two miles to a store to get some string. We tied the*

string on the neck of the snake and propped it's head up with a stick. When we got back on the bus we hid it in the front and carried the string to the back of the bus. Finally they got the bus ready to go and the driver turned the lights on and had everybody stick their heads out in the aisle so we could see if everybody was there. We started pulling the snake down the aisle then. Everybody went wild, guys jumped out the windows and climbed in the luggage racks and everything. It was a kick.

During the rough times in the Depression we thought of a lot of little ways to make some money. When Marcus Garvey was around New York he put on big affairs at the ball park and wanted me to play them for nothin'. I said, "No man, I can't eat on nothin'." Then this guy told me it was a nice deal and after you played you could walk up through the crowd and pass the hat. So I tried it. I played, then I passed my hat as I went on up the stairs. When I got to the gate I had about $7.00 and I just kept going. It was a nice touch but I got too many guys doing it. They caught one guy and put him in jail for thirty days and that killed it.

Bob White from New Orleans and I got another thing going on the numbers. All the colored people all over thought everybody from New Orleans knew Voodoo and could work great things for them. Bob and I bought ten cents worth of incense and some envelopes, got a frog, a green rag, and a table and chair. We set up the table and chair on the corner with a bunch of envelopes with numbers in them. Bob wrapped the green rag around his head like a turban. We put a sign on the table "Lucky Numbers." When somebody would want a lucky number, Bob would hold the frog and say some French then let him jump on one of the envelopes. I'd burn a little incense under the envelope and we'd sell it to the guy for a quarter. Then we'd give it to him and say don't forget us when you win. We had to pay the cop on the beat $2.00 a week to keep the table there, but he took his payoff in lucky numbers.

*Around this time I had one of the best jobs I ever had.
It was a little four-piece string band of Joe Venuti, Eddie
Lang, Dick McDonough, and me that played on the radio.
A violin, two guitars, and string bass — it was beautiful,
even at rehearsals people crowded around to hear us. It
was so good I knew it wasn't going to last. Man, we were
really doing some stuff. Joe sure could play violin; he was
really good. Eddie played guitar just like you play piano.
He knew the chords and his instrument. Eddie was about
the best guitar player around. Dick was very good too.
Eddie and Dick were the only two white guitar players I
knew up to that time. The radio program folded after a
couple of weeks.*

*At 131st Street and 7th Avenue there was a place called
the Band Box where all the guys used to go to have battles.
The owner had piano, drums, and bass. Then other guys
would come in with their instruments like sax, clarinet,
trumpet, trombone, and what have you trying to cut each
other. We'd usually go there in the morning after work. I
usually didn't stick around. It was just one room with guys
all packed in. Luckey Roberts, James P., Fats, Teddy
Wilson, and all the piano players used to come around.
Jelly would come in the evening sometimes, but he'd hang
around the corner outside talking to his gang. They would
all be listening to Jelly. As long as you stood there and
laughed and agreed, he'd talk all day. Nothing he said
sounded right to me.*

*Jelly had some good men on his records, and he had a
guy who did the arrangements for him. Jelly would say the
music goes something like this and the guy would write it
down. Then the guy would say, "What do you want going
in the first chorus, what do you want in the second," and
so on. It was like having a guy write a book and you
telling him what to put in it. They'd figure out the changes,
the first ending, the second ending, and the coda. Jelly
played some tough tunes like* King Porter Stomp *and* The

Pearls. *A lot of bands won't play them because they're too tough, they have too many changes.*

Bill "Bojangles" Robinson and Wellman Braud were like Jelly; they'd talk as long as anyone would listen and hung around outside the Band Box. After Braud got written up in Ripley's "Believe It or Not" column, he was too big for anybody. Ripley said he could pick faster than any bass player. He quit Duke's band and started one of his own. He got a nice little band together to play a place over in Jersey. He talked so much to the man who owned the place about where to put the tables and how things were in the wrong place, the man told him to get his band together and get the hell outta there. He was always talking himself in by showing the clipping from the column and then he'd talk himself right out again.

I know Braud couldn't pick as fast as I could, and I never knew anyone else who could. A couple of guys were better at playing melody than me, Jimmy Blanton and Junior Raglin. They could both play a whole lot of melody but had trouble keeping a rhythm foundation. Raglin was a guitar player and Blanton was a cello player before they switched to bass. Blanton played string bass like he played the cello.

A lot of guys who'd come to New York heard about the Band Box and they would come in there with their horns when they hit town, wanting to battle with the guys. We'd get one of the hotshots like Coleman Hawkins or Chu Berry to come down and they'd go at it. Albert Morgan, Sam's brother, hit town from New Orleans one day and started shooting his head off about how he could play bass. The guys came and got me out of bed to come down for a little cutting contest. When he saw me come in he told everybody he knew me in New Orleans and I was his friend and he wouldn't play against me. I went along and said, "No, I won't play against Morgan, he's my friend,"

*and I wanted to see him get some work around there. He
was a very nice kid.*

*I usually hung out at the Rhythm Club where the musicians
got together to play poker and gamble. At three or four in
the afternoon you could find nearly every musician in town
there. You could catch a gig there for the night, or a
recording date for later on. Lester Lanin used to have six
or seven bands going around New York, and he'd come
there and hire you for Jewish, Italian, or any kind of
music. I played a lot of different gigs like that for him.
The old musicians around New York used to hang out at
the Amsterdam Club. You had your own key and went
right on in. Mostly the guys gambled there. I met Scott
Joplin's nephew in there about 1929. I just shook his hand
and said hello.*

*I never had much to do with a lot of guys around New
York. Coleman Hawkins was one; he was on a different
kick than we were. He was also a sometimes guy,
sometimes he'd look right at you and didn't know you and
sometimes he did. After a while I started doing the same
thing to him. Tommy Ladnier was the same way. One
night he'd come in and look at me, then walk right on by
like he didn't know me. The next night he'd come in and
say, "Hello, George Foster, I saw you last night." I'd say,
"I know you did, you looked right at me, how did you
recognize me tonight?" It used to make me mad and if I
wanted to get him, I'd say, "Tommy you been knowin me
ever since Biloxi." He'd say, "Aw, man, let's not go into
that." I'd say, "Don't go into what? Biloxi's your home ain't
it?" He'd get hot and walk away. He didn't claim Biloxi; he
wanted everyone to think he was from New Orleans.
Tommy was a very fine trumpet player.*

*Some bandleaders when they have trouble with a guy or
with the union will call the whole band together. Luis
Russell used to do that a lot. He'd be having trouble with
a guy and would talk to all of us about the trouble. When*

times were rough and we were chargin' less than union scale, Louis would get in trouble with the union. He'd call us together and say, "We got trouble with the union." I'd say, "Man, we ain't got no trouble, you got trouble." Then he'd say, "We got to go before the union board." Someone would say, "We don't gotta go before no board." Earl Hines was another leader that way. He used to have a lot of trouble with Muggsy Spanier and Darnell Howard. He'd call us together and get goin' about the problem when someone would pipe up and say, "What did you call all of us down here for when you want to talk to Darnell?" And he'd say, "I'm gonna do that right now."

Wilton Crawley was a character. The way he played clarinet was standing on his head. He'd keep screwing around in a circle while he was playing. That was part of his act on the stage. When we were cutting records for Victor, Crawley wanted to stand on his head to record. Mr. Watson of Victor said "No." Crawley was just nuts. He played clarinet like Ted Lewis, not too good.

There were two Jabbo Smiths that I knew. One was the famous one from around Chicago and New York. He could play trumpet and trombone very good. He drank a lot and got in trouble. He was in Joliet [prison] for awhile. The last time I heard about him the law wanted him. Most of the time he was in and out of jail. The other Jabbo also played trumpet and was from around Boston. He was very bad too, maybe worse than the famous Jabbo. He'd fight, get cut up, drink, and get in trouble.

Shows are the hardest thing to play, especially for toe dancers. They're counting beats all the time and the musicians got to be following the music very close. The drummer has got to read and be very good because he hits the drums on catches and jumps. If he misses, the whole thing looks silly. A lot of leaders, like Cab Calloway and Noble Sissle, couldn't even wave their sticks for it. They were guys who were singers or had some kind of reputation. When they rehearsed, the piano player, or the real leader, would lead the band and he'd show the stick waver how to get them started and stopped. Noble Sissle had a pretty good ear for this. They let them in the musician's union even though they couldn't play a note, and Noble Sissle even ran for president of the union in New York and lost. Tiny Bradshaw and Lucky Millinder were another couple of these guys. They could play a little honky-tonk drums and led bands. As soon as the bands broke up on those guys, they went right out of the music business.

I played some shows and made some records with Bessie Smith in New York. After the shows I used to go to her dressing room, eat candy, and talk a lot of trash. She was nice, very nice. She knew what she was doing and she was my favorite blues singer. All of the big stars like Bessie, Clara Smith, Snakehips, Stepin Fetchit, were so easy to get along with. It was the little stars that just came up, and the mediocre stars and chorus dancers that were the hardest to get along with. They didn't know the music and couldn't get it. They would scream and be nasty to the musicians and try to blame everything that went wrong on them.

In New York going to a recording session was like going on a picnic. The most fun was with Fats Waller. He'd pack up a suitcase like he was going on a trip but it would be full of whiskey. When he'd get to the recording studio he'd pass bottles out to the guys. Then Fats would sit at the piano with his bottle and a big glass to drink out of. Him and James P. Johnson would sit down and fool around on the piano. They'd write and arrange the number right there in the studio. Then Fats would say something like, "Let's time this chorus." He'd have them time one chorus of what he was doing. As fast as Fats would play it, Jimmy would write it out. When Fats finished he'd go get a drink. Jimmy would write the music out and pass it around to the guys. Sometimes if Jimmy needed a note

*he'd go over to the piano and find it. Fats would sit down
and say, "OK, fellas, b-flat we're gonna do this in." And
off we'd go.*

*I never did know what tunes I made with Fats. The
music just had numbers on them like 1A, 2A, 4B. Fats
would say 4B and we'd play it. When the number came
out on record it had a name but we didn't know nothin'
about it. I didn't make too many records with Fats because
he was very tough to get your money from. You never got
paid until you caught him, then he'd usually only give you
a piece of what he owed you.*

*James P. Johnson was the nicest guy you ever will meet.
He was well spoken and so kind. I used to love to stand
around and hear Jimmy talk. When he came to the West
Coast about 1941 or 1942, he couldn't get along with Albert
Nicholas. It was Albert Nicholas's fault because you couldn't
hardly find anything to get mad at James P. about. Jimmy
always talked very soft and tried to help guys with their
music. Jimmy would tell you when you were wrong, but if
he told you, you were wrong. Then he would tell you when
you were right.*

*Jimmy always wanted someone to come to the studio with
him when he cut piano rolls or made records just to have
some company. He'd want you to go out and get his
booze and you'd sit and drink and joke. He used to come
by the house and get me when he was going to the studio.
I used to go so I could look out the top floor where the
studio was and see the girls sunbathin' naked on the roof
tops. The girls would wave and say, "Hello there, fellas."
The studio was at 113 57th Street. The only person around
the studio was the recording controller and he didn't mind
all the stuff goin' on. Sometimes Jimmy would bring four or
five people with him.*

*Jimmy made a lot of player piano rolls. The first time I
saw him recording rolls I thought he'd blowed his top. He
was playing a regular piano but no sound was coming out.*

I asked him what he was doing. He stopped, ran the roll back and played it for me. You play the piano just like a regular one but every time you hit it, it punches a hole.

Jimmy could write music very fast. He's the fastest one I know of. If you told him to arrange something, when you finish playing he'll sit down at the piano and play it and say, "This what you want?" Then he'd write it out. Bingie Madison was very fast too. If he heard an arrangement twice, he could write it out on his shirt cuffs. Jimmy wrote good so you could read it when he finished, they weren't just scratches. Joe Steele went to the conservatory and you couldn't read nothin' he wrote.

James P. was a much better piano player than Jelly. Jelly was a good entertaining piano player, but he wasn't in the same league with James P. or Fats.

I didn't record with Jimmy until way late, right before he died. I'd been knowing him for a long time though. He used to stay at our house a lot. He would be rehearsing one of those big shows or something like that and wouldn't get through till way late. He'd come by our house and I wouldn't let him go all the way out to Long Island. Sometimes he'd have Duke or someone else with him, and they'd stay too. We'd usually call Lil and let her know where he was. Sometimes she'd come to town and stay at our place with him. We used to go out to Jimmy's place and play a lot too. Jimmy never talked much except about music. He was always writing it, playing it, and talking about it. He taught Fats how to play. They lived right across from each other on Long Island, and Clarence Williams lived right there too. Jimmy was a very fine musician.

Willie the Lion Smith used to live in the same apartment house I did in Harlem. Willie is what you call a born musician. He was a very slow reader and couldn't play in

the big bands but was very good with the small ones.
Willie could play in more keys than anyone except James P.

Willie and I used to play with Leadbelly. I think we were
the only two guys who could play with him. Leadbelly
didn't know which key he was going to play in. He'd play
in all naturals and sharps. We'd have to listen to him then
search around to find the key. Then when we found it,
we'd take off. Josh White and most of them guitar players
aren't good musicians. They just play the blues. When
Willie and I would play with them kinda guys, he'd come
around to say, "We got a hard date today, Pops." A lot of
those guys can't even tune their instruments.

Leadbelly didn't know when to start or stop. The recording
companies always had to go and splice his endings on.
Leadbelly's wife's name was Irene and the tune of his
"Irene" got to be a big hit. As soon as it did he died.
Leadbelly was a mean and evil guy. He was in the
penitentiary three times for killing guys and every time he
played his way out. I was at his house one day with one
of the partners of Asch Records talking about making some
records, when he nearly killed a guy. Leadbelly's son-in-law
insulted this guy's wife and he chased the son-in-law up to
Leadbelly's door. They were fighting in the doorway when
Leadbelly picked up an iron poker and started hitting the
guy in the head with it. Me and the guy from Asch got
out of the place and took off. When Leadbelly went
before the judge for beating the guy we had to go to court
with him. The judge knew about Leadbelly's singing and
that he was on parole, and he didn't want to send him
back to jail. So he told the guy he nearly killed that he
had no business in Leadbelly's house and fined him, and
withdrew the charges against Leadbelly.

When Leadbelly would get mad he'd just sit and grit his
teeth. One time I told him he'd have to play a chord up
on his guitar or we couldn't make no record. He just sat
and started gritting his teeth. I told him he could grit his

teeth all day, but if he didn't play the chord we couldn't play with him. He finally played it. Another time the government told him he had to pay taxes, and he was mad because he'd never paid before. He just sat and gritted his teeth; I told him to have the man take it out before he got paid. Leadbelly was just a mean and evil man. I just made records with him and never hung around with him at all.

Willie the Lion was always getting a band up for rehearsal and no job showed up. In the Depression this was OK because we wasn't doin' nothin' anyway. One time after I married Alma we were getting ready to go to her home in South Carolina for a visit. I had my clothes all packed and sent to have them put on the train. Willie came around and said we had a job starting the next day. I stayed, turned in my ticket, and didn't have no clothes until Alma got back. That job ain't come up yet.

Perry Bradford was from Memphis. He wrote a whole lot of blues. He was one of those old honky-tonk piano players that played with one finger. I got to know him some around New York. He played like George Thomas, Eudell Wilson, and Manny Johns and his wife. Manny Johns and his wife were the only man and wife team I know of that played around New Orleans. One would sing and one would play the piano. If it got so they weren't making any tips, they'd switch off. In New Orleans most piano players made their money working in the whorehouses, but around Chicago and New York they made most of their money at house rent parties or what we called fish frys in New Orleans. In Chicago and New York they'd serve chitlins, pigs' feet, and gin. Sometimes they'd call them "birthday parties." You'd get an invitation to a birthday party and when you got there you had to pay to get in and then buy your own food and booze. Guys like Bradford, Jimmy Yancey, and Luckey Roberts used to make good money playing those affairs. They also played the tonks. Along State Street in Chicago there used to be a whole lot of them. Luckey Roberts was a fine piano player. I played a couple of shows with him. He was a little bitty guy but he was very strong. One night a couple of guys tried to hold him up. He grabbed them and knocked their heads together and then started whipping them something awful. By the time the police arrived the two robbers were hollering for the cops Luckey was beating them up so bad. Luckey used to do all the big piano jobs around New York.

I played with Teddy Wilson at the French Casino in New York. That was the old Earl Carroll Theatre at Fifty-first Street and Seventh Avenue. Upstairs they had a bar where Teddy and I played. Downstairs they had two bands, one that played the shows and Noble Sissle's that played the dances. Teddy was a very quiet guy and very nice. About all he'd ever say was, "Hello, how're you doin?" Teddy was a very good piano player and had a different style of playing than the other players. He played very good with a band or all by himself. He played all over the piano. He wasn't as good as Art Tatum. Tatum was out there all by himself but he was a liquor head. Even that didn't stop Tatum. He was so good he could walk out of a place or get fired and walk right into another place and the people would be glad to have him, juice head and all. He was a genius. If you're playing with him and he takes a solo, you can't play for listening to him.

The arrangement that rejoined Louis Armstrong, then the biggest name in jazz, with Pops and other old New Orleans comrades came about as the result of booking agency maneuvering. In 1935 Armstrong signed a personal management contract with the aggressive and astute Joe Glaser of Chicago. Glaser's first move was to refurbish the Armstrong orchestral image, somewhat tarnished by a succession of weak accompanying orchestras. Louis had not recorded since January, 1933, except for an unimportant session made in Paris with a pickup group of European musicians. The new team — Louis backed by the settled, sonorous, and powerful Luis Russell Orchestra — began auspiciously with a series of record sessions in New York starting in October, 1935, for the new Decca label, a thirty-five-cent seller that was moving aggressively into the jazz and pop field. The emphasis was on standard and current material — *La Cucaracha, On Treasure Island, Red Sails in the Sunset, You Are My Lucky Star.* These performances, trimmed to less than three minutes to meet jukebox demands, were dominated by Armstrong's vocals and high note trumpet playing. Louis had long since ceased to play cornet. Besides the standard tunes a few interesting originals were recorded: *Swing That Music* and a new version of the New Orleans favorite, *Mahogany Hall Stomp.* The band was heard to greater advantage on tour. There were many of these, long and short, to various parts of America, often with incredible jumps between the one-nighters that Joe Glaser had been able to book, like the one mentioned by Pops, from Bangor to New Orleans. Pops's salary of $77.00 a week was expected to cover maintaining a home for Alma in New York as well as his own expenses while on the road. These trips were always stimulating enough

but replete with hardship: lack of accommodations, hasty
and missed meals, catnaps caught between engagements
in the jolting bus, and Jim Crow conditions.
The chance discovery of Bunk Johnson in New Iberia,
Louisiana, in 1937, led to a rehabilitation movement to
bring the veteran trumpet player back to the jazz scene,
although this did not take place until the war years.
Fitted with new teeth, Bunk made a triumphant return to
music in San Francisco and later led his own bands in
New York. A currently available LP (*Bunk Johnson and his
Superior Jazz Band*) contains a long recorded interview
with Bunk and interesting examples of re-created New Orleans
small band style.
The wholesale firing in 1940 of the men in the Louis
Armstrong-Luis Russell Orchestra by Joe Glaser was typical of
the dubious practices prevalent in the music business.
Thereafter Armstrong recorded with various pickup groups —
the Mills Brothers and Casa Loma Orchestra among them —
before forming a small seven-piece combo to play concerts.
Pops began one of the worst periods of his life. His fortunes
did not improve until after the war. He appeared on the
This is Jazz Show produced by jazz authority Rudi Blesh,
made a successful tour of Europe with Mezz Mezzrow in 1948
and recorded for Mezzrow's King Jazz label. Then he returned
to the West Coast to join Earl Hines for a long, steady,
artistically rewarding stay at the Club Hangover in San
Francisco. That was in 1955. Thereafter Pops made San
Francisco his home and worked there almost continually with
small bands playing in the authentic prewar style (New
Orleans, Dixieland, Main Stream) until his death in 1969.

10. TRAVELING WITH ARMSTRONG — AND AFTER

Louis Armstrong tried all of the bands around New York but none of them would give up their name permanently for him. In 1935 Luis Russell gave up our name to Armstrong and we were known as Louis Armstrong's band after that. Before that, Louis had used our band a lot of times for recording dates and different gigs, but we always went back to Luis Russell's name. I was with Armstrong from 1935 until I got fired in 1940.

We worked a lot more under Russell than we did under Armstrong. When we went with Armstrong, we were all real glad and thought we'd make a lot more money. But Joe Glaser, his manager, wanted a lot of money for Louis. He wanted guarantees, advances, and a percentage. People just didn't have a lot of money in those days, and they wouldn't come out enough to afford big prices. So we didn't get as many dates. I was making $77.00 a week when we worked. When we made it, we spent it. Before I got married I gambled a lot and drank some. When you hit a new town everybody was glad to see you because they knew you spent a lot of money. I'd gamble on anything — poker, blackjack, tonk, fantan, craps, or anything else. If Joe Glaser didn't have any work, we'd loaf. We didn't get any

*pay but Joe would loan us money. After I married Alma she'd
send me money to live on so I wouldn't owe Joe.
everything when we got to working.*

*One time in 1937 we were loafing in Chicago and I was
playing gigs with some outlaw guys on the South Side. I'd
seen some of Benny Goodman's boys around town.
Benny had a recording date and they couldn't find Harry
Goodman so they went out to get me. When they got me
and got back, I got there about the same time Harry did,
so we both played on the records.*

*The guys in the band sure were glad I was getting a little
work because they were all broke and I'd share what I
had with them. We all shared when we were broke except
Louis Bacon. Louis Bacon had money and he never asked
nobody for nothing and he never gave nothing. When I got
sick with pneumonia all the guys gave some money to
help except him. He said, "I'm not giving those New
Orleans cats nothin'." When he got sick in New Orleans,
I was the only one in the band that went to the hospital
to see him. I carried some soup up to him that Alma
made. He sat up in the bed and cried.*

*With Armstrong we traveled a whole lot. Once we jumped
from Bangor, Maine, to New Orleans for a one-nighter, then
to Houston, Texas, for the next night. Traveling never
worried me like it did the other guys. We'd take off and
they'd start saying how far we had to go. I knew how far
it was so there wasn't any point thinking about it. Armstrong
always traveled by bus because it would take you right to
where you were going. Some of the bands like Duke's and
Cab's traveled by train, but they were always switching
connections and taking cabs to hotels and so on.*

*It was tough traveling through the South in those days. We
had two white guys with us — the bus driver and Joe Glaser.
If you had a colored bus driver back then, they'd lock
him up in every little country town for "speeding." It was
very rough finding a place to sleep in the South. You*

*couldn't get into the hotels for whites, and the colored didn't
have any hotels. You rented places in private homes,
boarding houses, and whorehouses. The food was awful
and we tried to find places where we could cook. We
carried a bunch of pots and pans around with us.*

*Charlie Holmes and I palled around together and we always
found some way to have a good time. The rest of the
guys were always watching to see what we cooked up. One
time the two of us were broke in Texas and wanted to
have a drink. We decided to get Bobby Austin, who was
the vocalist with the band and was Sonny Woods's girlfriend.
When we'd travel they'd fight all the time. He'd knock her
down, she'd lay there a while, then get up and hit him
with a shoe or something, then he'd knock her down again.
We always had to move our card game to keep out of
their fights. We started telling Bobby how bad Sonny was
and how awful he treated her. Every time we'd come up
with something else: "It's a shame how bad Sonny treats
you, you're so good to him and he's such a bum." She'd
say, "Have another drink boys." We had a nice little thing
going there for awhile until Sonny caught us. He got real
hot.*

*One time we were stuck in Tulsa, Oklahoma, and hadn't
had any work for about a month. Sonny Woods, Midge
Williams, and myself got a crap game going. Midge had
gotten to know the local sheriff and he gave us protection.
We'd get a few guys to play with Midge at one end in a
very low cut dress and Sonny or me at the other end.
When Midge would shoot she'd bend real low so everybody
could see her titties. All the guys would be looking at
them and we'd call whatever number we wanted and pick
up the dice. We got enough money to get us to Kansas
City and then Memphis for a week's work.*

*I never fooled around with none of the show girls we
worked with. To me they were just like a bunch of horses.
I just never paid them any mind. Sometimes I'd hustle a*

bottle to introduce some guy to one of them. He'd want to meet one and I'd tell him to bring me a taste and I'd try to fix it up. Then I'd tell the girl and I'd give her a taste. Besides that, when we got off they went one way and I went another. If you want to get along, don't fool with no girls you work with. They expect too much out of you. If you're going on the road they always try to team up with you. They know you're going to pay the rent and they're going to eat. If they'd come around I'd tell them my landlady don't allow no company. Some of the guys fooled around with them. Most of the guys were looking for a place to sleep and eat for nothin' just like the girls. I used to gamble with the girls sometimes and beat them out of their money.

When two bands would meet on the road, we'd all get together and make a whole gang of noise and get thrown out of hotels. In 1936 our band, the Isham Jones Band, and the Benson Band all met in Iowa, and all three bands got thrown out in the street for cuttin' up.

When I was on the road with Armstrong and we'd get close to New York, I'd call Alma and she'd meet me, like in Chicago, and we'd stay together there a week or so. Sometimes when the band would take off she'd go with me for a month or two, and sometimes she'd just go on back to New York. Alma is my second wife and the best thing I ever locked up on. I always say the reason I lived so long isn't because I took care of myself, because I didn't. The reason is, I locked up on a good wife. I never was what you call a corner bum though. Those are guys that stand around a certain street corner all day or hang around a saloon. Even if I went gambling I'd take $10.00 with me, or whatever I was going to play with, and if I'd lose I'd take off. I couldn't stand to just hang around swallowing bets like some of the guys. Some of them would play your hand harder than you did. Most musicians don't eat right and don't even go home at night. It kills them off.

Louis's second wife Lil sure was good to him. She still loves him after all these years. The reason she took off was Louis's pot smoking. There wasn't any woman or nothin', she just got tired of Louis smoking that stuff. He smoked pot just like you smoke regular cigarettes. The band was playing Jack Sheen's in New Orleans when she left. Jack's was a wide open place in St. Bernard's Parish. Louis smoked pot all the time I was with him and as far as I know never quit.

Louis should give more credit to Lil than anyone for teaching him how to play. She was a great piano player and a great musician. Lil's a nice girl too, not wild or mean at all. Louis should also give a lot of credit to old man Joe Oliver for teaching him how to play tunes and arrangements.

I knew all of Louis's wives. His first wife was a rough gal, Daisey. Daisey used to go with Eddie Atkins, the trombone player, before she married Louis. She used to work all over New Orleans and she used to come down to the Come Clean Hall every Sunday night to dance when I was playing there. She finally went to Chicago and I never heard no more about her.

Louis's third wife Alpha used to travel around with the band before they were married. They lived together for about ten years before they got married, then when they got married it only lasted about four years. When they fought they really went after each other.

I've had a good time in my life playing music and traveling around the world. It's kicks man! You really learn people. I can look at a guy right now and tell you, "That guy is no good, he's a rat," or "That cat's alright." When I see a guy come up to the stand I can tell you if he's going to start trouble or not. You sure learn a lot from traveling and meeting people.

I remember Bob Smiley, Louis's valet and bodyguard, and how I dealt with him once when he owed me a quarter

Louis Armstrong in the 1930s.

The Louis Armstrong Orchestra, about 1936. From left: Henry Allen, trumpet; Lee Blair, guitar; Louis Bacon, trumpet; Pops Foster, string bass; unknown; Luis Russell, piano; Gus Aiken, trumpet; Bobby Caston, vocals; Louis Armstrong, trumpet; Sonny Woods, vocals; Jimmie Archey, trombone; Charles Holmes, reeds; Greely Walton, reeds; Paul Barbarin, drums; Bingie Madison, reeds; Henry Moon Jones, reeds; Leonard Horn Davis, trumpet.

Rhythm section of the Louis Armstrong Orchestra, about 1936. From left: Luis Russell, piano; Paul Barbarin, drums; Pops Foster, string bass; Lee Blair, guitar.

Louis Armstrong in the 1930s.

Sonny Woods, about 1935.

Midge Williams, late 1930s.

Barney Bigard, late 1940s.

Pops Foster, about 1936, after recovering from a long illness.

Part of the Louis Armstrong Orchestra about 1936. From left: Paul
Barbarin. drums; Louis Armstrong, trumpet; Henry Jones, reeds; Lee Blair,
guitar: Pops Foster, string bass.

Alpha and Louis Armstrong and Alma and Pops Foster on outing to
Coney Island, about 1934.

Willie Bunk Johnson, San Francisco, about 1945, shortly after his discovery and rehabilitation.

Jimmie Archey and His Jazz Band, New York, about 1945. Sidney de Paris (?), trumpet; Tommy Benford, drums; Jimmie Archey, trombone; Dick Wellstood, piano; Darnell Howard, clarinet; Pops Foster, string bass.

Pops and Willie Foster, about 1950.   Pops and Alma, 1945, Boston.

The Foster family, about 1945. From left: Alma, Annie, Elizabeth, and Pops.

New Orleans musicians' get-together, 1944. From left: Big Eye Louis
Nelson Delisle, clarinet; Louis Nelson, trombone; Peter Bocage, cornet; Paul
Barbarin, drums; unknown, banjo; Pops Foster, bass; Sidney Bechet,
clarinet and soprano saxophone; Alphonse Picou, clarinet.

The Sidney Bechet Band in Boston, 1945. From left: George Thompson,
drums; Pops Foster, string bass; Bunk Johnson, trumpet; Sidney Bechet,
soprano saxophone; Ray Parket, piano.

Pops in 1945

Pops in 1967.

Pops in 1956, Zurich, Switzerland.

Pops at Club Hangover, Bush and Powell
Streets, San Francisco, about 1956. Band was
led by Earl Fatha Hines, piano, and featured
cornetist Muggsy Spanier. Joe Sullivan
was the intermission pianist.

Jimmie Archey and Pops Foster on European
tour, Sweden, 1956.

New Orleans Jazz Group on European tour, about 1958. From left: Alton Parnell, Jimmie Archey (with glasses), Darnell Howard, Alvin Alcorn, Josiah Frazier, Pops Foster.

Eddie Montudie Garland and Wellman Braud, about 1960.

Warren Baby Dodds, about 1950.

Minor Hall, about 1945.

Pops and Alma, 1960.

*and wouldn't pay me just to be nasty. We were playing
Little Rock, Arkansas, and were headed toward New
Orleans. I just started on him from the opposite direction
by saying, "Man, I don't want you to pay me, but wait
until we get to New Orleans where I can get some dust."
Louis Bacon said, "Man you wouldn't use none of that dust
on him would you?" And I said, "Man you don't know how
long he owed me a quarter, but I don't want it now. I'd
rather get some dust and turn him into a lizard." Smiley
followed me around for a week after that trying to pay me
the quarter and I'd just say, "No man, I gotta put the dust
on you now." Finally, just before we got to New Orleans
I took it and gave him a good warning.*

*We used to pull some bad tricks on Paul Barbarin because
he was so afraid of ghosts. Sometimes we'd go in his room
to call up spirits or pretend we were talking to ghosts.
When we were leaving the hotel in Chicago we stole some
sheets one time. That night out on the road we stopped for
a break. Paul had been drinking and was about half
gassed. A bunch of us put on the sheets across the road
from the bus, then one of us hit the side of the bus where
Paul was snoozing. He stuck his head up and we started
jumping up and down. He took off outta the bus and ran
down the road till we couldn't see him. When he came
back everybody was laughing and he wanted to fight.*

*Another time Paul met this girl and he told her he was in
the dress business. He took her up to his room at the
Douglas Hotel in Philly. My room was right next to his and
we listened to them. They decided to go get something to
drink and then come back. When they got back we had
Albert Nicholas under the bed with a fork to scratch on
the bed springs and a string tied to one of the chairs we
could pull from the next room. We'd look through the
keyhole and make sure the girl could see the chair move.
She said, "Mr. Barbarin, Mr. Paul, that chair's moving." Paul
said, "Don't worry, you're with a man, nothing's going to*

happen to you!" We pulled the chair again and Nick hit the bed springs with the fork. She wet all over the floor, ran out of the room and took off. Paul took off too. When he came back he came to my room and there were nine of us guys in there pretending like we were sleeping. He wanted to fight all of us.

From 1910 to 1937, I didn't see Bunk Johnson. In 1910 he left New Orleans with a minstrel show. In 1937 Louis's band was playing a Catholic dance in New Iberia, Louisiana, and I saw Louis talking to this old guy. After we started playing, I said to Louis, "Who's that old guy?"

Louis said, "That's Bunk Johnson."

I said, "I didn't even recognize him."

Louis said, "I didn't either, man."

The next intermission I went over and talked to Bunk for awhile. He said he'd been driving sugarcane wagons. He sure had changed in those twenty-seven years. He didn't have no teeth at all. He said he'd been with the minstrel show for a long time. Those minstrel show cars were really funny. They'd hook them on the back of the train and then put them off at the siding at the town where they were going. The show people would mostly live in the car because people wouldn't rent them rooms. Show people would steal anything they could carry and then not pay the rent. They'd steal chickens, rabbits, sheets, clothes, or anything.

After we met Bunk in New Iberia some guys from San Francisco found him and carried him to San Francisco. He played there for quite a while but he got to drinking and they sent him back to Louisiana. In 1945 Sidney Bechet and I met Bunk in New Orleans and carried him to Boston to play with us. The first night in Boston he got drunk and didn't show up. Alma went out looking for him. When she found him he was drunk and had lost his horn. After that he straightened up for awhile. Then Gene Williams wanted him to come to New York. Gene would get him drunk so Sidney would fire him, and it worked.

I've only missed a couple of gigs in my life. In 1937 I missed a movie gig with Armstrong. We were in New York and were going to leave for Hollywood. I was down with a mild case of pneumonia. Luis Russell came to the house and told me, "Pops, we're leaving for L.A. without you." I got worse then and went to the hospital the next day. I nearly died and it was two months before I caught up with them. Those movie deals were nice; you picked up a nice piece of change on them. When I finally caught up with the band, some of the guys were short of money, and so I asked them what they did with the money from the movie. They said they didn't make no picture. The movie outfit wanted the band to wear blackface and they wouldn't. Cab Calloway's band wouldn't either. They finally got Tommy or Jimmy Dorsey's band and they wore half-masks to make them look black.

I got my nickname from Louis Armstrong. He calls everyone "Pops." The name just stuck on me. In New Orleans some of the guys called me "the Fireman" or "Fireman George." We used to call Louis "Poppa."

Louis was always a happy-go-lucky guy about most things. I've seen him do a lot of crazy things like start on stage without any pants on. I remember one time a guy hit Louis for a handout. Louis gave him a quarter and the guy said, "Hey man, don't put me down like that!" Louis said, "OK man, let's have it back!" The guy did, thinking Louis was gonna give him more. Louis put the quarter in his pocket and took off.

Louis is real jealous of other players who put out. If you play bad you won't be in the band, and if you play too good you won't be there. When I'd get to romping along on the bass, he'd yell at me, "Hey, man, if you want to play trumpet come on down here and play." I'd say, "Go on man and blow your horn." He's lucky he's lived so long.

He works too hard because he don't want nobody to do nothing but him. Louis shouldn't be so jealous because he's an outstanding man.

In about 1935 or 1936 we started playing for audiences that just sat there. I never liked this, I always liked to play for an audience that dances. The kind of music I like to play is the faster stuff where you can really get to romping along. I don't really like to play many blues. They're slow and draggy. Some good ones like Basin Street Blues *you can rock along with.*

In 1940 Joe Glaser fired the whole band to get a cheaper band. I was making $77.00 a week when we worked and some of the guys were only making $66.00 and doing arrangements too. The reason they told me was I was too old and Jimmie Archey got told he was too short. Joe hired some of the guys back at a cheaper price. Some of the new guys he hired couldn't play the music and that was about the end of the band. They went downhill fast after that. Things really got rough for me, too.

Sometimes you have it good in life and sometimes rough. About the roughest time I've had was after I got fired from Armstrong's band. I made some records for a lot of little companies with different small groups and played a few gigs around New York. We were really scuffling to make it and then I got sick with pneumonia again. The finance company came and took all our furniture. Alma and me finally got my nephew to move us into a little room where he could help take care of us. Things finally started getting a little better and we wriggled out of it.

It was around this time I went to Chicago and recorded blues for a whole week. Panassié had set up the session so Mezz Mezzrow could record. They didn't put any name on the blues until later. Mezzrow claimed that he composed a lot of them. Panassié thinks that Mezzrow is the greatest. When Mezz is playing, he sits there rocking back and forth like Mezz is outta this world. Any little boy can play the clarinet or sax as good as Mezz can. He just stands up there and goes toot-toot-toot. Mezz sure is a good manager though and a very nice guy. I like him, but man he can't play no jazz.

In 1942 things got so bad in music I said I'd rather grab me a broom and start working. I went and took the test for subway work in New York. After the test I had my preference of a porter's job or workin' the change booth. One of the guys told me, "Pops, you'd better not take a job working the change booth because you can't sneak off. The best job around is the porter's, even though it don't pay a nickel, because you can slip off when you want to." I took the porter's job and stayed with it from 1942 to 1945 when I went with Sidney Bechet.

As soon as I started workin' I started slippin' off. I played all over New York and the other little places there are around there; I even slipped off to play gigs in Canada and Washington, D.C. My boss, Mr. Horton, was awful good to me. The most work I did was hiding from the Inspector. He'd come by to check if we were there, then get on the train. I'd get on the same train but the next car back. When I'd come back I'd bring Horton a box of those stinky old Cheroot cigars.

The water gigs I slipped off to and played in Washington, D.C., were great. They were kind of a symphony sort of thing. They'd take us out on boats to barges tied in the middle of the river, then we'd play for the people back on the bank. You get a different sound from music when you're playing on the water like that. It sure was beautiful.

One night I took off to play a big party in New York. Right in front of me one of the big shots on the subway, Mr. Bagley, sat down. He kept looking at me and I kept looking like I never saw him. The next day though the word came down for me to go to his office. When I got there, he said, "Why didn't you ever tell me you played music."

I said, "Who told you?"

He said, "I saw you."

I said, "Where?"

He said, "Last night, I kept passing you music to play all night on a little slip of paper, don't you remember?" I said, "Oh yeah, it was you!" Then he said I did a nice job and told me if I had to take off again just to tell the inspector he'd okayed it.

I used to play Minton's in New York before Dizzy Gillespie and Charlie Parker worked there. I was fronting a little group when Teddy Hill took over the management. Teddy was sore at me then and so he fired my band. I played with Diz and Charlie, both of them were great. Diz could do all that crazy stuff on his horn, and then stop and play a whole lot of trumpet. He'd do more crazy stuff on his horn than anybody. Diz and Charlie started all that stuff they're doing today. It was a symphony kind of music. Those two guys didn't overdo it, and they were the best that played that kind of music. Charlie used to drink a lot but I never saw him take dope. Diz always loves to get me to sit and talk to him about the old times.

I took a vacation down to New Orleans in 1945 and met Sidney Bechet on Perdido and Rampart. He came up to me and said, "What you doin around here, old man?"

I said, "What do you mean, dad?" While we were there we got some guys together and made some records for the USO at the Maison Blanche building. We got Louis Keppard, Alphonse Picou, Big Eye Louis Nelson, Peter Bocage, a guy named Henry on trombone, and a guy named Valcons on piano. We sure made a lot of music, but none of us ever heard the records. Sidney asked me if I wanted to play with his band he was gonna get for a Boston date he had. He said he was gonna get Bunk Johnson, so I said I'd do it too.

Before I left New Orleans I had a couple of sets of strings for my bass that were too light for my instrument, but I

*thought they were just right for Slow Drag Pavageau's. I
hadn't seen Slow Drag so I gave them to Jim Robinson,
the trombone player, to give to him. A few years later I
was back in New Orleans and I met Slow Drag. I asked
him how he liked the strings I'd sent to him, I also told
him I was kind of mad he hadn't written and thanked
me. He said, "I don't know, man, I never got them. Who'd
you give them to?"*

I said, "Jim Robinson."

*Slow Drag said, "That dirty bastard, he sold them to me!"
They didn't speak for a couple of years after that.*

*I went back to New York and took a six-month leave of
absence to go play with Sidney's band. From the time we
opened we had trouble with Bunk, but I've already talked
about it. Sidney fired Bunk and sent to New Orleans for
Peter Bocage. He came and started telling everybody how
to play so Sidney fired him and got a kid named Johnny
Windhurst to finish the job with us.*

*Some of the problems we had may have been Sidney's fault.
He is the most selfish, hard to get along with guy I ever
worked with. I saw him fire one trumpet player five times
in one night. You really had to try to get along with him.
From the time I played with him in Jack Carey's band in
New Orleans to making a bunch of Blue Note records
with him, he was a tough baby and all for himself.*

*After the Boston job gave out I went back to New York
and worked around with Art Hodes in the Latin Quarter at
a place called the Chicken Inn. It was owned by the guy
who owned Four Roses whiskey. When that job was
finished I went to Washington, D.C., with Sidney to play the
Brown Derby. Some guys wanted Sidney and I to come
to New York and go on the air with Louis Armstrong. But
Sidney said he was as big a name as Louis, so Louis
could come to Washington. Joe Glaser wouldn't go for that
and we didn't get the job.*

*When I finally got back to New York I went on the "This
Is Jazz" show for Rudi Blesh. They sent to Chicago for
Baby Dodds. He came out and him and I worked on the
show for almost its whole time on the air. We had guys
like Armstrong, Bechet, Muggsy Spanier, Wild Bill Davison,
George Brunies, Jimmy Archey, and a whole gang of guys.
That's how Jimmy got to be known. He played on the
show for a long time. There were a lot of good trumpet
players around Harlem in those days. When we first started
we'd try to get them to go on but they'd say they "didn't
want to play that old time stuff." After Baby, Jimmy, and
I started doing so well the same guys would come around
and say, "Hey, Pops, how about cutting me in on that show
you're on?" I'd say, "No man, this is that old time stuff you
don't wanta play."*

*Baby Dodds was really a good friend of mine, one of the
best I've had in a lifetime. We played a whole lot of jobs
together. He's also one of the best drummers. He never
overplayed his drums. I'd play a ilttle riff and he'd just
keep the beat instead of trying to drown me out. Baby used
to come around just so he could be with me and was
always passin' compliments to me. He used to say to Alma,
"I sure do love that old man." I always thought very high
of him.*

*When Baby and I were working together a lot in New York,
we started playing a lot of college jobs. I've been to
Columbia, Yale, Princeton, and lost my teeth at Penn State.
I got so drunk I dropped them in the toilet and flushed
them down before I knew what happened. It was when I
was with the college kids I started to drink whiskey heavy.
Before that I drank and even got drunk sometimes but with
the college kids every one of them wanted to buy you a
drink. They seemed to be so crazy about me, I couldn't
say no. So if there were twenty-five kids, I'd try to have
twenty-five drinks.*

*When I did get drunk, I didn't do anyone any harm.
Mostly I'd want to sleep, play music, or try to cut up and*

*be funny. I think colored musicians mostly drank booze and
the white guys started taking dope. Some young colored
musicians did start taking dope after that. The only real
trouble I ever had in my life was the drinking I did
around New York and that was all harm to myself.*

*One time I remember we went over to Rhode Island to
play a college date. Jimmy Archey, Art Hodes, me, and a
couple of other guys. Art brought a whole suitcase full of
whiskey. We all got pretty well loaded but Art couldn't even
stand up. It was wintertime, so we took him outside and
laid him out in a snowbank to cool him off. We forgot
him. When we finally remembered him, he was nearly
frozen stiff. It took us a long time to thaw him out; we
worked on it all the way back to New York. He lived, so
I guess it didn't do him too much harm.*

*Another time a bunch of us were playing a boat job on
the Hudson River. There was Marty Marsala, Baby Dodds,
Albert Nicholas, James P., and myself. Marty and I were
drinking up a storm that night and we kept passing glasses
of whiskey up to the boat pilot all night. He got pretty
drunk, and when we came into the pier that night he missed
his shot and rammed it. James P.'s piano stool broke and
James P. came down on his butt. He just sat there smoking
his cigarette and all of us laughing. The pilot backed up
and then rammed the pier again before he made it.*

*Baby Dodds and me used to have some wild times in
those days. Baby and I used to drive downtown in his car
and then get so drunk we'd lose the car. We'd have to
sober up so we could go down all the streets looking for it.
Drinking sure makes you act funny. Alma has never asked
me about money and has always been the best of wives.
One night I came home from a gig with the money they'd
paid me. I told Alma she was getting too smart so I was
going to hide my money. I set a mousetrap and put my
money in it in a drawer so if Alma tried to take it she'd
get caught. When I woke up the next day I asked her to
give me some money. She said I didn't give her none. I*

remembered hiding my money but I forgot about the mousetrap. I stuck my hand in to get it and nearly got a couple of broken fingers.

In 1948 I made my first trip to Europe with Mezz Mezzrow. Before I could go I had to go to the doctor to get an OK. He told me to lay off the whiskey for fifteen days. I went back after fifteen days and told him I'd laid off the stuff. He said I'd live a lot longer if I never touched it again. I said, "I quit," and I haven't touched it since. Alma didn't think I'd make it, but I did. In 1959 when my ticker started kicking up, I quit cigarettes.

Before I left New York in about 1954 I was down talking to Spool Head Clarence Williams at his pawnshop on 125th Street between Fifth Avenue and Lennox Avenue. He was the only colored man in the country to have a pawnshop at that time. I used to go down there to talk to him sometimes. This time I was saying, "There was one band I'd like to come to New York and play, and that was Clairborne Williams's band, my cousin!"

Clarence said, "What do you mean, your cousin?"

I said, "My cousin, man, they sure ain't your cousins even with your name." He said, "They were my cousins. All of the family was musical, I even had an aunt who had three young kids that played. I always wondered what happened to them." I said, "You're looking at one of them!" Clarence said, "I been knowing you for over forty years since New Orleans and I didn't know that. Why didn't you make yourself known?" I said, "Why didn't you make yourself known?"

We had a big laugh and talk about finding out we were related after all those years.

Around Harlem and Chicago's South Side all the white people used to come for entertainment. They used to leave their car and walk around from spot to spot. They don't do that anymore; they're scared to even come around. I'm even

afraid to walk around those places at night now. In 1955 I
took five dollars and went out to get Alma some medicine.
As soon as I hit the end of the steps two doped-up kids
grabbed me and choked me till I passed out. They took
the five dollars and my cigarettes. Both of them were from
the neighborhood and I knew them. I figured I was lucky
to be alive and I'd better get out of Harlem, so I came
out here to California to join Earl Hines at the Club
Hangover. We had a nice bunch of guys there. Muggsy,
Darnell Howard, Ory, sometimes; Earl, Zutty, and other guys.
Earl Hines really knew a lot about music. He taught me
more about music than anybody else. He would show me
chords I didn't know existed and how you could fit so
many different chords together. He's great. Muggsy and I
were great friends. The thing he liked to do most was
come over and eat Alma's red beans and rice. He was
always asking Alma to cook some up for him. The last
time he was here he ate two serving bowls full.

A lot of the old guys are gone now. There's only a couple
of us left. Montudie and I are about the only ones. I've
played with a lot of guys in my life and had a lot of good
times. Most of the guys I've played with the last thirty-five
years think I'm a lot older than I am. They remember I
played with Freddie Keppard, Manuel Perez, Joe Oliver,
and guys like that. That makes you old in their eyes. Some
of them think I'm about 150 years old. Well, when I
started I was always the youngest one in the band and
now I'm always the oldest. It's been kicks.

EPILOGUE

On October 30, 1969 at about 3:00 p.m. George Murphy
"Pops" Foster quit the scene. That was the day after I
finished the Foreword to this book. After a long illness, Pops
died of complications due to blood clots, a tumor found in
his stomach, and a weak heart that just gave out. Pops
was the kindest, gentlest man I have ever known. I know
of no one who has ever spoken against Pops. With me he
was tops.

Pops died knowing his life story had been written. I had
only the chronology and some of the pictures to go over
with him for some final data. Most of the chapters had
been delivered to him and the final four were on the way
to the typist when he died. He had read most of the
chapters and had said, "It sounds great, just the way
I told it." He had misgivings about two items — meeting the
woman at George Hooker's house and Jelly's left hand. I
told him if he would like, I would pull them out. He said,
"They were the truth so leave them in, and I didn't call the
woman's name anyway."

Some will claim that Pops says some nasty things about
Armstrong, Jelly, Bechet, and others. He always thought
Armstrong and Bechet were great musicians, and he liked
Jelly. When he discussed them it was as a friend. There is
nothing said in these pages Pops probably had not told the

people to their faces. He had such an elfish way of saying things, they never sounded cruel or nasty.

On October 30, 1969, at seventy-seven years and a few months, the world lost a great jazzman and I lost a close friend. I would like to say what Baby Dodds said about him. I loved that old man.

Tom Stoddard

CHRONOLOGY OF MUSICAL
GROUPS, 1899-1969

Below is a list of the principal musical groups with whom
Pops Foster played during his lifetime.

Pops and I had not completed the chronology when he
passed away. In the book he does not refer to some of the
groups listed in the chronology. These are, however, groups
he mentioned to me in conversation prior to his death. The
list is not all-inclusive, since there were numerous other
groups he played with occasionally. For example, he
toured Europe with the Mezz Mezzrow Orchestra in 1948,
Jimmy Archey in 1952, and Sammy Price in 1955. These
were really pickup groups for the tours or in the case
of the Archey trip, they were to play with local groups. In
some cases where I have put "gigged" (played a specific
performance from time to time), Pops may have played
with the group regularly for a month or so but I am
unaware of a permanent connection. In other cases, like the
Tuxedo Orchestra, Pops gigged with them for many years
before he finally took a regular job.

Wyatt Foster Band, McCall Plantation, La.—1899-1900
The Fosters, McCall Plantation, La.—1900-1902
Pickup groups and string trios at lawn parties and fish frys, New Orleans,
  La.—1902-1906
Rozelle Orchestra, New Orleans, La.—1906-1908

Magnolia Orchestra, New Orleans, La.—1908-1912
Frankie Dusen's Eagle Band, New Orleans, La.—1908-1910 (gigged)
Ory Band, New Orleans, La.—1908-1920 (gigged)
Manuel Perez Band, New Orleans, La.—1908-1915 (gigged)
Freddie Keppard's Olympia Orchestra, New Orleans, La.—1908-1909 (gigged)
Silver Leaf Band, New Orleans, La.—1910-1912 (gigged)
Bab Frank's Peerless Orchestra, New Orleans, La.—1910-1920 (gigged)
Hamp Benson's Primrose Orchestra, New Orleans, La.—1910-1911
    (gigged)
Gold Leaf Band, New Orleans, La.—1910-1912 (gigged)
Jack Carey's Crescent Band, New Orleans, La.—1909-1915 (gigged)
Toots Johnson Band, Baton Rouge, La.—1911-1912 (gigged)
Edward Clem Band, New Orleans, La.—1911-1912 (gigged)
Alphonse Picou Orchestra, New Orleans, La.—1912-1915 (gigged)
Tuxedo Orchestra, New Orleans, La.—1912-1920
Thornton Blue Band, New Orleans, La.—1912-1913 (gigged)
John Robichaux Orchestra, New Orleans, La.—1912-1913 (gigged)
Dutrey Brothers Band, ship to British Honduras—1914
Buddy Petit Band, New Orleans, La.—1915
Tig Chambers Band, New Orleans, La.—1915-1916 (gigged)
Armand Piron Orchestra, New Orleans, La.—1915-1917
Amos Riley Band, New Orleans, La.—1917 (gigged)
The Jazz Syncopators (Fate Marable and the Streckfus Lines)
    S.S. Belle of the Bend, New Orleans, La.—1917-1918
Fate Marable and His Jazz Maniacs, S.S. Capitol on Mississippi River—
    1919-1921
Charlie Creath's Jazz-O-Maniacs, S.S. St. Paul on Mississippi River and
    at St. Louis, Mo.—1921, 1923-1925
Eddie Allen's Gold Whispering Band, Mississippi River—1921
Ory's Sunshine Orchestra, Los Angeles, Calif.—1922
Curtis Mosby Band, Los Angeles, Calif.—1922 (gigged)
Oran Lips Page Band, Los Angeles, Calif.—1922 (recorded)
Dewey Jackson's Peacock Orchestra, St. Louis, Mo.—1925, 1928-1929
Sidney Desvignes Orchestra, New Orleans, La.—1926-1927
Mutt Carey's Liberty Syncopators, Los Angeles, Calif.—1927-1928
Elks Brass Band, Los Angeles, Calif. to Chicago, Ill.—1928
Luis Russell and His Orchestra, New York, N.Y.—1929-1935
Duke Ellington Orchestra, New York, N.Y. and Philadelphia, Pa.—1931
    (gigged)
Fletcher Henderson Orchestra, New York, N.Y.—1931-1933 (gigged)
Horace Henderson Orchestra, New York, N.Y.—1931-1933 (gigged)
Fats Waller and His Buddies (and his Rhythm), New York, N.Y.—1929-1935
    (recorded and gigged)
Jelly Roll Morton Orchestra, New York, N.Y.—1932-1935 (rehearsed)
Willie the Lion Smith Band, New York, N.Y.—1933-1945 (recorded and
    rehearsed)

*Louis Armstrong and His Orchestra, home base New York, N.Y., but
    traveled all over U.S.—1935-1940*
Bennie Goodman Orchestra, Chicago, Ill.—1937 (recorded)
Mezz Mezzrow Orchestra, Chicago, Ill.—1941 (recorded)
James P. Johnson Orchestra, New York, N.Y.—1942-1955 (gigged)
Pickup groups and various musicians in New York—1940-1955
Pops Foster Band, New York, N.Y.—1944
*Sidney Bechet Band, Boston, Mass, Washington, D.C., and New York, N.Y.—
    1945-1946*
This Is Jazz house band, New York, N.Y.—1947-1948
Earl Hines's Club Hangover Orchestra, San Francisco, Calif.—1955-1960
Pickup groups, concerts, and one-night gigs—1960-1969

SELECTED DISCOGRAPHY

Long-playing 33 rpm reissues available when this book went to press. (*Note:* Single cuts of particular interest are listed in parenthesis.)

The Louis Armstrong Story, vol. IV, Columbia ML 54386 ("I Can't Give You Anything But Love").

The Blues and All that Jazz, Decca DL 79230 ("Cousin Joe," "Box Car Shorty," with Sammy Price).

Sidney Bechet, Blue Note 81201-2-3-4.

Earl Hines Swingmasters, International Polydor 673-006.

Earl Hines, VJM-LC-2, VJM-LC-10 (Hangover Club sessions).

King Jazz, Storyville 136, 137, 141, 142, 153 (reissues).

New Orleans All Stars, International Polydor 623-217 (includes Archey, Howard, Purnell, et al.).

Art Hodes Blue Five, Blue Note BN B-6508 (includes Mezzrow, Kaminsky, et al.).

Sammy Price, Jazztone 1260.

Jelly Roll Morton: Hot Jazz, Pop Jazz, Hokum & Hilarity, RCA LPV-524.

Dewey Jackson, Origin #9 (1926 St. Louis recordings).

New Orleans style jazz available on long-playing 33 rpm reissues.

The Louis Armstrong Story, Columbia CL 851-2-3-4.

Louis Armstrong, An Early Portrait, Milestone 2010.

Sidney Bechet of New Orleans, Victor RCA LPV-510.

Baby Dodds: Drum Solos, Folkways 2290.

Johnny Dodds,Victor RCA LPV-558.

The Immortal Johnny Dodds, Milestone 2002.

Bunk Johnson and His Superior Jazz Band, GTJ 12048.

Freddie Keppard, Jazz Treasury 1002 (with Doc Cooke and Erskine Tate).

The Immortal Jelly Roll Morton, Milestone 2003.

Recorded in New Orleans, GTJ 12019 (Sharkey Bonano, Paul Barbarin, George Girard, Bill Mathews Band, 1956).

New Orleans Today, vols. I & II, 77 records LA 12-29.

New Orleans Jazz, Decca 8283.

Papa Joe (1926-1928), Decca 79246.

The Immortal King Oliver, Milestone 2006.

Kid Ory: Tailgate!, GTJ 12022 (1944-45).

Kid Ory, Vault LP 9006.

Piano Roll Ragtime, Sounds 1201.

POPS FOSTER DISCOGRAPHY
1924–1940
by Brian Rust

ABBREVIATIONS — Instruments

a arranger
as alto saxophone
bb brass bass (sousaphone or tuba)
bj banjo
c cornet
cel celeste
cl clarinet
d drums
g guitar
ldr leader

p piano
sb string bass
ss soprano saxophone
t trumpet
tb trombone
ts tenor saxophone
v vocal
vib vibraphone
vn violin
wb washboard

Record labels

Ban Banner
BB Bluebird
Bm Biltmore
Br Brunswick
Cam Cameo
CBS Columbia Broadcasting System
    (LP only)
Col Columbia
Cor Corona
Cq Conqueror
Davis Joe Davis
Dec Decca
El Electrola

Elite Elite
Fonit Fonit
HJCA Hot Jazz Clubs of America
HMV His Master's Voice
HRS Hot Record Society
Imp Imperial
JCI Jazz Classic
Je Jewel
Kr Kristall
Lin Lincoln
Mt Melotone
Od Odeon
OK Okeh

Or Oriole

Par Parlophone

Per Perfect

Phil Philharmonic

Pol Polydor

Ristic Ristic

Ro Romeo

Swing Swing

UHCA United Hot Clubs of America

Var Varsity

Vic Victor

Voc Vocalion

X LVA X LVA

Further details regarding the origins of record labels can be found in *Jazz Records 1897-1931* and *Jazz Records 1932-1942* by Brian Rust. Records numbered in italics indicate a dub of the original.

CHAS. CREATH'S JAZZ-O-MANIACS: *Leonard Davis-t/Charlie Lawson-tb/Sam Long-Thornton Blue-William Rollins-reeds/Cranston Hamilton-p/Pete Paterson-bj/Pops Foster-bb/Floyd Campbell-d-v.*

St. Louis, December 2(?), 1924

8781-A	Pleasure Mad	OK 8201
8782-A	Market Street Blues	—

St. Louis, March 1925

9018-A	I Woke Up Cold In Hand-1	OK 8217
9019-A	King Porter Stomp	OK 8210
9020-A	Every Man That Wears Bell-Bottom Britches	—
9021-A	My Daddy Rocks Me (With One Steady Roll)	OK 8217

Note: Some copies of the last title labeled "My Baby Rocks Me . . ."

CHAS. CREATH'S JAZZ-O-MANIACS: *Leonard Davis-t/Sonny Lee-tb/Sam Long-William Rollins-reeds/Horace Eubanks-cl-as/Cranston Hamilton-p/Lonnie Johnson-vn/Pete Paterson-bj/Pops Foster-bb/Zutty Singleton-d.*

St. Louis, November, 1925

9426-A	Market Street Stomp	OK 8280, Od 49161
9427-A	Won't Don't Blues-2	—
9428-A	Way Down In Lover's Lane	OK 8257
9429-A	Grandpa's Spell [*sic*]	—

DEWEY JACKSON'S PEACOCK ORCHESTRA: *Dewey Jackson-c/Albert Snaer-t/William Luper-tb/Thornton Blue-cl-as/Cliff Cochran-ss-as/Willie Humphrey-cl-ts/Burroughs Lovingood-p/Pete Robinson-bj/Pops Foster-bb/Floyd Campbell-d-v.*

St. Louis, June 21, 1926

E-3415	She's Cryin' For Me	Voc 1040, Or 1006	
E-3417	Capitol Blues	—	Br 80039
E-3419	Going To Town	Voc 1039	

CHAS. CREATH'S JAZZ-O-MANIACS: *Dewey Jackson-t/Albert Wynn-tb/Sam Long-Horace Eubanks-cl-as/William Rollins-ts/Burroughs Lovingood-p/Pete Paterson-bj/Pops Foster-bb/Zutty Singleton-d.*

St. Louis, May 2, 1927

80823-B	Butter Finger Blues	OK 8477
80824-A	Crazy Quilt	—

LOUIS ARMSTRONG AND HIS SAVOY BALLROOM FIVE: *Louis Armstrong-t-v/J. C. Higginbotham-tb/Albert Nicholas-Charlie Holmes-as/ Teddy Hill-ts/Luis Russell-p/Eddie Condon-bj/Lonnie Johnson-g/Pops Foster-sb/Paul Barbarin-d.*

New York, March 5, 1929

401690-C	I Can't Give You Any-thing But Love — vLA	OK 8669, 41204, UHCA 36, *Col 38052, 38221*, Par R-753, 22382, B-28512, B-35616, TT-9054, Od 165683, 279743, 284474, A-2302, A-286021, D-3109, ONY-41204, 028388
401691-B	Mahogany Hall Stomp	OK 8680, Voc 3055, Col 35879, Par R-571, A-7409, B-27391, B-35616, PZ-11268, Od 279743, A-2310, A-286008

Note: Odeon ONY-41204 as EDDIE GORDON BAND; all other issues except Okeh as LOUIS ARMSTRONG AND HIS ORCHESTRA

HENRY ALLEN, Jr. AND HIS (NEW YORK) ORCHESTRA: *As last, but Henry Allen replaces Armstrong; the saxes all double cl (Holmes also plays ss); Will Johnson-bj-g replaces Condon and Lonnie Johnson; Russell doubles cel and Barbarin vib.*

New York, July 16, 1929

55133-1	It Should Be You	*X LVA-3033, HMV 7EG 8112*
55133-2	It Should Be You	*VIC RA-5317*
55133-3	It Should Be You	Vic V-38073, BB B-10235, HMV B-6487, K-6949, K-8524, El EG-1598
55134-1	Biff'ly Blues	*X LVA-3033, Vic RA-5317, HMV 7EG-8112*
55134-2	Biff'ly Blues	Vic V-38073, HMV K-6949, El EG-1598

New York, July 17, 1929

53929-2	Feeling Drowsy	*HMV JK-2524*
53929-3	Feeling Drowsy	Vic V-38080, BB B-10702, HMV B-4970, BD-103, EA-2908
53930-1	Swing Out	*X LVA-3033, Vic RA-5317, HMV 7EG-8112*
53930-2	Swing Out	BB B-10702
53930-3	Swing Out	Vic V-38080, HMV B-4970, B-6500, EA-2908, JK-2524, El EG-3090, EG-3707

LUIS RUSSELL AND HIS ORCHESTRA: *Bill Coleman-t added to last; Allen and Higginbotham-v as noted*

New York, September 6, 1929

402938-C	The New Call Of The Freaks — vHA-JCH?	OK 8734, Col 35960, DO-2229, Par R-1645, Od A-286079, B-35635
402939-C	Feelin' The Spirit (Savoy Stomp*) — vJCH	OK 8766, *Voc 3480**, Par R-1882, A-3992, B-27607, TT-9064, Od A-2322, *HJCA HC-103*

| 402940-B | Jersey Lightning | OK 8734, Col 35960, DO-2229, Par R-740, Od A-286020, B-35628, 028397 |

LOU AND HIS GINGER SNAPS: As above

New York, September 13, 1929

| 9006-1 | Broadway Rhythm | Ban 6536, Cam 9319, Je 5730, Lin 3343, Or 1728, Ro 1107, *Ristic 15* |
| 9007-1-2 | The Way He Loves Is Just Too Bad | Ban 6540, Cam 9320, Je 5729, Lin 3344, Or 1726, Ro 1108, *Ristic 15* |

Note: Jewel and Oriole issues as DIXIE JAZZ BAND. Ristic uses 9007-1.

HENRY ALLEN AND HIS (NEW YORK) ORCHESTRA: *As for July 16, 1929, plus Victoria Spivey and the Four Wanderers (Herman Hughes-Charles Clinkscales-tenors/Maceo Johnson-baritone/Oliver Childs-bass)-v added*

New York, September 24, 1929

55852-1	Make A Country Bird Fly Wild — vFW	X LVA-3033, Vic RA-5317, HMV 7EG-8136
55852-2	Make A Country Bird Fly Wild — vFW	Vic V-38107, 760-0000, HMV JF-57
55853-1	Funny Feathers Blues — vVS	X LVA-3033, Vic RA-5317, HMV 7EG-8136
55853-2	Funny Feathers Blues — vVS	Vic V-38088, BB B-6588, HMV JF-57
55854-1	How Do They Do It That Way? — vVS	X-LVA-3033, Vic RA-5317, HMV 7EG-8136
55854-2	How Do They Do It That Way? — vVS	Vic V-38088
55855-1	Pleasin' Paul	X LVA-3033, Vic RA-5317, HMV 7EG-8136
55855-2	Pleasin' Paul	Vic V-38107, 760-0000, BB B-10235

MOUND CITY BLUE BLOWERS: *Red McKenzie-comb-v/Jack Teagarden-tb-v/Eddie Condon-bj-v/Jack Bland-g/Pops Foster-sb/Josh Billings-d.*

New York, September 25, 1929

| 56151-1 | Tailspin Blues — vRM-JT-EC-JB | Vic V-38087, BB B-6456, B-10209, HMV B-6252, BD-5758, EA-3040, JK-2877, K-6951 |
| 56152-3 | Never Had A Reason To Believe In You — vRM | Vic V-38087, BB B-6270, B-10209, HMV BD-187, K-6951 |

VICTORIA SPIVEY: *Vocal, acc. by Henry Allen-t/J. C. Higginbotham-tb/Charlie Holmes-ss/Teddy Hill-ts where shown/Luis Russell-p/Will Johnson-g/Pops Foster-bb-sb where noted.*

New York, October 1, 1929

56732-1	Blood Hound Blues — tsTH	Vic V-38570, BB B-8619
56733-	Dirty T.B. Blues — tsTH	—
56734-1	Moaning The Blues — tsTH	Vic V-38546, BB B-8619
56735-1	Telephoning The Blues — bbPF	—

WILTON CRAWLEY AND HIS ORCHESTRA: *Henry Allen-t/unknown-tb/*
Wilton Crawley-cl-v/Charlie Holmes-as/unknown-ts/Luis
Russell-p/Will Johnson-g/Pops Foster-sb/Paul Barbarin-d.

New York, October 3, 1929

56747-2	Snake Hip Dance	Vic V-38094, HMV R-10382
56748-2	She's Driving Me Wild	— —

JELLY ROLL MORTON AND HIS RED HOT PEPPERS: *Henry Allen-t/J. C.*
Higginbotham-tb/Albert Nicholas-cl/Jelly Roll Morton-p/Will
Johnson-g/Pops Foster-sb/Paul Barbarin-d.

New York, November 13, 1929

57080-1	Sweet Peter	Vic 23402, *Bm 1061, HJCA HC-34*
57080-2	Sweet Peter	*HMV JK-2860*
57081-1	Jersey Joe	Vic 23402, *HMV JK-2862*
57081-2	Jersey Joe	*Bm 1061, HJCA HC-34*
57082-1	Mississippi Mildred	Vic 23424, *HMV JK-2862*
57082-2	Mississippi Mildred	*Bm 1060, HJCA HC-35*
57083-1	Mint Julep	Vic 23334

MOUND CITY BLUE BLOWERS: *Red McKenzie-comb/Glenn Miller-tb/Pee*
Wee Russell-cl/Coleman Hawkins-ts/Eddie Condon-bj/Jack
Bland-g/Pops Foster-sb/Gene Krupa-d.

New York, November 14, 1929

57145-3	Hello, Lola	Vic V-38100, 62-0058, BB B-6270, B-10037, HMV B-6168, B-8952, EA-2963, JK-2260, JO-149, K-6501, K-8525, EI EG-7729
57146-3	One Hour	Vic V-38100, 62-0058, BB B-6546, B-10037, HMV B-6150, B-8952, EA-2963, JK-2260, JO-149, K-6501, K-8525, EI EG-7729

Note: Bluebird B-10037, HMV B-8952 and JO-149 as RED McKENZIE AND
THE MOUND CITY BLUE BLOWERS.

WILTON CRAWLEY AND HIS ORCHESTRA: *2 unknown-t-tb/Wilton*
Crawley-cl/Johnny Hodges-as/Jelly Roll Morton-Luis Russell-p/
Unknown-bj-g/Pops Foster-sb/?Sonny Greer-d.

New York, December 2, 1929

57565-2	You Oughta See My Gal	Vic V-38136
57566-1	Futuristic Blues	—
57567-2	Keep Your Business To Yourself	Vic V-38116, BB B-5827
57568-1	She's Got What I Need	— —

LOUIS ARMSTRONG AND HIS ORCHESTRA: *Louis Armstrong-t-v/Otis*
Johnson-Henry Allen-t/J. C. Higginbotham-tb/Albert Nicholas-Charlie
Holmes-cl-as/Teddy Hill-ts/Luis Russell-p/Will Johnson-g/Pops
Foster-sb/Paul Barbarin-d-vib.

New York, December 10, 1929

403493-A	I Ain't Got Nobody — vLA	OK 8756, Voc 3102, Par PNY-34026, R-1261, PZ-11204, Od ONY-36027, A-286065, Col 20505, J-2022

| 403494-C | Dallas Blues — vLA | OK 8774, Voc 3025, Par R-973, B-35608, Od 279485, A-2368, A-286040, *HJCA HC-110* |

Note: Parlophone PNY-34026 as TED SHAWNE AND HIS ORCHESTRA. *Hoagy Carmichael-v added, where shown.*

New York, December 13, 1929

| 403495-B | St. Louis Blues — vLA | OK 41350, Voc/OK 3008, Cq 9124, Par R-618, B-28506, B-35600, PZ-11113, TT-9052, Od 165975, 193651, 298096, A-2300, A-286013, Col 2727-D, 20505, J-2022, *HJCA HC-90* |
| 403496-C | Rockin' Chair — vLA-HC | OK 8756, Col 2688-D, Voc 3039, Par PNY-34027, R-785, B-28507, B-35631, Od ONY-36027, A-2301, A-286023 |

Note: Parlophone PNY-34027 as TED SHAWNE AND HIS ORCHESTRA.

LUIS RUSSELL AND HIS ORCHESTRA: *As for September 6, 1929, but Otis Johnson-t replaces Coleman.*

New York, December 17, 1929

| 403524-C | Doctor Blues | OK 8766, *Voc 3480*, Par R-1273, A-3688, Od A-286066, B-35635, 028245, *HJCA HC-103* |

FATS WALLER AND HIS BUDDIES: *Henry Allen-Leonard Davis-t/Jack Teagarden-tb-vib/J. C. Higginbotham-tb/Albert Nicholas-Charlie Holmes-cl-as/Larry Binyon-ts/Fats Waller-p/Will Johnson-bj Pops Foster-sb/Kaiser Marshall-d/Orlando Roberson-v.*

New York, December 18, 1929

57926-1	Lookin' For Another Sweetie — vOR	Vic V-38110
57927-3	Ridin' But Walkin'	Vic V-38119, *1AC-0135*, HMV B-4971, B-6390, EA-3265, SG-431
57928-1	Won't You Get Off It, Please?	Vic V-38119, *1AC-0135*, HMV B-4971, B-6549, EA-3713, SG-464
57929-2	When I'm Alone — vOR	Vic V-38110

LUIS RUSSELL AND HIS ORCHESTRA: *As for December 17, 1929, plus three vn and Louis Armstrong-t-v; Barbarin-vib only; unknown-d.*

New York, January 24, 1930

403680-A	Saratoga Shout	OK 8780, Par R-2225
403681-A	Song Of The Islands — vLA	OK 41375, Voc 3026, Par PNY-34032, R-909, A-3217, B-27329, B-28519, B-35601, TT-9057, 80313, Od 238995, A-2315, A-286035, ONT-36039
403682-C	Song Of The Swanee	OK 8780, Par R-1669, Od A-286080, B-35622, OR-1669

Note: Parlophone PNY-34032 as TED SHAWNE AND HIS ORCHESTRA

LOUIS ARMSTRONG AND HIS ORCHESTRA: *As for January 24, 1930, but vn omitted; Barbarin resumes on d; William Blue-cl-as replaces Nicholas.*

New York, February 1, 1930

403714-B	Bessie Couldn't Help It — vLA	OK 8774, Voc 3025, Par R-698, A-3046, B-28506, B-35600, TT-9052, Od 279485, A-2300, A-286017
403715-B	Blue, Turning Grey Over You — vLA	OK 4678, 41375, Voc 3124, Par PNY-34033, R-1494, 80313, A-6176, B-27329, B-35632, Od 238995, A-286071, ONY-36039, *JCL 536*

Note: Parlophone PNY-34033 as TED SHAWNE AND HIS ORCHESTRA
Okeh 4678 was originally issued in 1922 as the American edition of the first laughing record, which was made by Beka in Germany. This was subsequently used as a backing for the above Armstrong recording.

J. C. HIGGINBOTHAM AND HIS SIX HICKS: *Henry Allen-t/J. C. Higginbotham-tb/Charlie Holmes-as/Luis Russell-p/Will Johnson-g/Pops Foster-sb/Paul Barbarin-d.*

New York, February 5, 1930

403736-B	Give Me Your Telephone Number	OK 8772, HRS 14, Od PO-67, *A-2417, 028512, Par R-2799, A-7387, PZ-11121*
403737-C	Higginbotham Blues	OK 8772, HRS 14, Col 36011, *Od A-2417, 028512, Par R-2799, A-7387, PZ-11121*

HENRY ALLEN AND HIS ORCHESTRA: *As for December 17, 1929, but William Blue-cl-as replaces Nicholas; Will Johnson-v.*

New York, February 10, 1930

58581-2	Sugar Hill Function	Vic V-38140, 62-0060, HMV B-8409, JW-3, El EG-3707
58582-2	You Might Get Better, But You'll Never Get Well — vWJ	Vic V-38140, 62-0060, HMV B-8409, JW-3
58583-2	Everybody Shout	Vic V-38121, BB B-6588
58584-2	Dancing Dave	—

LIZZIE MILES: *Vocal, acc. by Porter Grainger-p/Teddy Bunn-g/Pops Foster-sb.*

New York, February 27, 1930

58676-1	The Man I Got Ain't The Man I Want	Vic 23281
58677-1 or 2	Yellow Dog Gal Blues	*Camden CDN-147* (LP)
58578-2	Too Slow Blues	Vic 23298
58579-	Done Throwed The Key Away	Vic 23306

LUIS RUSSELL AND HIS ORCHESTRA: *Henry Allen-t/J. C. Higginbotham-tb/ Albert Nicholas-cl-as-ss/Charlie Holmes-ss-as/Teddy Hill-ts/Luis Russell-p-ldr/Will Johnson-bj-g/Pops Foster-sb/Paul Barbarin-d-vib/ unknown-v; J. C. Higginbotham suggests Andy Razaf, but Walter Pichon suggests Paul Barbarin.*

New York, May 29, 1930

404047-A	Louisiana Swing	OK 8811, Par R-795, Od A-2322, A-286024, B-35638

404047-C	Louisiana Swing	OK 8811
404048-C	Poor Li'l Me — v	OK 8830, Par R-2212
404049-A	On Revival Day — v	OK 8811
404049-B	On Revival Day — v	OK 8811, Par R-2186

WILTON CRAWLEY AND HIS ORCHESTRA: *Henry Allen-t/Wilton Crawley-cl-v/Charlie Holmes-as/Jelly Roll Morton-p/Teddy Bunn-g/Pops Foster-bb/Bruce Johnson-wb.*

New York, June 3, 1930

62188-2	Big Time Woman — vWC	Vic 23292
62189-2	I'm Her Papa, She's My Mama — vWC	Vic 23344
62190-1	New Crawley Blues	—
62191-1	She Saves Her Sweetest Smiles For Me — vWC	Vic 23292

Note: Victor V-23344 as WILTON CRAWLEY AND THE WASHBOARD RHYTHM KINGS

LUIS RUSSELL AND HIS ORCHESTRA: *As for May 29, 1930, but Greeley Walton-ts replaces Hill; David Bee-a*

New York, September 5, 1930

404428-B	Muggin' Lightly	OK 8830, Par R-934, Od A-286037, 028397
404429-A	Panama	OK 8849, Par R-963, Od A-286039, B-35622, *HJCA HC-117*
404430-B	High Tension — aDB	OK 8849, Par R-1064, CO-148, Od A-286050

New York, ca. October 15, 1930

E-34924	You're Lucky To Me	Br rejected

Dick Robertson-v added

New York, ca. October 21, 1930

E-35024-	You're Lucky To Me — vDR	Rejected
E-35025-	I Got Rhythm	Mt M-12000
E-35026-	Memories Of You — vDR	Rejected

Unknown-t/Vic Dickenson-v added.

New York, December 16, 1930

E-35758-C	Saratoga Drag	Voc 1579, *Br 80038, 02508, A-500323*
E-35759-C	Case On Dawn (correct title: Ease on Down)	— — 02002, A-9734
E-35760-	Honey, That Reminds Me — vVD	Br 6046, A-9365

Note: Brunswick 6046 as THE SAVANNAH SYNCOPATORS

HENRY ALLEN AND HIS ORCHESTRA: *Henry Allen-t-v/Robert Cheek-Gus Aiken-t/Dicky Wells-tb/Albert Nicholas-cl-as/Henry Jones-as/Greely Walton-ts/Luis Russell-p-ldr/Will Johnson-g/Pops Foster-sb/Paul Barbarin-d-vib/Chick Bullock-v.*

New York, August 28, 1931

70195-1	You Rascal, You — vHA	Vic 22793, HMV B-4881

70196-1	Goin' To Town — vCB	Vic 22789, BB B-7367, HMV B-4907, K6439
70197-1	Say The Word — vCB	Vic 22789, HMV K6439
70198-1	Freakish Blues	Vic 22815, HMV B-4897, EA-3040

Note: Bluebird as THE SOUTHERN SERENADERS; so is the reverse, but this is of no interest.

THE RHYTHMAKERS: *Henry Allen-t/Jimmy Lord-cl/Pee Wee Russell-ts/Fats Waller-p-v/Eddie Condon-bj/Jack Bland-g/Pops Foster-sb/Zutty Singleton-d/Billy Banks-v.*

New York, July 26, 1932

12119-1	I Would Do Anything For You — vBB	Mt M-12457, Per 15651, Br A-500316
12119-2	I Would Do Anything For You — vBB	Ban 32530, Or 2534, UHCA 105, Br 02508
12120-1	Mean Old Bed Bug Blues — vBB-FW	Ban 32502, Mt M-12457, Or 2554, Per 15669, UHCA 105, Voc S-20, V-1021, Br A-500315, Imp 6003, 18012
12120-2	Mean Old Bed Bug Blues — vBB-FW	Col 35882
12121-2	Yellow Dog Blues — vBB	—
12121-3	Yellow Dog Blues — vBB	Ban 32502, Mt M-12481, Or 2554, Per 15669, UHCA 107, Voc S-20, V-1021, *Par R-2810, A-7399, DPE-9, P7-11148,* Br A-500315, Imp 6003, 18012
12122-2	Yes Suh! — vBB&ch	Ban 32530, Mt M-12481, Or 2534, Per 15651, UHCA 107, Br 02078, A-9940, Par R-2810, A-7399, DPE-9, PZ-11148

Note: Perfects as JACK BLAND AND HIS RHYTHMAKERS; Brunswick 02078, A-9940 as EDDIE CONDON AND HIS RHYTHMAKERS; Brunswick A-500315, A-500316 and Vocalion S-20 as CHICAGO RHYTHM KINGS; Vocalion S-9 and Imperials as BILLY BANKS' CHICAGO RHYTHM KINGS; UHCA and Vocalion V-1021 as BILLY BANKS' RHYTHMAKERS; all others as THE RHYTHMAKERS.

JACK BLAND AND HIS RHYTHMAKERS: *Henry Allen-t-v/Tommy Dorsey-tb/Pee Wee Russell-cl/Happy Cladwell-ts/Frank Froeba-p/Eddie Condon-bj/Jack Bland-g/Pops Foster-sb/Zutty Singleton-d/Chick Bullock-v/the chimes heard occasionally are probably played by Singleton.*

New York, October 8, 1932

12452-1	Who Stole The Lock (On The Hen House) — vHA&ch	Cor 35841
12452-2	Who Stole The Lock (On The Hen House) — vHA&ch	Ban 32605, Mt M-12513, Or 2593, Per 15694, Ro 1966, UHCA 104, Br 01737, A-500317, Par R-2812, B-71147, PZ-11142, Kr 21182
12453-1	A Shine On Your Shoes — vCB	Mt M-12510, Per 15689, UHCA 111

12454-2	It's Gonna Be You — vCB	—	—	Br A-500316
12455-1	Someone Stole Gabriel's Horn — vHA	Ban 32605, Mt M-12513, Or 2593, Per 15694, Ro 1966, UHCA 104, Br 01737, A-500317, Par R-2812, B-71147, PZ-11142, Kr 21182, Pol 580007		

Note: Columbia as THE RHYTHMAKERS; Brunswicks, Parlophones, and Polydor as CHICAGO RHYTHM KINGS.

MEZZ MEZZROW AND HIS ORCHESTRA: *Max Kaminsky-Freddy Goodman-Ben Gusick-t/Floyd O'Brien-tb/Mezz Mezzrow-cl-as-a/Benny Carter-t-as-v-a/ Johnny Russell-ts/Teddy Wilson-p/Jack Sunshine-g/Pops Foster-sb/ Jack Maisel-d.*

New York, November 6, 1933

14272-A	Free Love — aBC	Br 7551, A-9527, A-500369
14273-A	Dissonance — aMM	Br 7551, 02509, A-9527, A-500369, Par R-2881, PZ-11006, Col 291564, Pol 580008
14274-A	Swinging With Mezz — aMM-FO'B	Br 6778, 01762, A-500370, Par R-2881, PZ-11006, Col 291564, Pol 580008
14275-A	Love, You're Not The One For Me — vBC	Br 6778, 01762, A-500370

LUIS RUSSELL AND HIS ORCHESTRA: *Leonard Davis-Gus Aiken-t/Rex Stewart-c/Nathaniel Story-James Archey-tb/Henry Jones-Charlie Holmes-cl-as/Bingie Madison-Greeley Walton-cl-ts/Luis Russell-p-ldr/Lee Blair-g/Pops Foster-sb/Paul Barbarin-d-vib/Sonny Woods-the Palmer Brothers-v.*

New York, August 8, 1934

15571-1	At The Darktown Strutters' Ball — vSW	Ban 33179, Mt M-13146, Or 2981, Per 15995, Ro 2355, Voc C-0009, Imp 6056
15572-1	My Blue Heaven — vSW	Ban 33399, Mt M-13366, Or 3125 Per 16103, Ro 2499, Voc C-0009, Imp 6056, 18019
15573-1	Ghost Of The Freaks — vPB	Ban 33367, Mt M-13334, Or 3104, Per 16086, Ro 2478, Voc S-2, Imp 6004, 17042, 17500
15574-1	Hokus Pocus	Ban 33367, Mt M-13334, Or 3104, Per 16086, Ro 2478, Voc S-2, Imp 6042, 17042
15575-1	Primitive	Ban 33399, Mt M-13366, Or 3125, Per 16103, Ro 2499, Voc S-13, Imp 6040, 18006
15576-1	Ol' Man River — vSW	Ban 33179, Mt M-13146, Or 2981, Per 15995, Ro 2355, Voc S-13, Imp 6004, 18006

HENRY ALLEN AND HIS ORCHESTRA: *Henry Allen-t-v/Pee Wee Erwin-t/ George Washington-tb/Buster Bailey-cl/Luis Russell-p/Danby Barker-g/Pops Foster-sb/Paul Barbarin-d.*

New York, January 23, 1935

16671-1	Believe It, Beloved — vHA	Ban 33337, Mt M-13304, Or 3087, Per 16071, Ro 2461
16671-2	Believe It, Beloved — vHA	*Epic LP-3252*
16672-1	It's Written All Over Your Face	Ban 33337, Mt M-13304, Or 3087, Per 16071, Ro 2461
16681-1	(We're Gonna Have) Smooth Sailing — vHA	Ban 33355, Mt M-13322, Or 3097, Per 16080, Ro 2471, Voc C-0011
16682-1	Whose Honey Are You? — vHA	Ban 33355, Cq 8474, Mt M-13322, Or 3097, Per 16080, Ro 2471, Voc S-18, Imp 18010

Note: Matrices 16673/80 inclusive are by other artists on the previous two days. Copies of Vocalion S-17 exist, using matrix 16682-1 in error.

LOUIS ARMSTRONG AND HIS ORCHESTRA: *Louis Armstrong-t-v/Leonard Davis-Gus Aiken-Louis Bacon-t/Harry White-James Archey-tb/Henry Jones-Charlie Holmes-as/Bingie Madison-cl-ts/Greeley Walton-ts/Louis Russell-p/Lee Blair-g/Pops Foster-sb/Paul Barbarin-d.*

New York, October 3, 1935

60021-A	I'M In The Mood For Love — vLA	Dec F-5785, M-30382
60021-E	I'M In The Mood For Love — vLA	Br A-9902, A-505025, 80107
60021-F	I'M In The Mood For Love — vLA	Dec 579, 3796
60022-A	You Are My Lucky Star — vLA	Dec 580, F-5785, Br A-9902, 80107
60022-E	You Are My Lucky Star — vLA	Dec 580, M-30382, A-505025
60023-E	La Cucaracha — vLA	Dec 580, F-5835, Br A-9930
60024-B	Got A Bran' New Suit — vLA	Dec F-5836
60024-E	Got A Bran' New Suit — vLA	Dec 579, Br A-9931, A-505032

Note: Some copies of Decca 580 are marked 60022-E, but are aurally the same as 60022-A, and the same is true of Brunswick 80107; similarly, Decca 3796 shows 60021-G, but it is exactly the same as 60021-F. It is likely these higher "takes" are merely dubbings.

New York, November 21, 1935

60155-D	I've Got My Fingers Crossed — vLA	Dec 623, F-5869, Y-5042, Br A-9946, Fonit 1604, Pol A-61109
60156-A	Old Man Mose — vLA&ch	Dec F-5895, Br A-9962
60156-D	Old Man Mose — vLA&ch	Dec 622, Y-5051, Br A-505044, A-505265, Fonit 1603, Pol A-61080
60157-C	I'm Shooting High — vLA	Dec 623, F-5869, Y-5042, Br A-9946, Fonit 1604, Pol A-61109
60158-D	Falling In Love With You — vLA	Dec 622, F-5961, Y-5051

New York, December 13, 1935

60227-A	Red Sails In The Sunset — vLA	Dec 648, F-5835, Br A-9930
60228-A	On Treasure Island — vLA	Dec 648, F-5836, Br A-9931, A-505032

New York, December 19, 1935

60249-A	Thanks A Million — vLA	Dec 666, F-5868, B-9060, M-30387, Br A-9926, A-505034
60249-B	Thanks A Million — vLA	Dec 666, BM-1072, Pol A-61071
60250-A	Shoe Shine Boy — vLA	Dec 672, F-5936, BM-1083, Br A-9978, A-505049
60251-A	Solitude — vLA	Dec 666
60251-B	Solitude — vLA	Dec 666, F-5868, B-9060, M-30387, Br A-9926, A-505034
60252-B	I Hope Gabriel Likes My Music — vLA	Dec 672, F-5936, Br A-9978, A-505049, Fonit 1603, Pol A-61070

New York, January 18, 1936

60362-A	The Music Goes 'Round and Around — vLA	Dec 685, F-5895, Y-5069, Br A-9962, A-505044
60363-A	Rhythm Saved The World — vLA&ch	Dec 685, 824, F-5961, Y-5069
60363-B	Rhythm Saved The World — vLA&ch	Swaggie JCS-33774 (7" LP)

LOUIS ARMSTRONG AND HIS ORCHESTRA: *Same as above but Snub Mosley-tb replaces James Archey.*

New York, April 28, 1936

61058-A	I Come From A Musical Family — vLA	Dec 797, F-5995
61075-A	Somebody Stole My Break — vLA	Dec 797, F-5995

Note: Matrices 61060/72 inclusive are by other artists on other dates; 61073/4 are blank in the Decca files, and 61059 is listed below. Various members of the band speak on 61075-A

New York, April 29, 1936

61059-A	If We Never Meet Again — vLA	Dec 906, F-6202, Br A-81095, Fonit 1606, Pol A-61083

James Archey-tb replaces Mosley.   **New York, May 18, 1936**

61106-A	Lyin' To Myself — vLA	Dec 835, F-6040, Br A-505067
61107-A	Ev'ntide — vLA	Dec 835, F-6040, Br A-505067, Od 284232
61108-A	Swing That Music — vLA	Dec 866, F-6066, 8055, Od 284198
61109-A	Thankful — vLA	Dec 866, F-6066
61110-A	Red Nose — vLA	Dec 1049, Br 02514, A-91095, A-505265
61111-A	Mahogany Hall Stomp	Dec 824, 3793, 25154, F-6324, M-30673, MU-60455

Note: Decca 8055 is a Swiss issue.

MEZZ MEZZROW AND HIS ORCHESTRA: *Sy Oliver-t/J. C. Higginbotham-tb/ Mezz Mezzrow-cl/Happy Caldwell-ts/Sonny White-p/Bernard Addison-g/Pops Foster-sb/Jimmy Crawford-d/Mezz Mezzrow-Edgar Sampson-Larry Clinton-a.*

New York, June 14, 1937

010569-1	Blues In Disguise — aMM-ES	Vic 25636, A-1368, HMV B-8656, K-8028
010570-1	That's How I Feel Today — aES	As above
010571-1	Hot Club Stomp — aES	Vic 25612, A-1259, HMV B-8646, JK-2065, K-8100
010572-1	The Swing Session's Called To Order-aLC	As above

HENRY ALLEN AND HIS ORCHESTRA: *Henry Allen-t-v/? Glyn Paque-cl/Tab Smith-as/Harold Arnold-ts/Luis Russell-p/Danny Barker-g/?Pops Foster-sb/?Paul Barbarin-d.*

New York, June 19, 1937

21275-2	Till The Clock Strikes Three — vHA	Voc 3607
21276-2	The Merry-Go-Round Broke Down — vHA	Voc 3594
21277-1	You'll Never Go To Heaven (If You Break My Heart) — vHA	Voc 3594
21278-1	The Miller's Daughter, Marianne — vHA	Voc 3607

LOUIS ARMSTRONG AND HIS ORCHESTRA: *Louis Armstrong-t-v/Shelton Hemphill-Louis Bacon-Henry Allen-t/George Matthews-George Washington-J. C. Higginbotham-tb/Pete Clark-Charlie Holmes-as/Albert Nicholas-Bingie Madison-cl-ts/Luis Russell-p/Lee Blair-g/Pops Foster-sb/Paul Barbarin-d.*

New York, July 2, 1937

62328-A	Public Melody Number One — vLA	Dec 1347, 60497, F-6540, BM-1038, X-1484, Br A-81383, A-505118, Fonit/Pol (A)-61158
62329-A	Yours And Mine — vLA	Dec 1369, 60497, F-6540, Br A-81383, A-505118, Od 284324
62330-A	Red Cap — vLA	Dec 1347, F-6583, BM-1038, Br A-81400, A-505260

New York, July 7, 1937

62335-A	She's The Daughter Of A Planter From Havana — vLA	Dec 1353, F-6493, BM-1080, Br A-81290
62336-A	Alexander's Ragtime Band — vLA	Dec 1408, F-6583, BM-1074, Br A-81400, A-505260, Od 284383, Pol A-61111
62337-A	Cuban Pete — vLA	Dec 1353, F-6493, Br A-81290, Pol A-61111
62338-A	I've Got A Heart Full of Rhythm — vLA	Dec 1408, F-6915, F-49017, Br A-81904, Fonit 1609, Pol A-61193
62339-A	Sun Showers — vLA	Dec 1369, Od 284324

LOUIS ARMSTRONG AND HIS ORCHESTRA: *Louis Armstrong-t-v/Shelton Hemphill-Louis Bacon-Henry Allen-t/Wilbur de Paris-George Washington-J. C. Higginbotham-tb/Pete Clark-Charlie Holmes-as/Albert Nicholas-Bingie Madison-cl-ts/Luis Russell-p (-a unless otherwise shown)/Lee Blair-g/Pops Foster-sb/Paul Barbarin-d-vib/Chappie Willet-a.*

Los Angeles, January 12, 1938

DLA-1132-A	Satchel Mouth Swing — vLA	Dec 1636, 3794, F-7428, BM-1164, M-30353, Br A-505246
DLA-1133-A	Jubilee — vLA	Dec 1635, F-6765, M-30354, Br A-81718, A-505141
DLA-1134-A	Struttin' With Some Barbecue — aCW	Dec 1661, 3795, F-6814, BM-1039, M-30375, MU-60496, Br A-81782, A-81986, A-505155, Od 284383, Pol A-61187
DLA-1135-A	The Trumpet Player's Lament — vLA	Dec 1653, F-6814, M-30375, MU-60496, Br A-81782, A-505155
DLA-1136-A	I Double Dare You — vLA	Dec 1636, F-6619, M-30353, Br A-81451, A-505130, Pol 624136
DLA-1137-A	True Confession — vLA	Dec 1635, F-6619, M-30354, Br A-81451, A-505130, A-505141
DLA-1138-A	Let That Be A Lesson To You — vLA	Dec 1661, F-6655, F-49015, Br A-81520, A-505140, Fonit 1607, Pol A-61142
DLA-1139-A	As Sweet As A Song — vLA	Dec 1653, rest as for DLA-1138-A

MEZZROW-LADNIER QUINTET: *Tommy Ladnier-t/Mezz Mezzrow-cl/Teddy Bunn-g-v/Pops Foster-sb/Manzie Johnson-d.*

New York, December 19, 1938

030450-1	Royal Garden Blues	BB B-10087, HMV B-9416, EA-2597, SG-354, Swing 57
030450-2	Royal Garden Blues	X LVA-3027, Vic RA-5324, HMV DLP-1110
030451-1	Everybody Loves My Baby	BB B-10090, HMV B-9447, HN-2943, SG-355, Swing 209
030451-2	Everybody Loves My Baby	X LVA-3027, Vic RA-5324, HMV DLP-1110
030452-1	I Ain't Gonna Give Nobody None O' This Jelly-Roll	BB B-10090, HMV B-9447, HN-2943, SG-355, Swing 209
030452-2	I Ain't Gonna Give Nobody None O' This Jelly-Roll	X LVA-3027, Vic RA-5324, HMV DLP-1110
030453-1	If You See Me Comin' — vTB	BB B-10087, HMV B-9416, EA-2597, SG-354, Swing 57
030453-2	If You See Me Comin' — vTB	X LVA-3027, Vic RA-5324, HMV DLP-1110
030454-1	Gettin' Together	X LVA-3027, Vic RA-5324, HMV DLP-1110
030454-2	Gettin' Together	BB B-10088, HMV B-9470, HN-2953, JK-2174, SG-350, Swing 78

LOUIS ARMSTRONG AND HIS ORCHESTRA: *Louis Armstrong-t-v/Shelton Hemphill-Otis Johnson-Henry Allen-t/Wilbur de Paris-George Washington-J. C. Higginbotham-tb/Charlie Holmes-Rupert Cole-as/Albert Nicholas-Bingie Madison-ts/Luis Russell-p-a/Lee Blair-g/Pops Foster-sb/Sidney Catlett-d.*

New York, January 18, 1939

| 64907-A | Jeepers Creepers — vLA | Dec 2267, F-6990, BM-1041, Y-5332, Br A-82031, A-505216, Pol A-62148 |
| 64908-A | What Is This Thing Called Swing? — vLA&ch | As above, but Dec BM-1080 |

Joe Garland-ts replaces Nicholas   *New York, April 5, 1939*

65344-A	Heah Me Talkin' To Ya	Dec 2405, 25155, F-7110, Y-5407 Br A-82125, A-505222
65345-A	Save It, Pretty Mama — vLA	Dec 2405, 3516, 25155, F-7110, M-30718, Y-5407, Br A-82125, A-505222
65346-A	West End Blues — vLA	Dec 2480, 3793, 25154, 60455, F-7127, BM-1042, M-30673, Y-5713, Br A-82208, Od 286198, Pol 624084, A-61275
65347-A	Savoy Blues	Dec 2538, F-7177, BM-1138, Y-5713, Br A-505228

Dernard Flood-t replaces Johnson   *New York, April 25, 1939*

65460-A	Confessin' — vLA	Dec 2615, 3795, 60774, 333328, F-7213, Y-5913
65461-A	Our Monday Date — vLA	Dec 2615, F-7213, Y-5461
65462-A	If It's Good Then I I Want It — vLA	Dec 2480, F-7127, BM-1042, Y-5913, Br A-82208, Pol A-61275, 624084
65463-A	Me And Brother Bill — vLA (no tLA)	Dec 2538, F-7177, Br A-505228

New York, June 15, 1939

65824-A	Baby, Won't You Please Come Home — vLA	Dec 2729, F-7388, BM-1156, Br A-505247
65825-A	Poor Old Joe — vLA	Od 284649
65826-A	Shanty Boat On The Mississippi — vLA	Dec 2729, F-7388, BM-1156, Y-5461, Br A-505247, Od 284649

JIMMY JOHNSON AND HIS ORCHESTRA: *Henry Allen-t/J. C. Higginbotham-tb/Gene Sedric-ts/James P. Johnson-p/Eugene Fields-g/Pops Foster-sb/Sid Catlett-d/Anna Robinson-v.*

New York, June 15, 1939

24776-	Memories Of You	CBS CL-1780, BPG-62090
24777-	Old-Fashioned Love	Col DZ-545
24778-	Swingin' At The Lido	CBS CL-1780, BPG-62090
24779-	Havin' A Ball	— —
24780-	Hungry Blues — vAR	— —

LOUIS ARMSTRONG AND HIS ORCHESTRA: *As for April 25, 1939*
                                     New York, December 18, 1939

66984-A	Poor Old Joe — vLA	Dec 3011
66985-A	You're A Lucky Guy — vLA	Dec 2934, 60810, F-7567
66986-A	You're Just A No Account — vLA	— — —
66987-A	Bye And Bye — vLA&ch	Dec 3011, 3946, 25153, 60665, Br A-82695

W. C. HANDY'S ORCHESTRA: *W. C. Handy-c-v/J. C. Higginbotham-tb/ Edmond Hall-cl/Bingie Madison-ts/Luis Russell-p/Pops Foster-sb/Sidney Catlett-d.*
                                     New York, December 26, 1939

US-1223-1	St. Louis Blues	Var 8163, Davis DA-22, Elite 5039, Phil FR-81
US-1224-1	Loveless Love — vWCH	Var 8162
US-1225-1	Beale Street Blues	Var 8163
US-1226-1	'Way Down South Where The Blues Begin — vWCH	Var 8162

LOUIS ARMSTRONG AND HIS ORCHESTRA: *As for April 25, 1939*
                                     New York, March 14, 1940

67321-A	Hep Cats' Ball — vLA	Dec 3283, F-7700
67322-A	You've Got Me Voodoo'd — vLA	Dec 3092, F-7598
67323-A	Harlem Stomp	Dec 3092, 60811, F-7598
67324-A	Wolverine Blues	Dec 3105, F-8099, F-8055 (Swiss)
67325-A	Lazy 'Sippi Steamer — vLA	Dec 3283, F-7700

                                     New York, May 1, 1940

| 67648-A | Sweethearts On Parade — vLA | Dec 3235, 25440, 60442, Y-5861 |
| 67649-A | You Run Your Mouth, I'll Run My Business— vLA | Dec 3204, F-7849 |

SIDNEY BECHET'S BLUE NOTE QUARTET: *Sidney Bechet-cl-ss/Teddy Bunn-g/Pops Foster-sb/Sidney Catlett-d.*
                                     New York, March 27, 1940

709-	Lonesome Blues	BN 13, *JS 533*
710-	Dear Old Southland	— —
711-	Bechet's Steady Rider	BN 502
712-	Saturday Night Blues	—

RED ALLEN AND HIS ORCHESTRA: *Henry Allen-t/Benny Morton-tb/ Edmond Hall-cl/Lil Armstrong-p/Bernard Addison-g/Pops Foster-sb/Zutty Singleton-d.*
                                     New York, May 28, 1940

| 67839-A | Down In Jungle Town | Dec 18092, 25101, MU-03166, *Br 03166* |
| 67840-A | Canal Street Blues | As above |

ZUTTY SINGLETON AND HIS ORCHESTRA: *Henry Allen-t/Benny Morton-tb/ Edmond Hall-cl/Lil Armstrong-p/Bernard Addison-g/Pops Foster-sb/Zutty Singleton-d.*

New York, May 28, 1940

67841-A	King Porter Stomp	Dec 18093, M-30320, *Br 03167*
67842-A	Shim-Me-Sha-Wabble	— — —

SELECTED BIBLIOGRAPHY

Asbury, Herbert, *The French Quarter.* New York: Alfred Knopf, 1936.

Blesh, Rudi, and Harriet Janis. *They All Played Ragtime.* New York: Oak, 1966.

Charters, Samuel. *The Bluesmen.* New York: Oak, 1967.

———. *The Country Blues.* New York: Holt, Rinehart and Winston, 1959.

———. *The Poetry of the Blues.* New York: Oak, 1963.

Feather, Leonard. *Encyclopedia of Jazz.* New York: Horizon, 1960.

Handy, W. C. *Father of the Blues.* New York: Macmillan, 1941.

Hentoff, Nat, and Albert MacCarthy. *Jazz.* New York: Rinehart and Co., 1959.

Hodeir, Andre. *Jazz: Its Evolution and Essence.* New York: Grove, 1956.

Schuller, Gunther. *Early Jazz.* New York: Oxford University Press, 1968.

Stearns, Marshall. *The Story of Jazz.* New York: Oxford University Press, 1956.

Ulanov, Barry. *A History of Jazz in America.* New York: Viking, 1952.

INDEX

Albert, Don, 16

Allen, Eddie (Gold Whispering Band), 90, 104, 111, 116, 119-120

Allen, Henry (Red), 102, 135, 137, 139

Allen, Tin Can Henry, 131

Ammons, Albert, 95-96

Anderson, Tom, 24

Anderson's Annex (tonk, New Orleans, La.), 19, 24

Arbuckle, Fatty, 131

Arcadia Ballroom (Chicago, Ill.), 117, 124

Arcadia Ballroom (New York, N.Y.), 140, 144

Archey, Jimmy, 81, 115, 130, 166, 170-171

Armstrong, Alpha, 141, 162

Armstrong, Daisey, 162

Armstrong, Lil, 115, 152, 162

Armstrong, Louis, xi, xxii, 1, 22, 29, 32, 40, 48, 51, 59-60, 67, 70, 72, 74, 77, 81-82, 85, 88, 95, 100, 102, 104, 107, 110, 113, 115, 117, 127, 137-138, 141-143, 156-166 passim, 169-170

Atkins, Eddie, 27, 162

Audubon Club (New Orleans, La.), 43

Austin, Bobby, 160

Austin, Willie, 123

Bacon, Louis, 159, 163

Band Box (club, New York, N.Y.), 146, 147

Baptiste, Albert (Silver Leaf Band), 36, 51, 84

Baptiste, Rene, 47

Baquet, Achille, 62

Baquet, George, 43, 55, 62, 87

Barbarin, Louis, 128, 129

Barbarin, Paul, 136, 139, 163, 164

Barrett, Emma, 119

Bartlett, Buddy, 1

Basie, Count, xx

Bechet, Sidney, xi, 22, 28, 40, 52, 72, 81, 88, 98, 102, 117, 164, 167-170 passim

Beidorbecke, Bix, 104, 117, 124

Belle of the Bend (Mississippi steamship), 102, 103, 107

Benson, Hamp, 26, 27, 84

Benson, Ralph, 110, 161

Benton, Tom, 35, 77, 99, 102

Berry, Chu, 147

Berry, Parker, 131

Bigard, Barney, 28, 49, 135

Bigard, Emille, 28, 49, 81

Big Bob, 125

Big Easy Hall (Gretna, La.), 26, 79

Billy Phillip's (cabaret, New Orleans, La.), 18, 29, 32, 37

Black and Tan Orchestra, 120, 122, 130, 131

Black Benny, 88-89

Black Joe, 85-86

Black Pete, 18, 96, 98

Blake, Eubie, 72

Blanton, Jimmy, xvii, 102, 147
Blesh, Rudi, xviii-xix, 157, 170
Blind Freddie, 92
Blue, Thornton, 85
Bocage, Peter, 47, 48, 105, 106, 109, 168, 169
Bolden, Buddy, xi, 16, 17, 22, 25, 42, 46, 47, 51, 77, 78
Bonner, Theodore, 121
Bostic, Earl, 102
Bowman, Euday, 72
Boyd, George, 81, 82
Bradford, Perry, 154
Bradshaw, Tiny, 150
Braud, Wellman, xvi, xx, xxi, 125, 147
Brown, Johnny, 52, 53
Brown, Ray, xix
Brown, Tom, 62
Brundy, Walter, 43, 44, 47
Brunies, George, 49-50, 62, 170
Budour, Louis, 3
Bulls Club (New Orleans, La.), 64
Burley, Dan, xix
Butler, Billy, 121
Butts, Frank, 91

Calb, Albert, 95, 98
Caldwell, George, 86
Calloway, Cab (The Missourians), 143-144, 149, 159, 165
Campbell, Arthur, 105
Campbell, Floyd, 111
Capitol (Mississippi steamship), 110, 111
Carey, Jack (Crescent Band), 16, 36, 44, 48, 51, 55, 62, 81, 86, 87, 88, 90, 169
Carey, Papa Mutt (Liberty Synco-pators), 86, 102, 117, 118, 120, 121, 129-130, 131
Carney, Harry, 143
Carter, Benny, 138, 139
Carter, Jack, 128
Casa Loma Orchestra, 157
Casey, Floyd, 119
Cato, Pineleg, 99

Celestin, Papa Oscar, 53, 77, 81, 107, 119
Chambers, Tig, 85, 86, 98
Cherie, Eddie, 128
City Golf Club (New Orleans, La.), 43
Clay, Sonny, 131, 132-133
Clem, Edward, 46, 87
Clerk, 54
Cless, Rod, 124
Club Hangover (San Francisco, Calif.), 121, 157, 173
Coltrane, John, xi
Come Clean Hall (Gretna, La.), 26, 89, 162
Cooper, Elzy, 122
Cooper, U. S. Grant, 115
Cornish, Willie, 17
Cotton Club (New York, N.Y.), 143, 144
Cottrell, Louis, 89, 106
Coycault, Ernest (Nenny), 122, 131
Coyault, Pills, 122
Crackter, 125
Crawley, Wilton, 97-98, 149
Creath, Charlie (Jazz-o-Maniacs), 40, 74, 111, 115, 117, 118, 119, 122-123, 125, 126-127
Creole Jazz Band. See Oliver, Joe
Crescent Band. See Carey, Jack
Crow, Bill, xvii

Darensbourg, Joe, 129
Davis, Miles, 104
Davis, Richard, xix
Davison, Wild Bill, 170
DeLisle, Baptiste, 43
De Paris, Wilbur, 140
Desvignes, Sidney (Original Tuxedo Band), 118, 119, 127-129
Dixon, Cal, 138
Dodds, Johnny, 40, 48, 50, 52, 53, 87, 98, 102, 104, 106, 113, 117, 138
Dodds, Warren (Baby), 40, 77, 84, 102, 104, 105, 106, 115, 170, 171
Dorsey, Jimmy, 165
Dorsey, Tommy, 165

Drag Nasty, 18, 98
Drag Nasty Hall (Gretna, La.), 26
Dragonetti, Domenico, xi
Duhé, Laurence, 37
DuMaine, Louis, 83
Dunn, Johnny, 120
Dupas, Arnold, 28, 81
Dupas, Dave, 28, 81
Dupree, 144
Dusen, Frankie (Eagle Band), 17, 19, 22, 28, 29, 36, 38, 41, 44, 46, 47-49, 51, 64, 78, 105, 106, 122
Dutrey, Honoré (Nora), 19-20, 27, 48, 56, 102
Dutrey, Jimmy, 19-20, 48, 56
Dutrey, Pete, 19-20, 48, 56, 85
Dutrey, Sam, 19-20, 48, 53, 56, 81, 87, 106, 115
Duvivier, George, xii

Eagle Band. *See* Dusen, Frankie
Eagle Saloon (New Orleans, La.), 46, 47
Elks Brass Band, 45, 118, 133
Ellington, Duke, xi, 102, 125, 135, 143, 147, 152, 159
Eubanks, Horace, 118
Europe, Jim, 44

Fasco, 81, 85
Fewclothes' (cabaret, New Orleans, La.), 18, 37
Filhe, George, 87
Fisher, 62
Foster, Alma (wife), 130, 140-141, 154, 156, 159, 161, 164, 170, 171-172, 173
Foster, Annie (mother), 5, 6, 8, 9, 14, 15
Foster, Bertha (first wife), 64-65, 120
Foster, Charley (father), 2, 3, 4, 8, 9, 14, 15
Foster, Chinee, 81
Foster, Elizabeth (sister), 3, 8, 9, 14, 21
Foster, Martha (grandmother), 5, 8, 9, 14

Foster, Willie (brother), 2, 3, 8, 9, 14, 19, 20, 28, 77, 79, 82, 84, 127, 128
Francs Amis Hall (New Orleans, La.), 65
Frank, Alcide, 45, 46
Frank, Bab (Peerless Band), 44-46, 61, 119
Freeman, Bud, xxii
French Casino (New York, N.Y.), 155
Funky Butt Hall (New Orleans, La.), 19, 46, 87

Garland, Eddie (Montudie), 21, 51-52, 120-121, 173
Garland, Johnny, 27
Garvey, Marcus, 145
Gaspard, Oke, 45-46, 61
Gaspard, Vic, 45
Gillespie, Dizzy, 168
Glaser, Joe, 156-159 *passim*, 166, 169
Globes Hall (New Orleans, La.), 18
Gold Leaf Band, 84
Gold Whispering Band. *See* Allen, Eddie
Goodman, Benny, 159
Goodman, Harry, 159
Goughe, Harrison, 28
Groshey, Eddie, 32, 34
Guaraldi, Vince, xvi
Gyp the Blood's (cabaret, New Orleans, La.), 32, 37

Hadlock, Richard, xii
Haggart, Bob, xii, xxii
Halfway House (cabaret, New Orleans, La.), 62
Hall, Jim, xviii
Hall, Minor (Ram), 129-130
Hampton, Lionel, 131
Handy, W. C., 90-92
Harmony Club (New Orleans, La.), 43
Harper, Claude, 142
Hawkins, Coleman, 123, 137, 147, 148
Henderson, Fletcher, 123, 135, 137, 139, 140, 143

Henderson, Horace, 143
Herriford, Leon, 131
Higginbotham, J. C., 135, 137, 139
Hightower, Willie, 84, 85, 106
Hill, Teddy, 133, 135, 139, 168
Hines, Earl (Fatha), xi, xvii, 97,
    149, 157, 173
Hinton, Milt, xii
Hite, Les, 131, 132
Hodes, Art, xxii, 169, 171
Hodges, Johnny, 143
Holmes, Charlie, 135, 139, 160
Honis, Ralph, 19
Hooker, George, 68-69
Howard, Darnell, 120, 128, 149, 173
Howard, Joe, 16, 103, 106, 115
Howard, Paul, 131
Humphrey, Jim, 86
Humphrey, Little Willie, 86
Humphrey, Willie, 85, 86
Huntz & Nagels (cabaret, New
    Orleans, La.), 18, 29, 32, 37

Imperial Band, 42, 87
Island Queen (Mississippi steam-
    ship), 129

Jackson, Dewey (Peacock Orchestra),
    74, 86, 104, 111, 117, 118, 123,
    125, 127, 133, 134
Jackson, Jim, 131
Jackson, Ovette, 19
Jackson, Spencer, 46
Jackson Square Gardens (New
    Orleans, La.), 43
Jackson, Tony, 18, 72, 95
Jackson, Willie, 42
Jacobs, Walter, 73, 78, 132
Jazz-o-Maniacs. See Creath, Charlie
Jazz Syncopators. See Marable, Fate
Jefferson, Isaac, 114-115, 119
Johns, Emmett, 85
Johns, Manny, 154
Johnson, Bill, xvi, xxi, 37
Johnson, Buddy, 47, 85
Johnson, Bunk, 25, 47-48, 77, 157,
    164-165, 168, 169

Johnson, Dink, 54, 120
Johnson, Ernest (Young Olympia
    Band), 51, 114, 131
Johnson, Jack, 74
Johnson, James P., 97, 98, 146,
    150-152, 153, 171
Johnson, Jesse, 133
Johnson, Jim, 16, 114
Johnson, Joe, 19, 20, 27, 48,
    64, 82, 84
Johnson, Lonnie, 92, 118
Johnson, Nookie, 37
Johnson, Otis, 144-145
Johnson, Pete, 95-96
Johnson, Toots, 69
Johnson, Yank, 85
Jones, David, 104, 106, 115
Jones, George, 96
Jones, Hank, xviii
Jones, Isham, 161
Jones, Jo, xx
Jones, My Knee, 99
Joplin, Scott, 11, 43, 70, 72, 73,
    74, 78, 148
Josephs, Kayser, 85
JS (Mississippi steamship), 110

Keely, Frank, 17, 83, 95, 98
Kelley, Peck, 117
Kelly, Guy, 69
Kendalls, Oscar, 85
Keppard, Freddie, 1, 17, 22, 25, 27,
    29, 37-40 passim, 54-55, 57, 77,
    78, 83, 84, 86, 95, 102, 104, 117, 173
Keppard, Louis, 21, 27, 37, 81, 168
Kimball, Andrew, 45
Kimball, Henry, 14, 77, 114
King, Martin Luther, 6
Kyle, Buddy, 18

Ladnier, Tommy, 148
LaFaro, Scott, xix
Lala, Johnny, 62-63
Lamb, Joseph, 72
LaMenthe, Ferdinand Joseph. See
    Morton, Jelly Roll
Lang, Eddie, 63, 146

Lanin, Lester, 148
Lankford, Harry, 119
La Rocca, Nick, 38-39
Ledbetter, Huddie (Leadbelly), 52, 153-154
Lesberg, Jack, xii-xiii, xvii
Lewis, Alexander, 105-106
Lewis, Dandy, 46
Lewis, Frank, 17
Lewis, Meade Lux, 95-96
Lewis, Steve, 99-100
Lewis, Ted, 149
Liberty Dance Hall (Los Angeles, Calif.), 129
Liberty Syncopators. See Carey, Papa Mutt
Lindsay, Herbert, 53-54
Lindsay, John, xvi, xviii, 53
Lomax, Alan, 72
Love and Charity Hall (New Orleans, La.), 64
Lovingood, Burroughs, 114-115, 118
Lyons, Bob, 46

McCullen, George, 84
McCurdis, Charley, 45, 87
McDonough, Dick, 63, 146
McKenzie, Red, 114
McKinney's Cotton Pickers, 141
MacMurray, 89
Madden, Arnie, 140
Madison, Bingie, 142, 152
Madison, Chiff, 50, 51
Madison, Kid Shots, 82
Madison, Stone, 50, 51
Magnolia Band, 21, 22, 25-38 passim, 41, 44, 48, 49, 74, 80
Mahogany Hall (New Orleans, La.), 24, 93
Manetta, Fess, 54
Marable, Fate (Jazz Syncopators), 36, 48, 102-104, 106-115 passim, 120
Marrero, John, 128
Marsala, Marty, 171
Marshall, Kaiser, 137
Martin, Coochie, 43

Martin, Henry, 83
Mason, Norman, 120
Masonic Hall (New Orleans, La.), 18, 41, 46
Metcalf, Louis, 133, 135
Metoyer, Arnold, 37, 77, 98, 107
Meyers, 131
Mezzrow, Mezz, 139, 157, 166-167, 172
Millinder, Lucky, 150
Mills Brothers, 157
Mingus, Charles, xix
Minton's (cabaret, New York, N.Y.), 168
Missourians, The. See Calloway, Cab
Monk, Thelonius, xii
Moran, Billy, 47
Morgan, Albert, xvi, 102, 114, 147-148
Morgan, Isaiah, 129
Morgan, Sam, 16, 114, 129, 147
Morgenstern, Don, xxi
Morton, Jelly Roll, xii, xviii, 33, 40, 59, 72, 91, 93-98 passim, 100, 102, 137, 146-147
Mosby, Curtis, 131, 132
Moten, Bennie, 117
Mound City Blue Blowers, 137
Mumford, Brock, 16
Mumphrey, Brock, 64

Nation, Carrie, 31
Nelson, Big Eye Louis Delisle, 33-34, 45, 47, 54, 82, 87-88, 168
Nicholas, Albert, 49, 82, 87, 128, 135, 137, 139, 151, 163-164, 171
Nicholas, Wooden Joe, 87
Nichols, Red, 142
Nunez, Roy, 33

Oliver, Joe (King), 1, 19, 21, 25, 28, 29, 34, 37, 40, 48, 52, 60, 72, 74, 77-81 passim, 83, 84, 95, 102, 104, 117, 118, 128, 143, 162, 173
Olympia Orchestra, 87
Olympic Band, 42
One-Eleven Dance Hall (Los Angeles, Calif.), 116-117, 121
Onward Band, 60, 68

Original Dixieland Jazz Band, 39, 54-55, 62, 102
Original Tuxedo Band. *See* Ridgley, William; Desvignes, Sidney
Ory, Kid, 21, 38, 42, 44, 49-53 *passim*, 65, 78, 85, 90, 102, 107, 115-122 *passim*, 138, 173

Page, Oran P. (Hot Lips), (Papa Midnight and His Band), 118, 133
Page, Walter, xx
Palao, Jimmie, 54, 57
Palmer, Roy, 19, 84-85
Panico, Louis, 110
Papa Midnight and His Band. *See* Page, Oran P.
Parenti, Tony, xvii, xxi, 63
Parker, Charlie, xi, 168
Pavageau, Alcide (Slow Drag), 169
Peacock Orchestra. *See* Jackson, Dewey
Peer, Ralph, 117
Peerless Band. *See* Frank, Bab
Penerton, John, 46, 48, 77, 84
Perez, Manuel, 22, 29, 37, 47, 77, 83, 84, 98, 102, 173
Perkins, Dave, 61-62, 85
Perseverance Hall (New Orleans, La.), 55, 68
Petit, Buddy, 36, 77, 81, 82, 122
Petit, Joseph, 82
Picou, Alphonse, 22, 23, 28, 36, 45, 87, 168
Piron, Armand J., 38, 99-100, 105
Plantation Club (Chicago, Ill.), 143
Ponts, Henry, 34
Porter, Willie, 131
Primrose Band, 26, 84
Pryor, Arthur, 71
Purvis, Jack, 140

Raft, George, 140
Raglin, Junior, 147
Rappolo, Leon, 62
Real Tom Anderson's (tonk, New Orleans, La.), 19, 82
Reinhardt, Django, 92

Rena, Kid Henry, 82, 86
Rhythm Club (New York, N.Y.), 148
Rice's (cabaret, New Orleans, La.), 18, 29, 37
Ridgley, William (Bebe) (Original Tuxedo Band), 53, 104, 106, 115, 119
Riley, Amos, 62, 84
Roberts, Luckey, 146, 154-155
Robertson, Zue, 27
Robichaux, John (orchestra), 13-14, 25, 38, 41, 43, 44, 47, 51, 84, 85, 86, 90, 93, 99
Robinson, Bill (Bojangles), 147
Robinson, Jim, 169
Roseland Ballroom (New York, N.Y.), xxii, 139, 140
Ross, Miles, 46
Rozelle Orchestra, 17, 19, 20, 21, 48
Rucker, 19
Rumsey, Howard, xvii n. 19
Russell, Luis, xx, xxi, 97-98, 118, 133, 135-137, 138, 140-144 *passim*, 148-149, 156, 157, 158, 165
Russell, Pee Wee, 117, 124, 137

Safranski, Eddie, xii n. 4
St. Catherine's Hall (New Orleans, La.), 84, 105
St. Cyr, Johnny, 22, 35, 44, 102, 104, 105, 106, 107, 112, 113, 119, 120, 125, 133
St. Dominic's Hall (New Orleans, La.), 64
St. Paul (Mississippi steamship), 109, 110, 111, 119
Santiago, Willie, 87
Saratoga Club (New York, N.Y.), 140, 141, 143
Savoy Ballroom (New York, N.Y.), 138, 139
Savoy Sultans, 142
Schoffner, Bob, 123, 125-126
Schuller, Gunther, xii-xiii, xv, xviii
Scott, Bud, 44, 121
Scott, James, 70, 72
Sedric, Gene, 102, 120

Shaw, Milt, 140
Shields, Larry, 62
Sidney (Mississippi steamship), 104, 110
Silver Leaf Band. See Baptiste, Albert
Simeon, Omer, 135
Singleton, Zutty, 44, 50, 55, 118, 173
Sissle, Noble, 128, 149-150, 155
Skinner, June, 3
Smiley, Bob, 162-163
Smith, Alec, 84
Smith, Bessie, 137, 150
Smith, Clara, 150
Smith, Jabbo, 149
Smith, Joe, 143
Smith, Stuff, 53
Smith, Willie the Lion, 152-153, 154
Snakehips, 150
Snowden, Elmer, xii, 18
Sore Dick, 18, 98
Souchon, Edmund, 63
Sousa, John Philip, 11, 71
Southard, Harry, 131
Spanier, Muggsy, 149, 170, 173
Spikes, Reb, 131
Stall, Lorenzo, 89-90
Starr, Henry, 131-132
Steele, Joe, 143, 152
Stepin Fetchit, 150
Stewart, Rex, 135, 140
Streckfus, family, 77, 103-115 passim, 119, 127
Streckfus, John, 105, 107, 112
Sugar Johnny, 37, 83, 95
Suggs, Percy, 110
Sullivan, Joe, 61
Superior Band, 42, 44, 47, 85
Sylvester, Bob, 142

Tatum, Art, 155
Teagarden, Jack, 117, 124, 137
Thomas, George, 154
Thomas, Walter, 119-120
Tio, Lorenzo Jr., 22, 28-29
Tony and His Iowaians, 110
Tony's Saloon (New Orleans, La.), 64

Tranchina's (cabaret, Spanish Fort, La.), 36, 105
Trippania, Ernest (Quank), 28, 53
Trumbauer, Frankie, 117, 124
Turpin, Tom, 72, 73-74, 78
Turtles, The (club, New Orleans, La.), 64
Tuton, 128
Tuxedo Band, 22, 38, 44, 53-54, 93, 99, 119
Tuxedo Dance Hall (New Orleans, La.), 18, 30, 37, 53
Twenty-Five Club (New Orleans, La.), 33, 34, 57, 93-94

Umphrey, Ory, 128

Valcons, 168
Venuti, Joe, 146
Vigne, Jean, 28, 45, 89
Vigne, Sidney, 89
Vinson, Eddie, 54, 57

Waller, Fats, 137, 146, 150-151, 152
Ware, Gene, 128
Warner, Willie, 16-17
Washington (Mississippi steamship), 108
Washington, Benny, 125
Washington, Fred, 121
Washington, George, 81
Weiss, Sid, xii n. 4
West End Golf Club (New Orleans, La.), 43
White, Bob, 145
White, Coochie, 45
White, Josh, 153
White, Leon, 129-130, 131
White, Lulu, 24, 32, 93
Wild Ned, 46, 48, 77, 78
Williams, Charlotte, 5
Williams, Clairborne, 5-6, 172
Williams, Clarence, 6, 40, 95, 98, 100-101, 117, 118, 126, 152, 172
Williams, Cootie, 143
Williams, Fess, 139
Williams, Gene, 164-165

Williams, George, 90
Williams, James, 43, 85
Williams, Little James, 85
Williams, Lucy, 6
Williams, Michael, 6
Williams, Midge, 160
Wilson, Alfred, 98
Wilson, Eudell, 95, 98, 154
Wilson, Teddy, 146, 155
Windhurst, Johnny, 169

Woods, Sonny, 160
Wright, Eugene, xxi
Wynn, Albert, 118

Yancey, Jimmy, 154
Young Olympia Band. *See* Johnson,
    Ernest

Zeno, Henry, 64
Zimmerman, Fred, xiii